"Having been frustrated by so many learned Old Testament commentaries, which may be full of good scholarship but offer little help to preachers, it is a joy to recommend such a fine book, which is so clearly the work of someone who is a very fine preacher himself. It is marked by careful exegesis, which reveals the main thrust of Joshua as a whole and each major section without getting lost in unnecessary details. All the big questions the preacher and congregation will ask are addressed and there are excellent pointers to application. It provides fuel, not only for our preaching, but for our hearts and lives."

Vaughan Roberts, Rector of St Ebbe's, Oxford, England; Director, The Proclamation Trust

"Here is another excellent commentary, which combines great insights of exegesis, theology, relevance, and pastoral application. Every page is enriched by David's extensive experience and wisdom in understanding and preaching the Bible. This commentary is ideal for those preparing to teach or preach the book of Joshua, and it is also invaluable for Christians who want to understand the book of Joshua and read it for personal encouragement. I praise God for David's ministry."

Peter Adam, Vicar Emeritus, St Jude's Church, Carlton, Australia; former Principal, Ridley College Melbourne; author, *Speaking God's Words: A Practical Theology of Preaching* and *The Message of Malachi*

"This is a fine addition to the Preaching the Word series. Jackman combines pastoral sensitivity, erudition, and an experienced feel for the text to give us a guide through the life-changing book of Joshua."

Josh Moody, Senior Pastor, College Church, Wheaton, Illinois; author, *Journey to Joy: The Psalms of Ascent*

"As a seasoned pastor and trainer of preachers, David Jackman has a long history of handling God's Word in ways that benefit the Church. This volume on Joshua only adds to his legacy of gospel usefulness. David's presentation of the text is clear and accessible. And the road he paves to Christ and the gospel can be trusted. Get it!"

David R. Helm, Pastor, Holy Trinity Church, Chicago; Chairman, The Charles Simeon Trust

JOSHUA

PREACHING THE WORD
Edited by R. Kent Hughes

(((PREACHING *the* WORD)))

JOSHUA

PEOPLE *of* GOD'S PURPOSE

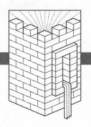

DAVID JACKMAN

R. Kent Hughes
Series Editor

::CROSSWAY®

WHEATON, ILLINOIS

Joshua

Copyright © 2014 by David Jackman

Published by Crossway
    1300 Crescent Street
    Wheaton, Illinois 60187

Cover design: Jon McGrath, Simplicated Studio

Cover image: Adam Green, illustrator

First printing 2014

Printed in the United States of America

ISBN-13: 978-1-4335-1197-4

ISBN-10: 1-4335-1197-5

PDF ISBN: 978-1-4335-2377-9

Mobipocket ISBN: 978-1-4335-1199-8

ePub ISBN: 978-1-4335-2377-9

Library of Congress Cataloging-in-Publication Data

Jackman, David.
Joshua : people of God's purpose / David Jackman.
    pages cm.—(Preaching the word)
    Includes bibliographical references and index.
    ISBN 978-1-4335-1197-4 (hc)
    1. Bible. Joshua—Commentaries. I. Title.
BS1295.53.J33   2013
222'.207—dc23   2013003647

Crossway is a publishing ministry of Good News Publishers.

VP		31	30	29	28	27	26	25	24	23	22	21
14	13	12	11	10	9	8	7	6	5	4	3	2

To
Ollie, Tom, Charlie, and Millie
"Cling to the Lord your God."
Joshua 23:8

Be strong and courageous, for you shall cause this people to inherit the land that I swore to their fathers to give them. Only be strong and very courageous, being careful to do according to all the law that Moses my servant commanded you. Do not turn from it to the right hand or to the left, that you may have good success wherever you go. This Book of the Law shall not depart from your mouth, but you shall meditate on it day and night, so that you may be careful to do according to all that is written in it. For then you will make your way prosperous, and then you will have good success.

JOSHUA 1:6–8

Contents

A Word to Those Who Preach the Word

There are times when I am preaching that I have especially sensed the pleasure of God. I usually become aware of it through the unnatural silence. The ever-present coughing ceases, and the pews stop creaking, bringing an almost physical quiet to the sanctuary—through which my words sail like arrows. I experience a heightened eloquence, so that the cadence and volume of my voice intensify the truth I am preaching.

There is nothing quite like it—the Holy Spirit filling one's sails, the sense of his pleasure, and the awareness that something is happening among one's hearers. This experience is, of course, not unique, for thousands of preachers have similar experiences, even greater ones.

What has happened when this takes place? How do we account for this sense of his smile? The answer for me has come from the ancient rhetorical categories of *logos*, *ethos*, and *pathos*.

The first reason for his smile is the *logos*—in terms of preaching, God's Word. This means that as we stand before God's people to proclaim his Word, we have done our homework. We have exegeted the passage, mined the significance of its words in their context, and applied sound hermeneutical principles in interpreting the text so that we understand what its words meant to its hearers. And it means that we have labored long until we can express in a sentence what the theme of the text is—so that our outline springs from the text. Then our preparation will be such that as we preach, we will not be preaching our own thoughts about God's Word, but God's actual Word, his *logos*. This is fundamental to pleasing him in preaching.

The second element in knowing God's smile in preaching is *ethos*—what you are as a person. There is a danger endemic to preaching, which is having your hands and heart cauterized by holy things. Phillips Brooks illustrated it by the analogy of a train conductor who comes to believe that he has been to the places he announces because of his long and loud heralding of them. And that is why Brooks insisted that preaching must be "the bringing of truth through personality." Though we can never perfectly embody the truth we preach, we must be subject to it, long for it, and make it as much a part of our ethos as possible. As the Puritan William Ames said, "Next to the Scriptures, nothing makes a sermon more to pierce, than when it comes out of the inward affection of the heart without any affectation." When a preacher's *ethos* backs up his *logos*, there will be the pleasure of God.

Last, there is *pathos*—personal passion and conviction. David Hume, the Scottish philosopher and skeptic, was once challenged as he was seen going to hear George Whitefield preach: "I thought you do not believe in the gospel." Hume replied, "I don't, but he does." Just so! When a preacher believes what he preaches, there will be passion. And this belief and requisite passion will know the smile of God.

The pleasure of God is a matter of *logos* (the Word), *ethos* (what you are), and *pathos* (your passion). As you preach the Word may you experience his smile—the Holy Spirit in your sails!

R. Kent Hughes

Preface

It has been both a privilege and a joy to accept the invitation from Dr. Kent Hughes to contribute this volume to his Preaching the Word series. We have worked together in a variety of contexts and locations over the years, especially in preaching workshops for pastors, and we have a shared passion to become better preachers of the Word ourselves and to help others develop their skills under God. We long to see a new generation of effective Bible expositors raised up by the Lord to teach and apply his unchanging truth to all the multiplying challenges and opportunities of contemporary life.

I first preached Joshua at the outset of my pastoral ministry in Above Bar Church, Southampton, England, back in the early 1980s, and it has been a favorite book of mine ever since. When this invitation came, I decided to start again from scratch, and my renewed study of this great book has been illuminating, convicting, and challenging, but hugely encouraging to me, as I trust it will prove to be to you too. I have preached it in many different contexts over the past two years or so in pastors' workshops and preaching conferences, in Bible conventions, and to several local churches in pulpit ministry or retreat weekends in several different parts of the world. I am grateful to many who have reacted with the material in question times and informal discussions, which has sharpened my understanding of both the text and its applications. I am also glad to express a special indebtedness to outstanding commentators and writers on the text of Joshua, from John Calvin onward, but in particular, among contemporary writers, to David Howard Jr. and to Paul Copan, whose scholarly and pastoral insights have benefited me greatly in my exposition. Very many thanks also to my good friend Nancy Olsen, who typed and checked the manuscript for me and whose secretarial skills have been such a help and support over many years.

"People of God's Purpose" is the subtitle of the book because I believe a large part of its lasting relevance and helpfulness for us in our generation is to be found in its instruction and challenge to us to enter into all the potential of the gospel blessings (our land of promise) secured for us by our Joshua. We too need to learn to trust God's promises more deeply and so to obey his commands more wholeheartedly. There are urgent and vital lessons in this text for the twenty-first-century church. But Joshua himself is not the focal point of the book that bears his name, and neither is Israel. That honor belongs to God himself, who is the hero of every Old Testament narrative and who is here revealed in all his dependable faithfulness as the eternal covenant Lord who makes and keeps his promises, the sovereign King of all creation who fulfills every one of his gracious purposes. "Not one word of all the good promises that the LORD had made to the house of Israel had failed; all came to pass" (21:45). How different the church today would be if we Christians would live in the light of that eternal reality!

Finally, I am grateful to dedicate this book to my four grandchildren, in the hope and prayer that they too will grow up to become people of God's purpose in their generation, in whatever ways he chooses for them.

David Jackman
London, England
February 2013

1

Overture and Beginners

JOSHUA 1:1, 2

THE BEGINNING OF THIS sixth book of the Bible is as stark as it is surprising. From Exodus onward, the last four books have been dominated by one giant human figure—Moses. For forty years he has been the constant factor, the mediator and deliverer of his people—always there, always dependable, the man who speaks face-to-face with God, "as a man speaks to his friend" (Exodus 33:11). It must have been almost impossible to imagine life without Moses, much as those of us who are British citizens find it hard to imagine our country without Queen Elizabeth II after her sixty wonderful years upon the throne. But "Moses my servant is dead" is the blunt beginning of this book (v. 2) and life, as always, must go on.

The words are spoken to Joshua, the son of Nun, by no means a young man at this stage, but with his real life's work just about to open up before him. The words are spoken by the sovereign Lord, Yahweh, whose name reveals his unchanging faithfulness to his covenant promises because of his immutable character and purposes. The words are not unexpected. They are like the starting pistol to a race that Joshua has always known he would one day run and for which he has been trained and has prepared for decades. But they must have come with awesome demand and challenge, and they must surely have provoked that mixture of excited anticipation and inner panic we all know when we stand on the threshold of a major new chapter of our life experience. "Now therefore arise, go over this Jordan, you and all this people . . ." (v. 2).

The time has come to enter the land, to possess in reality all that their covenant Lord had promised Israel through the centuries, since first he told their father Abraham, "I will give to you and to your offspring after you the land of our sojournings, all the land of Canaan, for an everlasting possession, and I will be their God" (Genesis 17:8). This was why he brought them out of their slavery in Egypt. This was what their forty years in the desert was always anticipating. This was how the sovereign Lord would now fulfill his often repeated promises.

The pattern had been set right back at the beginning of God's dealings with Abram, when, in Ur of the Chaldeans, he received the divine summons, "Go from your country and your kindred and your father's house to the land that I will show you" (Genesis 12:1). This clear command was accompanied by no road map, no detailed schedule, no explanation of how it would all happen, but Abram had all that he really needed—the promise from the sovereign Lord that he would show him the land and then later give it to him and his family (Genesis 12:7). The command and the promise run together throughout the Bible. So it is here for Joshua. The command is to cross the River Jordan, but the promise is that God is now giving his people their promised land. Both command and promise depend upon the sovereignty of God, expressed in his wise will and achieved by his irresistible power. So it is as God's people both believe the promises and obey the commands that they enter into the experience of fellowship with God at the deepest, relational level. The same is true for us today. Why do we so often fail to obey God's commands? Because we do not really believe his promises. The two always go together. Faith leads to obedience. Disobedience is always rooted in distrust. We will see this lesson worked out often in the book of Joshua; it is a continuing challenge that we shall often encounter in our contemporary experience of living the Christian life.

It is significant that the designation of Moses as "the servant of the Lord" in verse 1 is matched at the end of the book (24:29) with the same title, but this time it is assigned to Joshua. The story of the book, at one level, is the story of Joshua's progress and development from the description of him as "Moses' assistant" (1:1) to his own epitaph as the Lord's servant. But Joshua is not the hero of the book, as we shall see. That role is entirely occupied by the Lord himself, whom Joshua served. Nevertheless, Joshua features as the central human actor in the drama of the conquest of Canaan, and it is entirely appropriate for us to look at some of his earlier history before we delve into the details of the text.

The Apprentice

We are first introduced to Joshua in the early days of the exodus, before the nation is brought together to Sinai to receive the Law of God. Perhaps a better translation of the Hebrew word *torah*, translated as "law," would be "instruction" since this stresses the relational aspect of God's self-revelation as he reveals how his people are to live in covenant with him. Of course, this is interwoven with the binding effects and sanctions of his commands, which are not just advice but carry divine authority and inflict within them punishment for their infringement.

Just a few months out of Egypt the Israelites face an all-out assault from the Amalekites at Rephidim, where God has provided water from the rock. Without any words of introduction, Joshua is nominated by Moses to select an army and lead the battle, which he does (Exodus 17:8–10). After the great victory ("Joshua overwhelmed Amalek," Exodus 17:13), God commands Moses to record in writing and cause it to be read to Joshua that he, the Lord, will be at war with Amalek until he will "utterly blot out the memory of Amalek from under heaven" (Exodus 17:14). Joshua, previously unknown, is suddenly a successful military leader, but he needs constantly to be reminded that this was God's victory, not his, entirely dependent on Moses' symbolic raising of his hands to the throne of Yahweh in supplication and intercession. It is interesting that at this first recorded Joshua incident the written testimony is given a central place in encouraging his faith and reminding him where power really lies. The man of action is to be dependent on the word of the Lord and on the prayers of his people.

We next meet Joshua, described as Moses' "assistant," in Exodus 24:13, where he accompanies the great leader as he responds to God's call to come up Mount Sinai to receive the tablets of the Torah. There is nothing to indicate that Joshua was with Moses when he entered the cloud of God's presence, but he was certainly nearer to God's self-revelation "like a devouring fire" (Exodus 24:17) than any of his fellow Israelites. And when the protracted interview ends, it is Joshua who descends with Moses to witness the horrors of the golden calf idolatry in the camp. The young man assumes the noise of the people below to be a sign of war, but Moses knows better, and the orgy quickly becomes evident (Exodus 32:17–19). After the initial acts of judgment and the withdrawal of God's immediate presence from the camp, it is Moses who sets up a tent outside, a prototype "tabernacle" or "tent of meeting," where he alone can communicate with God, in personal intimacy. But the privilege of proximity again belongs to Joshua. "When Moses turned again into the camp, his assistant Joshua the son of Nun, a young man, would not depart from the tent" (Exodus 33:11). We don't know, of course, how much Moses passed on to the young apprentice, but such closeness to the action and his awareness of God's glory must have been enormously formative in the young warrior's thinking.

Still Learning

The next time we meet Joshua, God has called Moses to select seventy elders, upon whom he puts his Spirit so as to enable them to share in the burden of leadership that Moses has been shouldering alone. This unique visitation of the Spirit was evidenced by their speaking God's word (prophesying), a unique occurrence. Even though two of them had not left the camp, Eldad and Medad nevertheless prophesied as well, although so much to Joshua's consternation that he says to Moses, "My lord Moses, stop them" (Numbers 11:28). But Moses' response is, "Would that all the LORD's people were prophets" (v. 29). The meekest man in all the earth demonstrates not the slightest hint of jealousy. He has no concern for his own position or authority, but only for the well-being of the people. So the young Joshua has to learn that leadership is never an exclusive privilege, that he is not to glorify Moses, giant though he is, nor is he to seek to hedge God in to his own preferred agenda. These remain essential insights for godly leadership still today.

But then comes the greatest contribution Joshua has so far made in the purposes of God for Israel, when he is selected by Moses to represent his tribe, Ephraim, as one of the twelve spies commissioned to spy out the land of Canaan (Numbers 13:1–16). Only Joshua and Caleb return with a good report, urging immediate occupation, "for we are well able to overcome . . ." (Numbers 13:30). Not only so, but they plead with the whole congregation to trust in God's grace and favor to "bring us into this land and give it to us, a land that flows with milk and honey" (Numbers 14:8). They must not fear the Canaanites but rather trust God's promise and his presence with them. Yet the major report of rebellious unbelief prevails, the opportunity is lost, and Israel confines herself to the tragedy of forty more years in the wilderness as that whole generation is condemned to die outside the land, except Caleb and Joshua (Numbers 14:30). A plague removes the ten spies; only Joshua and Caleb remain alive (Numbers 14:37, 38).

Eventually the years pass, and God commands Moses to view, but not enter, the land of promise before his own death (Numbers 27:12, 13). Moses' concern is with the succession. Still, it seems, his dominating passion is the welfare of the nation. So he petitions God in specific terms that become increasingly significant as the mega-narrative of the Bible unfolds. He asks for a man "who shall go out before them and come in before them, who shall lead them out and bring them in, that the congregation of the LORD may not be as sheep that have no shepherd" (Numbers 27:17). He asks for a shepherd, doubtless influenced by his years tending the flock of Jethro, his father-in-law, as well as his years leading the flock of God. And God's answer is immediate: "Take Joshua the son of Nun, a man in whom is the Spirit, and lay your hand on him" (Numbers 27:18). Accordingly, Joshua is publicly commissioned with some of the authority Moses had. This is not perhaps a reference to job-sharing so much as a recognition that although Joshua is clearly God's man, his relationship will be different from that which Moses had with God. Joshua will not have the face-to-face fellowship Moses experienced. He has a written record by which God's will is made known, coupled with access to Eleazar the priest "who shall inquire for him by the judgment of the Urim before the LORD" (Numbers 27:21). In this sense he is the first Israelite leader who, although directly commissioned by God, is dependent on the word of God already spoken and written and the prayerful inquiry of the priest to provide the wisdom he needs to make godly decisions for the people.

From now on, until Moses' death, Joshua and Eleazar are included together in the government of the nation. So in Numbers 32:28 they are told to ensure that the people of Gad and Reuben will not inherit their assigned land east of the Jordan unless they enter Canaan with the rest of the tribes and play their part in its armed conquest, which they agree to do. The fulfillment of this command with its promise will have considerable prominence in the book of Joshua.

Heir Apparent

The book of Deuteronomy, the second giving of the Law, sees the nation of Israel encamped on the plains of Moab prior to their entry into the land, when Moses dies. But the old leader has much to pass on from God to the people before God calls him into his presence. Reminding them of the exclusion of their parents' generation through unbelief, Moses recalls not only God's promise to Caleb and Joshua that they would enter, but also God's instruction to him about the new leader: "Encourage him, for he shall cause Israel to inherit [the land]" (Deuteronomy 1:38). Two chapters later we are given more insight into Joshua's preparation, as well as encouragement he received for imminent future challenges. Moses relates how, under God's direction, he told Joshua at the time of their victory over Og, king of Bashan, and Sihon, king of the Amorites (Numbers 21), "Your eyes have seen all that the LORD your God has done to these two kings. So will the LORD do to all the kingdoms into which you are crossing. You shall not fear them, for it is the LORD your God who fights for you" (Deuteronomy 3:21, 22). And on this basis the instruction is renewed. "Charge Joshua, and encourage and strengthen him, for he shall go over at the head of this people, and he shall put them in possession of the land" (Deuteronomy 3:28).

This note of encouraging and strengthening Joshua now becomes increasingly persistent, serving as an introductory motif to the first chapters of the book of Joshua. Deuteronomy 31 records the passing of the baton from Moses to his assistant. Speaking of his own imminent departure, Moses assures the nation that they will possess the land, "and Joshua will go over at your head, as the LORD has spoken" (Deuteronomy 31:3). This succession planning is divine in both its origin and execution. But in his words to Joshua, Moses is more specific. He calls Joshua to be "strong and courageous," not fearful or easily discouraged, because of the sure and certain promises of God (Deuteronomy 31:7). "It is the LORD who goes before you. He will be with you; he will not leave you or forsake you" (Deuteronomy 31:8). This is clearly echoed by New Testament faith in the last chapter of Hebrews, where the writer quotes the same promise, given directly by God to the new leader in Joshua 1:5 and links it with the bold affirmation of the psalmist in Psalm 118:6: "The Lord is my helper; I will not fear; what can man do to me?" (Hebrews 13:5, 6). Here is the thread of faith in the promises of God as the antidote to fear, and these promises bind the whole Bible together.

Joshua is then commissioned by the Lord, in the presence of Moses, with the repeated message, "Be strong and courageous, for you shall bring the people of Israel into the land that I swore to give them. I will be with you" (Deuteronomy 31:23; cf. Deuteronomy 31:6, 7). At the end of the book everything is prepared and ready for the conquest. Along with the death of Moses there is also a sense of expectation about what is about to happen, since Joshua is "full of the spirit of wisdom, for Moses had laid his hands on him" (Deuteronomy 34:9). And then, as we turn the page, from the Pentateuch to the first of the historical narratives (or former prophets), we hear God's command, "Now . . . arise, go over this Jordan" (Joshua 1:2). Joshua's moment has arrived.

Reflections

Important principles can be derived from the Moses and Joshua narrative and are exemplified and expanded elsewhere in Scripture concerning the training of leaders and the ordering of succession. What comes across most clearly is the way in which Joshua's own knowledge of God and resulting dependence on him become the key equipping method for the work he has to do. As Moses' right-hand man, Joshua is privileged to share in some of the greatest moments of divine revelation, albeit at a distance. But this is not in order for him to learn how to be a leader as much as to learn how totally dependent on God he is. And then he learns the character of the God on whom he must depend.

It is quite clear that Joshua is far from being a person of superhuman qualities. Otherwise would he have needed so constantly to be exhorted to "Be strong and courageous"(1:6)? This doesn't seem to indicate that Joshua was a natural for leadership. But this is not an unusual selection for the God who chooses the foolish, the weak, the despised and "even things that are not, to bring to nothing things that are" (1 Corinthians 1:28). The root of the matter is that Canaan is not conquered by Joshua's superior military strategy or dominating heroism, but the Lord gives his people the land (1:2). That is why the land becomes Israel's. Joshua is the necessary and highly valued human agent at the heart of the process, but as he learned from his first encounter with the Amalekites, the battle belongs to the Lord. Contemporary Christian leadership badly needs to relearn that lesson. God is the hero of the book of Joshua. Everything is directly and categorically attributed to him, as the end of the book makes abundantly clear. The Lord gave Israel the land. The Lord gave Israel rest as he delivered their enemies into their hands. Every one of his promises was fulfilled (see 21:43–45).

The other factor to remember is how daunting and seemingly impossible this task must have appeared as Joshua and the people faced the crossing of the Jordan and the conquest of the land. That was why they needed constantly to be exhorted to listen to, remember, and put their faith in the word of their God, revealed in his promises. This was to be the first generation dependent on the written instruction of God in the Torah and on the requirements of faith and obedience recorded in the book of the covenant. Face-to-face conversation with the Lord was not Joshua's constant privilege, as it had been Moses'. He had to lead the people dependent on the written word and the spirit of wisdom, just as Christian leaders do today. When we face the daunting task of reaching our increasingly hostile culture with the good news of Christ, our equivalent dependence on the Word of God in the hands of the Spirit of God to accomplish the work of God is just as vital. That is our only means of advance too. So as we unpack the book of Joshua, we are not dealing with ancient history so much as with the living God who rules all history for the accomplishment of his eternal purposes of grace and glory. If we are to be people of those purposes in our desperately needy generation, we shall need to learn well the lessons of this magnificent book and put them into practice.

Perhaps the greatest incentive to do this is provided by the New Testament reflection on this whole episode of salvation-history as the writer to the Hebrews looks beyond Joshua to Jesus and the greater fulfillment in the gospel of all that was foreshadowed in the Old Testament.

> For if Joshua had given them rest [permanently], God would not have spoken of another day later on. So then, there remains a Sabbath rest for the people of God, for whoever has entered God's rest has also rested from his works as God did from his. Let us therefore strive to enter that rest, so that no one may fall by the same sort of disobedience. (Hebrews 4:8–11)

2

A Double Commissioning

JOSHUA 1:3–18

NATIONAL TRANSITIONS, from one leader or government to another, are always times of uncertainty and stress. The conventional wisdom is often for the new leadership to take its time to settle in, familiarize itself with the situation, and weigh the options before launching into any decisive action. That is especially so when either the previous leader has been greatly revered or when the future is unsettled and problematic. But Joshua is afforded no such luxury. As we have seen, God does not say, "Moses my servant is dead. Now take your time to settle in. Win the confidence of the people gradually. Don't take on anything too demanding just yet!" On the contrary, there is a peremptory command to get ready to cross the Jordan into the promised land "now" (1:2). It is as though the final barrier to the entry has been removed and God cannot wait to fulfill his promises.

Purpose and Structure

The structure of chapter 1 is significant and formative for our understanding of the rest of the book. This is a history book. Some scholars suggest that it should be attached to the Pentateuch,[1] as the conquest of the land is the natural climax of the sequence of covenant promises beginning with Abraham and stretching on through the exodus and the wilderness wanderings. But it is also persuasive to see it as the first of the historical narratives that lead from the period of the conquest through the judges to the institution of the monarchy and on through the division of the kingdom to Israel's ultimate defeat at the hands of the Assyrians and Judah's exile to Babylon. This unit runs from Joshua to 2 Kings. Clearly Joshua is not the author of the book of which he is the eponymous human "hero"; perhaps it was the work of Samuel or an unknown historian. But we have here a true record of events that really took place. At the start of the book Israel is still awaiting the crossing of the Jordan, and by the end much of the land has been conquered and all of it allotted to the twelve tribes. It really did happen.

Yet the arrangement of the Hebrew Scriptures categorizes Joshua as the first of the "former prophets." For us today it seems strange to call a history book prophetic. But Biblical prophecy is not history written in advance. Rather, it is the telling of what God has done and will yet do from the divine perspective. The task of the prophet is to declare the mind of God to the people, to "forth-tell" God's infallible word into their situation, and this is achieved by learning the theological implications of the history. Here is God's interpretation of what happened and why. This book of Joshua has its own unique contribution to Biblical theology as we see the work of God begun under Moses coming to fruition under Joshua, because he is the faithful covenant-keeping Lord who always keeps the promises he has made.

By extension, then, this is also a teaching book. Paul reminded the Christians in Rome that "whatever was written in former days was written for our instruction, that through endurance and through the encouragement of the Scriptures we might have hope" (Romans 15:4). That is why the book of Joshua is of such great potential benefit to the twenty-first-century church. The God of Joshua is our God. He does not change his purposes or renege on his promises. So we can learn from this book great principles of Christian life and faith, for our edification. Of course, we shall need to read and study the book as New Testament believers and preach it as followers of Christ, not as Jewish rabbis. But the Christ who is the center and focus of all the Scriptures (Luke 24:44) is not difficult to find in this book. Joshua means "savior," and Jesus is another form of the same name. Joshua points us on to the Lord Jesus Christ, the ultimate great fulfillment of all that the Old Testament deliverer foreshadowed. Similarly, we shall not find it hard to identify with the people of Israel in this book, because we are God's new Israel (Galatians 6:16), the universal community of the people of God's purpose. We too are in a battle fully to possess all that God has given to us. We too have not yet reached the fullness of rest in the heavenly kingdom, but we are set free to fight against the world, the flesh and the devil and so to enter into more and more of the blessings of the everlasting gospel. We too have life-changing lessons to learn about the priorities of faith and obedience.

Chapter 1 is all about receiving and passing on God's word. From verses 3–9 God is speaking directly to Joshua in a blend of promise and command designed to deepen his faith and nerve his obedience. In verses 10, 11 Joshua passes on the instruction to the people via their officers. There follows a special word to the two and a half tribes (Reuben, Gad, and half of Manasseh) reminding them of Moses' instruction that they are to cross the Jordan and fight in the conquest with their brothers, although their inheritance will be east of the Jordan, where their families can already settle (vv. 12–15). In return the tribal leaders assure Joshua of their obedience and loyalty, along with the hope that he will experience strength and courage through God's presence (vv. 16–18). The only conditional element in these exchanges is that Joshua will lead the people by his own example of faith in the promises and obedience to the commands.

God Commissions Joshua (1:3–9)

By Promise (vv. 3–5)

After the original command of verse 2, the next three verses are entirely promises. God is declaring his intentions and is relating them to his character as he proclaims the integrity of his covenant faithfulness. There are three things to which God unreservedly commits himself: (1) to give them the land to its fullest extent (vv. 3, 4); (2) to overcome their enemies (v. 5a); (3) to be with Joshua as he was with Moses (v. 5b). And each of these promises is guaranteed as fulfillment of the word already spoken ("just as I promised to Moses," v. 3) and continuation of the blessing already experienced ("as I was with Moses," v. 5b).

The Land (vv. 3, 4)

Note that although none of the land is yet in their possession, God can say, "I have given [it] to you" (v. 3), using the past tense to express the absolute certainty of a future occurrence. There is no doubt about who will receive the land, nor about its amazing extent. The area described in verse 4 is enormous, though very much in tune with the original promise to Abraham in Genesis 15:18–20. David Oginde comments, "In terms of current political boundaries, the promised land would thus cover modern Israel, the whole of Jordan, a large part of Saudi Arabia, half of Iraq, the whole of Lebanon, part of Syria and the whole of Kuwait!"[2] But as he points out, even at the height of the monarchy in the days of David and Solomon, Israel actually only occupied a small section of this total area.

This raises an important question for the expositor. If Joshua's forward advance was dependent on believing God's promises in detail, how is it that so much of this promise was never fulfilled? Preachers need to deal with such objections and queries or they will certainly undermine the faith of their hearers. There seem to be two important considerations to bring out. The first is that the actualization of what is promised is dependent on the wholehearted obedience of God's people. The sadness of the book is that the conquest was far from complete, that compromise and comfort took over, and that many of the inhabitants of the land were never dislodged. The same unbelief and lack of faith that precluded their entry to the land forty years earlier surfaced in the next generation in an unwillingness to push forward with the complete conquest after the initial gains had been secured. "They were unable to enter because of unbelief" (Hebrews 3:19)—that is said of the exodus generation, but by extension exactly the same weakness was revealed in their descendants.

But there is another more theological reason, to which John Calvin draws attention at the start of his commentary on Joshua.[3] He attributes their failure to press the conquest to these boundaries to their sloth, which was the product of unbelief. The liberality that God was offering them they refused to appropriate. Indeed, the full fruition of what God promised had to wait for its completion until Messiah came. Just as Christ offers a rest superior to that achieved by Joshua, so he offers a kingdom more glorious in its extent than any earthly empire ever has been or could be. That great land mass could have been Israel's had she risen to the challenge in faith and obedience, but like them we know only too well what it is to settle for the attainable and, doubtless, to miss vast dimensions of God's potential grace. Because there is never any shortage of power or depletion of God's purpose on his part, it must be true that none of us has less of God and his promised blessings than we truly desire.

The Conquest (v. 5a)

The promise of verse 5a is particularly personal to Joshua. It is a commitment of limitless divine power to overcome all merely human and therefore merely transitory and mortal opposition. No man can stand in opposition to God. But as Joshua viewed the prospect facing him, the innumerable tribal groups and city-states that occupied the land, their security and wealth, their cutting-edge technology and powerful war machines, he could surely be forgiven for thinking that this was "mission impossible." But with the promises of God, he was more than fully equipped to accomplish God's purposes. The parallels are striking with our contemporary challenges. The citadels of atheistic materialism and reductionist psychology seem impregnable. Indeed they are to human beings, but "if God is for us, who can be against us?" (Romans 8:31). The answer is that there are many enemies—tribulation, distress, persecution, famine, nakedness, danger, and sword, to name a few (Romans 8:35). Yet "in all these things we are more than conquerors through him who loved us" (Romans 8:37). Nothing can separate his people from the love of Jesus, and nothing can stand in the way of the fulfillment of his purposes. In the words of Horatius Bonar (1808–1889) in his hymn "Blessed Be God, Our God":

> Blessed be God, our God,
> Who gave for us His well-beloved Son,
> The gift of gifts, all other gifts in one;
> Blessed be God our God!
>
> Who shall condemn us now?
> Since Christ has died, and risen, and gone above,
> For us to plead at the right hand of Love;
> Who shall condemn us now?
>
> The victory is ours!
> For us in might came forth the mighty one;
> For us he fought the fight, the triumph won:
> The victory is ours![4]

The Presence (v. 5b)

Here is the greatest promise of all, which undergirds everything else the Lord has said. When God had threatened to withdraw his presence from his people after the incident of the golden calf, Moses had pleaded eloquently and persuasively that if God were to desert his people they would lose everything that was distinctive about them (Exodus 33:12–16). This was what made Israel unique. And now God graciously assures Joshua that this blessing will be his as well. He will never let him down and will never let him go—an assurance that is equally our own, sealed with the blood of Christ's cross. It is a wonderful strength to know that the Lord is more committed to his people than we ever can be to him. "Behold, I am with you always, to the end of the age" (Matthew 28:20) is still Christ's promise to his missionary church.

By Commands (vv. 6–9)

Personal Courage

We show that we really believe God's promises only when we begin to obey his commands. So three more times God exhorts his agent to "be strong and (very) courageous" (vv. 6, 7, 9). At the end of the chapter (v. 18), even the people are saying the same words to him. Clearly Joshua is no omnicompetent superhero. The same command had already been issued three times in Deuteronomy. And now, on the verge of Jordan, it would not be at all surprising if his knees were knocking and if the people were aware of it. There is no Moses now to fall back on. There is a good and glorious prize ahead—a land flowing with milk and honey—but the prospect of actually fighting the Canaanites with an almost untried army was terrifying. Moreover, Joshua knew only too well the weaknesses and fickleness of his people. Even God had spoken about giving them up! So we may certainly not claim any superiority over Joshua in these verses, as though he ought not to have needed the repeated exhortations. What we often tend to regard as natural courage is perhaps, in the last analysis, a self-discipline that resolves to overcome our all too natural fear in order to achieve a greater good. "You shall cause this people to inherit the land" (v. 6) is the promise, which generates the courage to obey.

Personal Faith

But while the will is certainly involved, the courage that Joshua is called to exercise is of divine origin, generated by the divine word. In God's economy there are no imperatives without indicatives, no commands without teaching as to how those commands can be obeyed and what it means actively to trust God's promises. Here is no exception. Verse 7 tells us that strength and courage are directly dependent on careful, detailed obedience to the written word of Yahweh, in the Law given to Moses. Joshua is to be under the authority of God, mediated by his written word, as is every believer who has become the recipient of direct revelation through the Bible writers. In this sense Joshua stands with us and for us as we face the spiritual battles and challenges of our time in history.

Notice what this personal faith looks like—an unswerving devotion to practice in detail everything God has commanded. Obedience like that keeps the channels of grace open, so that goals are achieved, ministries are effective, and God's purposes get fulfilled. In turn that means a deep and detailed acquaintance with the content of God's revelation. Day and night it is to be the subject of Joshua's meditation (v. 8). Clearly this cannot mean that he did nothing but study God's Law; he was a man of immense action and energy. But nothing is excluded from the comprehensive Hebraism "day and night"; it means there is never a moment when, whatever decision has to be made, the book of God is not in the driver's seat. It is to be constantly read aloud to Joshua and to others, constantly rehearsed and remembered, and constantly obeyed in action that is meticulous and enthusiastic (v. 8). Unswerving and unconditional obedience to the Lord's will is the guarantee of prosperity and success, which has nothing to do with the size of Joshua's bank balance and everything to do with the purposes of the living God being fulfilled. Mission impossible will then become mission accomplished.

If this was the case when only five of the sixty-six books of the Bible were as yet committed to writing, how much more must it be so for Christian believers who have been given the full and complete revelation? And yet, in the midst of all the confusion and debate about how the contemporary church is to meet the challenges of this generation, how little we hear about the centrality of daily, disciplined, and detailed obedience to all that the Lord has spoken in his word of truth! The quest for the bizarre and unusual, through visions, dreams, and "prophecies," has taken over the central place in many congregations today. Biblical teaching, we are told, is old hat, out-of-date, boring, ineffective. But "faith comes from hearing, and hearing through the word of Christ" (Romans 10:17). Without that word there will be no lasting faith. Without faith there will be no obedience. Without obedience there will be no fundamental change, no gospel advance. Accepting an alternative to the centrality of Scripture, in the church and in the Christian, producing fear and dismay, is forbidden to Joshua in verse 9. Such alternatives are not hard to find in the western church as major denominations continue to turn their backs on God's revealed Word and to embrace a compromise arrangement with the sinful world.

Personal Action

If God in his kindness has shown his people how we are to live in relationship to him, then obedience that is active, and not merely intellectual assent, is the only way to appropriate his goodness. If we want to know God's promises in practice and experience their growing potential in our lives, we must obey God's commands. That is what the life of faith is all about. The promises of God are unconditional in terms of God's own commitment, but their enjoyment depends upon our detailed obedience, and that means faith, which shows itself in works (James 2:21–26). Suppose you are given a check for 1,000 dollars. It is unconditional. It has the signature of the person who has written it. He has the money in his account to meet it. It's all there, with no condition entailed, except that you act in faith and go to the bank to cash it. When you believe that everything is above board and genuine, you enter into the promise by cashing the check, and the money is yours. But you don't get the benefit of the 1,000 dollars by framing the check, putting it up on your wall, and looking at it from time to time.

Similarly, we shall not get far in our Christian discipleship by listening to God's Word but never acting on it. All that will happen is that our hearts will harden (Psalm 95:7ff.). Knowing and walking with God requires faith and a willingness to act within the terms of the contract or agreement. And we have seen that those terms are trust and obedience. Martin Luther used to define faith as saying, "Yes, this is for me." That is the lesson we are being taught here, as Joshua was. We are called to say yes to God's resources—his grace and power, his constant presence—and appropriate them to the exact point of our conscious need. That is the source of strength and courage. "Be strong in the Lord and in the strength of his might" (Ephesians 6:10). "Be strengthened by the grace that is in Christ Jesus" (2 Timothy 2:1). "I can do all things through him who strengthens me" (Philippians 4:13).

Faith responds to promise by action. I can move forward through Christ. He is the dynamic, the energy, and he will take me where he wants me to be, if I trust him. Faith does not fear and give up. Faith does not underestimate the enemy and relax. Faith watches and prays, "Lord, help me now. Give me your courage, your strength to help in this time of my need." But this is faith in Christ as revealed in his Word, not faith in faith! Even well-taught congregations need to beware of an intellectualism that is theologically accurate and exact but never translates into active obedience, which is costly and totally dependent upon God.

Joshua Commissions Israel (1:10–18)

The first sign of Joshua's active faith and obedience appears in his unquestioning relay of God's word to the people through their tribal leaders in verses 10, 11. The instructions are very practical, and everyone is to be involved. They need food prepared for the crossing because in three days they will enter the land to take possession of it. Probably at this time Joshua does not know in detail how this crossing is to be achieved. He would certainly have known what we, the readers, are not made aware of until 3:15, that the river "overflows all its banks throughout the time of harvest." That is yet another impossible ingredient in a growingly terrifying commission. But the promise is in the driver's seat. It is "the land that the LORD your God is giving you to possess" (1:11). If Yahweh says that now is the time to go forward and cross the river, it is!

The final part of the chapter deals with Joshua's special instructions to the two and a half tribes who will settle east of the river in the lands that had been taken from Sihon and Og, kings of the Moabites (see Numbers 21:21–35). Moses had granted them permission to occupy this good grazing country provided they agree to join forces with the other tribes when they invaded Canaan (Numbers 32), and it is this recorded agreement, which Joshua and Eleazar had witnessed, to which he now recalls them. Their families could stay behind in what came to be called Gilead, but their fighting men are to be committed to the conquest (Joshua 1:14).

The last three verses of the chapter underline for us how God is already fulfilling his promises to Joshua. There is not only no opposition to his leadership, as promised in verse 5a, but not a whiff of resentment at the transfer of leadership. Indeed, not only do they affirm their unquestioning loyalty to Joshua as the new leader, they even agree that whoever rebels against his commands will be "put to death" (v. 18). There are, however, two provisos, each introduced in English by the word "only." In verse 17 we read, "only may the LORD your God be with you," and in verse 18, "only be strong and courageous." The first is covered by faith in the already expressed promises of God and the second by Joshua's commitment to do everything according to God's word. This concludes a very auspicious start to Joshua's ministry. God is with him. The people are with him. Plans are already afoot to cross the river, and soon they will be at Jericho, the fortress city that guards the entry to the land of promise. All this is guided and orchestrated by God himself. He is the central character of this chapter, as he is of the whole enterprise that the book will go on to describe.

Of course, we are not Joshua, and we cannot put ourselves precisely in his shoes. But as Jesus mediates to us, his rescued people, the mind and will of the unseen Father, through his teaching we do stand in a similar position—dependent on God's word to lead us and called to a life of faith and obedience. We all know what it is to need courage for an unseen future and faith in God's promises to generate obedience to his commands. What strikes me in this chapter is the divine urgency about it all. This day has been a long time coming, but when it dawns, there is no room for delay. Our problem is that we often fail to act as we know we should because we do not believe sufficiently to launch out on the bare word of our promising God. Yet nothing can be more certain or more secure. I'm not talking about bright ideas we have thought up or notions we like to entertain but about a clear word of God from Scripture. When God applies his word to our lives in regard to something he is calling us to do, we must begin to do it, in the strength that he supplies, as soon as we can. Our temptation is to wait and then ask for further light, without acting on the light he has already given us. But all I need to do for my heart to harden, after God has spoken his word, is . . . nothing! All progress in our discipleship begins by God speaking with clarity (and often persistence) through the Scriptures, commanding and promising, and then the Spirit of God applying that word of truth so relevantly and potently that we cannot escape its demand. This is the purpose of God's commission—a life that trusts and obeys, which is a life that he can use.

3

Inside Enemy Territory

JOSHUA 2:1–24

IT IS OFTEN SAID that the United States and Great Britain are two nations divided by a common language. In fact, cultural differences usually run deeper than their linguistic delineation, and presuppositions—certainly not articulated and often not even realized—dictate what we think we are hearing as much as what we think we are saying. But when the cultures are diametrically different, when not only the vocabulary but the very mind-set of the other side is bewilderingly opaque, we need firsthand testimony of what is actually going on and careful interpretation of what is being assumed. Enter the two spies of verse 1.

Joshua faces a quandary. Still based in Shittim (a Hebrew word for the wood from acacia trees) where Israel had succumbed to idolatry and immorality with the Baal of Peor and its Moabite devotees (Numbers 25:1ff.), Joshua is aware that across the Jordan the Canaanite city of Jericho stands, walled and defended, like a sentinel to bar Israel's progress into the land. As yet, though, he has no strategy for its conquest. He has divine assurance that God will most certainly give them "every place that the sole of your foot will tread upon . . . just as I promised to Moses" (Joshua 1:3), but no instructions as to how to defeat Jericho. So, like the good general he is in process of becoming, he does as Moses did and sends out spies (not twelve but two) on a reconnaissance mission of the land, "especially Jericho," which is challenge number one. This is wisdom rather than faithlessness, of which some accuse Joshua.

Consider the situation. Jericho is a well-defended garrison with trained troops in residence. First Israel has to cross the Jordan, in flood season, and then face an apparently impregnable citadel. Their position will be extremely vulnerable—an enemy in front of them and a river in full flood behind them.

In the absence of any direct divine instruction, Joshua is doing the responsible thing in sending out his scouts. He is using the means that are at his disposal. That is not an unspiritual course of action. Indeed, to pray without using the means that God has given us is almost as foolish as to use the means without praying. The two need to be combined together in all our battles. This was a lesson Israel learned throughout her history, finally enshrined in the post-exilic Psalm 126 celebrating the return of the captives to Zion. The situation is met with prayer—"Restore our fortunes, O Lord, like streams in the Negeb!" (Psalm 126:4)—but that has to be accompanied by dedicated action—"Those who sow in tears shall reap with shouts of joy" (Psalm 126:5). Praying and sowing belong together. So here Joshua's commonsense approach is evidence that he has great faith in the promises of God and not at all the opposite.

God's Unlikely Choice

The focus shifts, then, to Jericho and especially to one of its citizens, Rahab, a prostitute (v. 1), whose house the spies enter. Some translations and commentators want to designate her an "innkeeper," following the later rabbinic insistence that she be held in reverence by the Jews. Calvin's comment is typically forthright. "It is indeed a regular practice with the Rabbins [sic] when they would consult for the honor of their nation, presumptuously to wrest Scripture and give a different turn by their fictions to anything that seems not quite reputable."[1] Certainly the New Testament holds Rahab in great repute as a woman of faith in Hebrews 11:31 and James 2:25, but both references clearly refer to her as a prostitute. Her rescue is far more to the glory of God than any attempted whitewashing of her behavior. The point is that an immoral, pagan woman would never have been considered as a candidate for God's rescuing grace in the midst of the judgment that he was about to inflict on her city. Yet she and her family are the ones who are rescued when Jericho is destroyed, an example of God's compassion and mercy in response to faith. And they were not only rescued and brought into the covenant community but also were given an honored place in the genealogy of the Lord Jesus Christ (Matthew 1:5).

This is one of the great salvation stories of the Old Testament. Initially everything is stacked against Rahab. She has no family background of a knowledge of the living God. She lives as a pagan in a thoroughly pagan city. She is known as a prostitute, making her living in a way that is a constant offense against God. The Bible doesn't say this is the worst of sins because it doesn't deal in comparative evaluations as some Christians seem to do. But it certainly sees sin as alienating the sinner from a holy God, making every human being (for we are all sinners) subject to God's condemnation and righteous judgment. Yet this is the woman whom God chooses to rescue by what seems an almost accidental sequence of circumstances. She receives the spies and hides them from the king's investigation squad (vv. 2–4). The spies seem rather inept since they are spotted almost as soon as they enter the city (v. 2). But the king's men are equally naive since they are sent on a wild goose chase after the spies by Rahab's lies (vv. 4–7), while all the time their quarry lies hidden under the stalks of flax on Rahab's roof.

Clearly Rahab set no great store on honesty of speech. Her denial of knowledge about the spies and deliberate misleading of the pursuers seem both fluent and without any pangs of conscience. She is, after all, a pagan woman. But not surprisingly these verses have raised a considerable ethical debate, which is given a detailed treatment by David M. Howard in his very valuable commentary.[2] Her lies are neither condemned, nor are they commended in the text. The narrative does not teach that lying is justifiable or that the end justifies the means. Rather Rahab seems to have been trapped in a moral choice in which either option would involve sin. Either she could have disclosed the spies and almost certainly brought about their execution, or she could have denied that she knew their whereabouts, which was clearly untrue. A lie is a distortion or denial of the truth with the intention to deceive, and that is clearly what Rahab did. Probably it came quite naturally to her since, like us, she was a fallen human being living in a fallen world, as we need to remember before we are too eager to point the finger.

She had to choose the lesser of two evils, and as far as she was concerned that meant lying to save the spies' lives. It was, of course, motivated also by her growing spiritual awareness, as the next few verses show, but that does not exonerate her from her sin. All false witness calls out the judgment of God who is the Truth. So we cannot say that God saved her because she saved the spies. As James points out, that high-risk strategy constituted the "works" that demonstrated the reality of her faith (James 2:25). But it was her faith that saved her and her family. God did not need Rahab's lie to protect the life of his men. Had she told the truth, God could well have worked in other ways to deliver the spies, as the rest of the Bible frequently illustrates. God has total ability to confuse and redirect those who are seeking to abort his purposes. But this is only speculation. Rahab was being herself. Lying came naturally to her, as it does to every sinner. No one would have imagined that she could become the object of God's saving grace. But her story is wonderful evidence that no one is beyond the reach of divine mercy.

Rahab's Unlikely Faith

Undoubtedly, the focus of this wonderful chapter lies on Rahab's amazing confession in verses 9–11. This speech reveals a situation that not even the most optimistic Israelite could have imagined. Jericho, that impossible barrier to the people of God, is in fact already a defeated foe. Before the first feet are placed in the Jordan to bring the people into the land, the hearts of the inhabitants of Jericho are melting in fear (v. 9). The agent of that defeat is the word about what God has already done for his people and how this reveals his character. Look at Rahab's testimony. "I know that the LORD [Yahweh—the covenant name of God] has given you the land" (v. 9). How does she know? By what she and her fellow citizens have heard (v. 10) concerning the exodus from Egypt, the miraculous crossing of the Red Sea, and the destruction of Sihon and Og. That is what has caused hearts in Jericho to melt and their courage to fail. But more than past progress or military victories is involved, at least in Rahab's case. She traces these events back not to any inherent superiority of the sons of Abraham but to the reality she confesses in verse 11: "The LORD your God, he is God in the heavens above and on the earth beneath." For Rahab there is nowhere where God is not God, including Jericho.

The truth of who God is and what he has done for his people has already penetrated Jericho, and when the word of God gets into enemy territory, only two reactions are possible. Either there is faith in the greatness of the Lord and a casting of oneself entirely on his mercy (vv. 12, 13), or there is fear, which determines to resist God's supremacy, challenge his will, and continue to fight against his purposes. We shall meet the same pattern on at least three other occasions in the book. The same language is used in 5:1 regarding "all the kings of the Amorites who were beyond the Jordan to the west, and all the kings of the Canaanites who were by the sea." In 9:24 the Gibeonite deception is explained by the same mechanism. Again in 10:1, 2 Adoni-zedek, king of Jerusalem, reacts to the news of what God has done in Jericho and Ai in the same way. The mighty acts of God in Israel's history always serve to reveal the character of Israel's God, and once the uniqueness of his sovereign authority and power over the whole of creation is realized, the reaction can only be submission or resistance. In the face of God's purposes, neutrality is impossible.

Of course, the same is true today. Contemporary attacks on the reasonability of Christian belief often depend on ignoring the historical evidence of Biblical revelation, especially with regard to the incarnation, life, death, and resurrection of the Lord Jesus Christ. If Christianity can be reduced to religious speculation or an ethical code, it can be easily dismissed, which explains why the anti-supernatural and anti-historical destructive Biblical criticism of the past 150 years has emptied the churches of the western world. But the Biblical revelation is gloriously and stubbornly historical, which we must never tire of asserting. "The Word became flesh and dwelt [literally, pitched his tent] among us" (John 1:14)—that is a historical statement. Certainly it contains an explanation of the event that may be contested, but the factual existence of Jesus of Nazareth on the pages of history is beyond dispute. Refusal to acknowledge that Jesus Christ is Lord does not lead to neutrality; ultimately it leads to fear that fans the flames of denial and resistance.

Rahab has no other explanation for the astonishing event of the exodus and all that flowed from it, even though she seems a most unlikely candidate to come to faith in Israel's God and appears to stand entirely alone among her fellow citizens in Jericho. The sheer historical force of what God has done and what he will yet do generates within her the faith that is prepared to risk her life in order to save it and the lives of her family (vv. 12, 13). She is prepared to cut herself off from her background, to risk being charged as a traitor, and to do everything she can to help the spies because of her new faith-allegiance to the only true and living God. All her future now depends on this God; so she casts herself upon his mercy and on the faithfulness of his representatives (v. 14). Because it is the Lord who is giving his people the land, they will replicate his faithful character in the way in which they deal with this newest convert and her extended family.

Faith's Unlikely Test

Rahab's eventual rescue depends not only on her initial confession of faith leading her to seek God's mercy, but on her continuing obedience to the instructions that the spies give her about the scarlet cord (v. 18). This is why she is such an attractive example for James to use in his New Testament letter. In that key passage relating faith and deeds (James 2:14–26), James several times asserts their indivisibility. "Faith by itself, if it does not have works, is dead" (James 2:17). "I will show you my faith by my works" (James 2:18). Abraham's "faith was active along with his works, and faith was completed by his works" (James 2:22), in his being prepared to offer up his son Isaac. "You see that a person is justified by works and not by faith alone" (James 2:24). "Faith apart from works is dead" (James 2:26). Rahab is the other example James uses of this "faith revealed in actions" principle. The primary significant action is her provision for the spies and their protection, but the life of faith is always to be expressed in the activities of obedience. Indeed, obedience to what God commands is the only credible confirmation of belief in what he provides.

The obligation laid on her by the spies is to hang a scarlet cord in the window, through which she will let them down by rope to escape the city, since "her house was built into the city wall" (v. 15). It seems unlikely that the scarlet cord was the escape rope since verse 18 calls it "*this* scarlet cord," implying that the spies give it to her. Also different Hebrew words are used for "rope" in verse 15 and "cord" in verse 18. Woudstra suggests that they would have brought it with them, as they "probably came prepared for various eventualities."[3] The reason is practical. Expecting to attack the city by siege and bombardment, the Israelite forces would need to identify clearly the house whose occupants are to be spared. They will be faithful to their rescue promise provided Rahab keeps the terms of the agreement, gathering all her family into the house marked by the scarlet cord (vv. 17–20). Rahab agrees to the terms, the spies escape through the window, down the city wall, and make for the cover of the hills (v. 21). The scarlet cord remains tied in the window.

Many commentators have seen the scarlet cord as a replication of God's deliverance of Israel from Egypt. Back in Exodus 12, the only houses that were saved from the destructive judgment of the firstborn when God passed through the land were those where the shelter of the Passover lamb was demonstrated by its blood applied to the sides and tops of the doorframes. "The blood shall be a sign for you [instead of you], on the houses where you are. And when I see the blood, I will pass over you . . ." (Exodus 12:13). The color of Rahab's cord, scarlet, has sometimes been taken to illustrate that deliverance is only possible through the blood of sacrifice, projecting forward to the New Testament reality of rescue solely through Christ's blood shed on the cross. Taking seriously the unity of the sixty-six books of the Scriptures, we rightly identify recurring patterns or types of God's dealings with his people at different stages of redemption history. The danger is that connections become imaginative and fanciful rather than real and then become an imposition on the passage rather than an exposition of its significance. In this case the color alone would seem to be a weak ground on which to justify a typological link to the cross. But the principle of obedience as the outward expression of inner faith and even more the dependence on God's mercy as a guarantee for salvation are certainly principles that have New Testament currency, as we have already seen in James.[4]

To Rahab, it may have seemed strange to have to tie a red cord in her window, but she did it for what it symbolized of her faith in and obedience to Yahweh, Israel's God, not because the object itself had any greater power than that of a sign of unseen realities. Perhaps a useful reminder to us is the need to continue in trust and obedience even when we cannot see why it should be in certain terms or how things will work out. For the Christian believer, that same mercy of God is conveyed to us through Christ's death on the cross as our Passover lamb, under whose blood we find shelter from God's righteous wrath (1 Corinthians 5:7). But the cross is still the foolish stumbling-block it was to the Greeks and Jews of sophisticated first-century Corinth (1 Corinthians 1:23). "For the word of the cross is folly to those who are perishing, but to us who are being saved it is the power of God" (1 Corinthians 1:18). That is the urgent issue that the Rahab narrative presents to us.

The chapter ends (vv. 22–24) where it began, with the spies. The plan to evade their pursuers is successful, as is their crossing of the Jordan, and their consequent report to Joshua is triumphant. "Truly the LORD has given all the land into our hands. And also, all the inhabitants of the land melt away because of us" (v. 24). It is a striking contrast to the negativity of the ten spies and their report in Numbers 13—we came, we saw, we cannot. How different now and how like the content of the report that Caleb and Joshua had brought back to Moses! These two spies had not traveled extensively through the land or visited its settlements. Rather, their conviction was that if God could do this in Jericho, there could be no limit to what he would do in the rest of the land. It's a good lesson for us to bring away from this exciting chapter. As the church of Jesus Christ, we are never so strong as when we are recognizing and rejoicing in the sovereign grace of God.

If God can rescue a Rahab, no one is beyond his reach or his concern. He is no respecter of persons. This should teach us not to categorize our as yet unbelieving family, friends, or acquaintances according to how likely we think they will respond to the good news of grace. God is at work behind the scenes. The city of Jericho presented itself as a hard nut to crack, but within its shell it had already crumbled. So we should never write off anyone because of their background or record. God's delight is to save sinners. "The Son of Man came to seek and to save the lost" (Luke 19:10). "This man receives sinners and eats with them" (Luke 15:2). We must not fall for the lie that Christianity is for a few people who have a religious kink in their inadequate personalities. The truth of God is for every man and every woman, all made in his image, all needing to be redeemed and restored. There is no life so impervious that God's grace cannot break into it in transforming power. But neither must we ever imagine that the opposition is invincible. God's word can get into territory that the enemy holds, and when that word of God begins to work, strong citadels become vulnerable. The dynamic lies in the power of the Holy

Spirit taking the word of God and so penetrating minds and hearts that people cannot escape from God's truth, faith or fear being the alternative outcomes.

This chapter is a clarion call to have confidence in the mercy and grace of our God, in the gospel of his saving acts. When that is rooted deeply in us, we shall both pray and expect God to work—not one or the other but both. It means that we shall give weight to the word of the Lord over against all other human factors. In our technical and technique-dominated culture we are not short of sociological analysis about why Christianity is in decline in the twenty-first-century Western world. There may be considerable help in such diagnoses, but they do not provide a remedy. The answer lies in the Word of God in the hands of the Spirit of God and in the prayerful obedience of God's people. There is no reason why the Word of God should not "speed ahead and be honored" today (2 Thessalonians 3:1). God has conquered many Jerichos down the centuries and totally transformed situations, and he is well able to do it again. Perhaps he is waiting for us, his people, to demonstrate our faith in obedience and trust by dependent prayer. However, there is no doubt that God is mightily at work across the planet. "In the whole world [the gospel] is bearing fruit and increasing" (Colossians 1:6). He is rescuing Rahabs and their families, pulling down Satan's strongholds, calling whoever will to come and take shelter under the provision of the sacrificial death of his Son upon the cross.

4

Wonders among You

JOSHUA 3:1–17

THE TITLE I HAVE GIVEN THIS CHAPTER is a quotation from verse 5 where Joshua calls the people to renewed consecration: "for tomorrow the LORD will do wonders among you." The NIV translates this as "amazing things." Literally they are "things to be astounded at." All of this helps us catch the ethos of the chapter in the sense of amazement and awe at the way in which God provides a way through the Jordan for his people to enter the land. This is a major event in Israel's story seen in the promise given to Abram so long ago: "To your offspring I will give this land" (Genesis 12:7). Now at last they are moving into its fulfillment. It is also a major stepping-stone in salvation-history as the next stage in God's covenant relationship with Israel swings into action. Whatever we learn from this chapter and the next, we must never lose sight of the wonder of God's mighty acts and never stop recalling and proclaiming them.

Chapters 3, 4 of Joshua clearly belong together, dealing with the details of the crossing of the Jordan and its memorialization. But to a cursory reader the text can appear somewhat repetitive and even confusing. Part of this is intentional. The verb "to cross" is used no fewer than twenty-two times.[1] Also, the storyteller's technique sometimes involves returning to a part of the narrative that he closed earlier, so he can develop the instructional purpose of his writing. Moreover, there is a pattern to the units that form the whole. First, God takes the initiative by giving his word and commandments to Joshua. Next Joshua passes on the word of the Lord to the people, informing them of what God is going to do. Then the writer tells us just how God fulfills what he has promised, and at the end of each section there is a linking summary looking back to God's faithful fulfillment and forward to the next stage of the story line. In this way the excitement and astonishment are sustained as the details of the actual historical events are carefully described and unpacked. So in chapter 3 we have the preparations that the people had to make in order to cross the river, followed by the crossing itself and the astounding way God brought it about. Chapter 4 will similarly divide into two, with the focus of the lifting of the memorial stones from the riverbed being followed by the memorial at Gilgal.

Preparing for a Miracle

Behind the matter-of-fact description of verse 1, we are surely meant to sense the mixture of anticipation, excitement, and suspense that flowed through the camp. They have spent considerable time at Shittim, and now, at last, they are on the move, toward the river. But as yet there is no word about how it is to be crossed. So there is a three-day pause (v. 2), perhaps to allow the impossibility of what is about to happen, from a purely human point of view, to sink really deeply into their consciousness. Seeming delays frequently have the greater purpose of refining and deepening our faith. So we must not underestimate the challenge that the river presents to them. A little later (v. 15), there is a parenthetical comment, almost as though it is incidental, about an aspect of the situation that must have made a huge impact on them—"now the Jordan overflows all its banks throughout the time of harvest." This is not a babbling brook in which to paddle. It is a fast-flowing, swirling flood, probably between ten and twelve feet deep at this season and at this point. Fording or swimming are out of the question. Rafts are an impossibility, and engineering is not yet able to excavate a subterranean passageway. Remember too that this is a whole nation—wives and children, animals and baggage—on the move, with no obvious way to cross the swollen torrent. But they are on the move because God says to move forward. The command had been given in 1:2, and as soon as the spies returned, Joshua began to obey. They don't know how it will happen, but they take the next logical step forward in obedience to what God has already said and leave the outcome with him. This is a great lesson on how to live Christianly, in trust and obedience.

Alexander MacLaren,[2] whose expository thoughts have stimulated generations of Bible preachers since he ministered at Union Chapel in Manchester for over forty years, once said, "God often opens his hand one finger at a time." That is what is happening here. It is enough to see the next step and to trust God for what we cannot see yet. Indeed, it is the essence of true faith to trust where we cannot see, "for we walk by faith, not by sight" (2 Corinthians 5:7). The point is memorably made in Isaiah's commentary on the third

Servant Song where we see the suffering servant resolutely committing himself to God's will, trusting in his constant support and ultimate vindication through all the devastation of pain and grief. "Who among you fears the Lord and obeys the voice of his servant? Let him who walks in darkness and has no light trust in the name of the Lord and rely on his God" (Isaiah 50:10). This is a helpful reminder that two ingredients can and do coexist—walking in darkness and trusting in the Lord's name (his nature).

At last the instructions are given (v. 3). The focal point is to be the ark of the covenant, because this is the symbol of the Lord's presence among his people, here in the role of leader and guide. God's ark is carried, it is true, by human agents, but the one whose presence it symbolizes is the one who gives instructions to the bearers. Israel's responsibility is to follow. Again this provides us with a continuing principle for covenant fellowship. It is not our role to second-guess what God will do, any more than it is to argue about how he could possibly do it. We have to follow. Faith gathers up all our cares and anxieties in the knowledge that he has taken the responsibility for our future and every step ahead of us, and faith leaves it all with God (see Psalm 55:22; 1 Peter 5:7). We must never give up what we do know because of what we don't. Even though we don't know how God's faithfulness and power will be revealed or how he will order our circumstances, what we do know is that he is our God, committed to us by his unbreakable covenant promise, and "his love is as great as his power and knows neither measure nor end."[3]

In the verses that follow (vv. 4–6) our attention is drawn to three specific ingredients of their faithful waiting for and on God. The first is their submission to his instructions, which meant looking to the ark and not at the river. Within the gold-covered ark were the tablets of the Law, the covenant that God had made with his people—the outward and visible sign of the very terms on which God lived in the midst of his people. They had to keep their distance (v. 4) for reasons of visibility, but also perhaps as a reminder that God is holy and that sinners cannot freely come within the range of his presence. The detailed instructions for the setting up of the tabernacle contain similar prohibitions.

Secondly, they are to "consecrate" themselves (v. 5). In Exodus 19:10 this involved washing of garments as well as inner concentration and renewed dependence on God. They are about to have a totally new experience (Joshua 3:4b); so they have to be dedicated to God in submission and follow about half a mile back, with their eyes focused on the gold-covered ark. God does his wonders for people who are consecrated to him. And then, thirdly, there has to be specific obedience (v. 6). The priests exemplify this.

They do what Joshua tells them to do. There is a sanctity and deliberation about the whole process that is often lacking in our contemporary discipleship. We don't want to wait. Sometimes we don't want to set our lives apart to the Lord for his exclusive use. Often we don't want to allow any sort of distance because we imagine that we already know the way and don't need step-by-step guidance. These verses may well challenge us to some profound reassessments of our daily discipleship, especially in our instant generation where we want everything sorted out and guaranteed before we start. Perhaps this is why wonderful manifestations of God's glory are comparatively rare among us. This chapter reminds us that we are not writing the agenda. That is the Lord's prerogative. What he requires from us is submissive obedience that desires his glory rather than our own and is content to fulfill whatever role he is pleased to assign to us.

Understanding God's Ways

The past tense at the beginning of verse 7 ("said") probably places this more detailed instruction before the events we have just witnessed. The Lord had already said these words to his servant, as the basis for verses 3–6. Clearly he revealed more to Joshua than is recorded in these verses, but the emphasis is on his purposes in orchestrating events in this way. For Joshua, it is the further confirmation of the promises of chapter 1 that the Lord will indeed be with him as he was with Moses, which carries the assurance to the nation that he is certainly the divinely appointed successor as God "begin[s] to exalt" him (v. 7) in their estimation. For Israel it will be proof "that the living God is among you" and consequent upon that the assurance that "he will without fail drive out from before you the Canaanites" and other pagan peoples in the land (v. 10). He is going to part the waters of the Jordan to enable them to cross into the promised land, just as he parted the waters of the Red Sea to enable their exodus from Egypt (Exodus 14). But there is more to it than that. He could have brought them over in the dry season or at a different point where the fords would be comparatively shallow. But God chose the most improbable time and location because his deeper purpose was to develop his people's trust in him. They come into the land physically solely because of the miracle that is about to be described, and this is designed to teach them the essential principle that only by the same supernatural, divine power of their covenant Lord will the whole land be conquered and become their possession.

The priests, carrying the ark, are to advance to the river's edge and "stand still" there (v. 8). The people are now told that the ark of the Lord will be their trailblazer, going over the Jordan ahead of them. They will literally have to follow. They are taking the first steps in the long journey that will lead to the expulsion of the seven tribal groups named in verse 10. That might seem an even more impossible task, but the God who can get his people across the Jordan can most certainly give them the land. Remember too that driving out the nations was an act of righteous judgment. God had foretold to Abraham that his descendants would return to the land of Canaan centuries later when the iniquity of the Amorites had reached its completion (Genesis 15:16). So the Israelites are to be the instrument by which the land is judged and purged of the gross immorality and iniquitous occultism that characterized Canaanite culture. It is because the land belongs to God and because he has purposes of unimaginable grace for Abraham's seed and all the families of the earth that the time for the conquest has now arrived. He is, in practice as well as in affirmation, "the Lord of all the earth" (v. 11).

Finally, in verse 13 the nature of the forthcoming wonder, a manifestation of supernatural, creative power, is described. As soon as the priests' feet touch the river's flow, the waters "shall be cut off from flowing." For the first time we, the readers, are given a glimpse of what God is about to do, and it is awesome. By definition all miracles are extraordinary, but this is so beyond human ability or comprehension that it can have no explanation except divine power. The fact that it is announced before it happens is further confirmation of its divine origin. There is nothing to indicate coincidence or natural causes in this text. Trying to imagine the scene is stretching, but trying to account for it in human terms is impossible. As so often, John Calvin's comments are an enormous help to us. He writes, "The title Lord of all the earth here applied to God is not insignificant, but extols his powers above all the elements of nature, in order that the Israelites, considering how seas and rivers are subject to his dominion, might have no doubt that the waters, though naturally liquid, would become stable in obedience to his word."[4]

Experiencing the Impossible

We should certainly not underestimate the courage and faith of the priests as they advanced toward the river carrying the ark. The banks had been submerged by the overflowing river. They could so easily lose their footing, stumble into a hole, or be swept away by the current. But the greater the obstacles that faith encounters, the greater is the victory and assurance that come from continuing to act in trust and obedience. Verses 14, 15 record the facts so there can be no doubt as to what actually took place. Pressing on in faith and obedience, the priests reached the river. Nothing had changed. The river was still in full flood. But as soon as they took the next step of obedience and put their feet in the stream, the promised miracle occurred, exactly as predicted, and the ark went on into the river and "stood firmly on dry ground in the midst of the Jordan" (v. 17). So the whole nation passed over in safety as the waters remained heaped up. "There cannot be a doubt that this wonderful sight must have been received with feelings of fear, leading the Israelites more directly to acknowledge that they were saved in the midst of death. For what was that collected heap but a grave in which the whole multitude would have been buried, had the waters resumed their naturally liquid state?"[5]

Adam, the city beside Zarethan (v. 16), is thought to be about twenty miles upstream from Jericho, which would have left a very wide crossing for the whole nation to utilize. Even so it must have taken several hours at least to accomplish the crossing. The end of the chapter focuses attention on the centrality of the ark in the whole supernatural event. While the ark is in the river and the priests stand firmly on dry ground, the nation is safe, and so they swarm across. Don't you think spies from Jericho, doubtless hidden in the hills, would have rushed home that day to talk about seeing all those people crossing the impossible barrier on the dry riverbed? God does wonders for his people, and what he promises by his word, he accomplishes by his power and so seals his predictions by his actions. There could not be a more magnificent, God-glorifying beginning to the conquest of the land.

But what are the implications of the text for twenty-first-century Christian readers? I remember a song from my youth:

> Got any rivers you think are uncrossable?
> Got any mountains you can't tunnel through?
> God specializes in things thought impossible.
> He does the things others cannot do.

Yes, that is our God. He can and does perform miracles. But I want to add, don't presume that your particular set of difficulties will melt away by divine intervention. The fact that God *can* do the impossible does not mean that he always *will*. There is no unconditional promise here that will be valid for all God's people in all the varied challenges and complexities of life in this world. After the Israelites crossed the Jordan, they generally had to use normal human methods to carry on their lives. That particular miracle never recurred; it remains a miracle.

So often we read the Old Testament wrongly and then suffer disappointment, which if repeated can even begin to spell shipwreck for our faith. For example, we rush to interpret the story by looking for some point of similarity or coincidence with our present circumstances. Life will always present difficulties, and sometimes these seem intransigent and insoluble, like a river in full flood barring our way to the fulfillment and enjoyment that we tell ourselves must be God's best for us. We ourselves become the children of Israel in our interpretation of the story, and we put ourselves in their shoes (or sandals) on the brink of our river, claiming that God will miraculously intervene to remove the impassable barrier. But then he doesn't. So we ask why. *Perhaps I am not consecrated enough, or my record of obedience is not impressive enough, or perhaps he isn't really interested in me after all, or perhaps the promises have no real benefit for me.* You can see the perilous downward spiral that can result from this misunderstanding, all because we tried to draw the line directly from a unique salvation-history event for Israel to our everyday, individual experience. That's the wrong line to draw. The question we should be asking first and foremost in an Old Testament narrative like this is, what is God teaching us about God here? That is the strong and direct line from the Biblical text to our own lives, because whatever God reveals of himself in the narrative remains true for us today. His character is eternal and unchanging; so we are to allow the story to instruct us about God before we rush to put ourselves in the picture. The Bible is God's book about God before it is God's book about us. In their excellent introduction to Biblical interpretation, *How to Read the Bible for All Its Worth*, Gordon Fee and Douglas Stewart put it like this: "No Bible narrative was written specifically about you. . . . You can always learn a great deal from these narratives, but you can never assume that God expects you to do exactly the same things that Bible characters did, or have the same things happen to you that happened to them."[6]

It is not therefore a measure of our faith as to whether or not we can convince ourselves that God will part the waters of our "Jordan" by some divine intervention. That may not be his best purpose for us at all. New Testament promises clearly intended for God's people at all times are to be claimed in faithful prayer, expectant that the Lord will be faithful to his word. But we are not at liberty to construct promises of miraculous intervention for ourselves from a narrative like Joshua 3. What then does it have to say to us? The answer is, a very great deal!

It teaches us that this God, our God, is the Lord of Heaven and earth, of time and eternity. He works all things in the history of Planet Earth according to the purpose of his will, and "all things" includes every circumstance of our individual lives. Romans 8:28 is a precious verse often used to make the point: "And we know that for those who love God all things work together for good, for those who are called according to his purpose." But sometimes we fail to set the verse in its immediate context by reading on to verse 29 to see what "his purpose" actually is. We tend to assume that it must be our own well-being and happiness as his dearly loved children. But the next verse shows us that it is richer and deeper than that. "For those whom he foreknew he also predestined to be conformed to the image of his Son" (v. 29). His purpose is to restore the defaced image of God in us, his redeemed human creation, to make us more and more like the Lord Jesus Christ. That is how we are to face our crises and adversities—to see them as the transformation process that God knows we need to become increasingly dependent on him and so to produce the fruit of his life within us. Seeing our lives in that perspective, Joshua 3 is immensely strengthening, both in our understanding of God's purposes and our confidence in his total wisdom and total ability to bring them to a glorious and successful conclusion.

That will also change our perspective on the world around us, in our own moment of time, as we see our little lives caught up in something much greater than our immediate needs or circumstances. We are part of the universal kaleidoscope of the purposes of the sovereign Lord as he carries out the plans by which his eternal kingdom will be revealed and established. And he is the God of the impossible, as this chapter reveals. The tide of anti-God forces may be in full flood in our time and in our place, but it is not outside God's control. The same is true of the overwhelming problems and pressures that may impact any local congregation of God's people or indeed any individual believer. He still makes a way through for those who consecrate themselves to him and who trust and obey him. Perhaps our problem is that we are busily looking for wood to build a raft or are beginning to plan our bridge-building or our tunnel-digging but have lost sight of the God who does amazing things or are too impatient to wait for his will and his way. But the ark, the symbol of God's covenant mercy and faithfulness, still leads us in the person of our Lord Jesus Christ, who has promised never to leave us or forsake us (Hebrews 13:5). We are to follow him, "looking to Jesus, the founder and perfecter of our faith, who for the joy that was set before him endured the cross, despising the shame, and is seated at the right hand of the throne of God. Consider him . . . so that you may not grow weary or fainthearted" (Hebrews 12:2, 3).

For Israel, this is just the first step into the land, the beginning of a long journey to possess what God is giving them. There will be many more challenges, not least Jericho, threatening to bar their progress and to frustrate God's purposes. But nothing can stop the God who made and governs the whole created order, for whom the waters rise and stand in a heap. And that

God is with us, his people, throughout our lives and on into eternity. We need to trust him, and because we trust him, to obey him.

> When I tread the verge of Jordan,
> Bid my anxious fears subside;
> Death of death, and hell's destruction,
> Land me safe on Canaan's side.
> Songs of praises, songs of praises,
> I will ever give to thee;
> I will ever give to thee.[7]

5

A Memorial Forever

JOSHUA 4:1—5:1

REMEMBERING IS AN essential part of Christian discipleship. It is also a profoundly human activity. We remember and celebrate the anniversaries of our births, our marriages, or noteworthy events in the history of our home nation. Partly such times serve as signposts in the passage of time, but they also provide opportunities for reflection and reassessment and perhaps readjustment for the present in the light of the past. Annual ceremonies of remembering those who were killed in the service of their countries during the two world wars of the twentieth century, for example, and in the smaller conflicts since then serve to remind us of the price of freedom and help us honor the sacrifices of those who secured it and call us to its renewed valuation and wise use. The memorial stones taken from the bed of the Jordan and set up at Gilgal were designed to fulfill a similar purpose in the ongoing life of the nation of Israel.

Broadly this passage divides into two sections, of which 4:14 and 5:1 form the reflective summary conclusions. Following R. Polzin's analysis that the first section (4:1–14) is narrated from a vantage point outside of the promised land, whereas the second (4:15—5:1) from within it,[1] David Howard adds the observation that the first evaluative comment shows the effect of the events within Israel (4:14), while the second shows the effects outside Israel.[2] This is a helpful structure within which to work in a chapter that contains elements of backtracking and repetition in its close relationship to the events of chapter 3.

"What Do These Stones Mean to You?"

This question put into the mouths of the hypothetical future generations of Israelite children serves as a unifying theme for our consideration of what actually happened and why. The opening words of 4:1 would seem to be moving the action on, although they are an almost verbatim repetition of 3:17. In fact, we are taken back to what the Lord had already said to Joshua. We need to remember that the distinction between perfect and pluperfect past tenses with which we are familiar in classical and contemporary languages does not exist in Hebrew. So it is perfectly feasible to translate the end of verse 1 as "the Lord had said to Joshua." This helps us maintain the order of events more logically and credibly, and it also links the narrative back to 3:12, where the mysterious choosing of a man from each of the twelve tribes of Israel is now given purpose and significance.

The purpose, revealed in verse 3, is that each man is to take a stone from the middle of the Jordan's bed, where the priests' feet are anchored while the people pass over, and carry it across to the new campsite within the land. This instruction to Joshua is then conveyed to the twelve men who are commanded to fulfill the task (vv. 4, 5). The emphasis is upon the unity of the nation; every tribe is included on equal terms. Although the eventual settlement will see two and a half tribes back east of the Jordan, there is never a hint that the river is to divide the nation. They are one people under their one God. The purpose is for the stones to be a "sign," an always-present pointer to the great miracle by which God has brought them into the land and to the great God who performed it (v. 6a). The language is similar to that used about the Passover in Exodus 12:26, 27, which is to be an annual sign, reminder, or memorial of the miraculous deliverance of God's people from their slavery in Egypt and the execution of God's wrath. Future generations need to know that these things really happened—hence the twelve large stones from the riverbed—but also what they testify about the character and promises of God. Especially significant is the reference to the ark in verse 7, indicating that it was God who was in the midst of the situation with his people to deliver, protect, and guide them, not a remote or distant deity, unlike the gods of the pagans all around them. Twice in verse 7 the point is explained: "the waters of the Jordan were cut off." Look at the stones! There is the evidence. They are a memorial forever. And not just of the crossing but of the covenant Lord, Yahweh, who accomplished it all. As Woudstra comments, "The notion of remembering in Hebrew is more than a calling to mind. It involves a remembering with concern; it also implies living reflection and, where called for, a corresponding degree of action."[3]

In verses 8–10 the theological explanation naturally leads on to the record of obedience, noted twice for its detailed compliance. They did "just as Joshua commanded" and "just as the LORD told Joshua" (v. 8). This is a link to the later comment of verse 14 that "the LORD exalted Joshua in the sight of all Israel" on that day, just as he had promised he would back in 3:7. Verse 9 provides a well-known textual difficulty since it seems to imply a second set of twelve stones "set up . . . in the midst of the Jordan" in addition to those carried to the west bank. Woudstra, Polzin, and other commentators see the stones stood up in the riverbed as marking the very location where the priests had stood and the people had crossed. The Septuagint text, for example, refers to twelve "other" stones. But other commentators suggest that there was one set of stones set up by Joshua initially (as v. 9) to mark the place of the crossing but then taken out of the river once the crossing was complete.[4] However, whether there were stones solely at Gilgal or in addition a corresponding set in the Jordan, visible at low water levels, the narrative is clear about their purpose and the fact that "they are there to this day" (v. 9b). The section concludes with a note that the people crossed over quickly (v. 10b), perhaps because of their natural apprehension that the waters might return, but also to emphasize that there were no hitches or delays. Everything went smoothly, without complications, because the hand of God was at work.

Verses 11–14 serve as a summary of what we have witnessed from 3:1 onward and a reminder of its significance. Here is the Jericho perspective on what has happened, as is hinted by verse 13. "All the people" (v. 11) who had been east of the Jordan are now across the Jordan, confronting Jericho. However, verse 12 shows that this did not include the families of the tribes whose settlement remained to the east—Reuben, Gad, and the half-tribe of Manasseh. Joshua 1:14 has already told us that their families are to remain in the land allotted by Moses (see Numbers 32; Deuteronomy 3:18–20), but that the fighting men are to join their brothers in the conquest of the land across the river. Verse 13 highlights the obedience by the 40,000 warriors joining the Israelite forces "for battle," considerably less than the sons of Reuben and Gad listed in Numbers 26:7, 18. So this section ends with a united nation across the Jordan, ready for battle, and recognizing Joshua as the true successor to Moses. The crossing of the Jordan is clearly a parallel to the crossing of the Red Sea, after which "the people feared the LORD, and they believed in the LORD and in his servant Moses" (Exodus 14:31). The parallel is clearly intentional. God had established Moses and now establishes Joshua as Israel's human leader, and the people are united in their "awe" (Joshua 4:14) or fear of him as their divinely appointed chief man, just as it had been with Moses.

Hearts Melting for Fear

As we revert back now to the main narrative (v. 15ff.), the focus shifts from what the event of the crossing meant to Israel to what it meant to the people outside of the covenant community—the kings of the Amorites and Canaanites "beyond the Jordan to the west," whose reaction is noted in the concluding summary verse at 5:1: "Their hearts melted and there was no longer any spirit in them because of the people of Israel." Once again the narrative pattern is followed. God initiates the next stage by commanding Joshua to instruct the priests bearing the ark to come up out of the river (v. 16). Joshua passes on the instruction to the priests, being the agent of God's word (v. 17), and the priests obey (v. 18). There is also a repeated emphasis on the miraculous at this point in the timing. No sooner had the feet of the priests touched the dry ground on the west bank than "the waters of the Jordan returned to their place and overflowed all its banks, as before" (v. 18b). When the presence of God, symbolized by the ark, is removed from the river, the normal conditions of the creation are resumed. Only God's power could have brought about this miraculous chain of events. The people there were to learn that lesson, and the record of it in the stones and in the story was to be preserved for all the generations yet to come.

The dating of the event in the calendar to the tenth day of the first month (v. 19), Nisan, is also indicative of divine control. The significance of the day is that it was when the Passover lamb was selected, in preparation for its sacrifice on the fourteenth day of the month (Exodus 12:3, 6). Clearly the timing underlies the connection of the entry of the land with the exodus from Egypt some forty years earlier. The resting place chosen for their first night in the land is Gilgal (Joshua 4:19), where the memorial stones are set up (v. 20). It has been commented that the name of the place is derived from the Hebrew verb "to roll," with the suggestion that implicit in the name is the rolling away of the shame of their Egyptian slavery and their wandering in the desert as at last they cross the frontier and enter the land of promise. As Joshua rehearses to the people the purpose of the memorial, he refers firstly to the historical event (v. 22), then to its explanation (v. 23), and finally to its purpose (v. 24). The emphasis is entirely on Yahweh, "your God," mentioned four times, as the heart of the story. He dried up the Jordan just as he had done to the Red Sea, and he did it "for us," his people (v. 23).

However, the outstanding insight comes in verse 24, which reveals the two great reasons for the entry to the land being done in such a miraculous manner. First, God wants all the world to know that all power is in his hands. Because he is the only true and living God, Creator of everything and everyone, it was never his purpose to restrict this knowledge to Israel alone. It was always his design that the relationship of covenant love and faithful devotion between Yahweh and his people should be evangelistic—a testimony to the nations of his own magnetic appeal. Sadly, as the Old Testament progresses we witness the accumulated failures and ultimate refusal of Israel to be this servant light-bearer to the nations. But here God acts upon the international, political stage to demonstrate his reality and his mighty hand. Second, it is for Israel's benefit, "that you may fear the LORD your God forever" (v. 24b). He wants them to know, as they settle down for their first night in the land of promise, which will become the land of rest, that they are there only because of him. Were it not for Yahweh, their God, they would still be slaves to Pharaoh in Egypt. Were it not for him, they would have died in the wilderness. Were it not for him, they would still be stranded, homeless, east of the Jordan. Therefore, their only proper response must be a continuing reverent awe and submission to God, because he is God. That will be the one unchanging factor in all the unknown future about to open up before them. He is the mighty God who alone can do wonders, so he is to be feared. We cannot manipulate him, deceive him, or hide from him; but we can trust and obey him, and we can love him because he has first loved us. That is what the Israelites were to recall whenever they saw the twelve stones at Gilgal. It was to be "a memorial forever" (v. 7) to the faithful provision of a loving God, who was to be the object of his people's love and trust forever. If the hearts of his people melt in loving gratitude and faithful service, they will never melt with the terror like that of the pagan kings (5:1), who know they are on a collision course with Israel's mighty God of all the earth.

And for Us Today?

What are we to derive for our instruction from this amazing chapter, Joshua 4? Doesn't it show us primarily that all our hope is founded upon the God who does mighty things and that we constantly need to be reminded of what they are and why they happened? This is even more the case for us at our period in the history of Planet Earth, when we can look back at the finished work of the Lord Jesus Christ and the sufficiency of God's revelation in the sixty-six books of Scripture. We too need to remember.

Our spiritual memories are very short, so that often in the busy flow of life we forget the spiritual realities on which we are grounded. But just as God knew their needs, so he knows ours, and one of the reasons why we have the Scriptures in their permanent written form is so we can come back to them day after day to be reminded. It is one of the reasons also why we gather together with fellow believers in regular times of corporate worship, instruction, and fellowship. In a culture like ours, addicted to novelty, it is easy to fall into the temptation of judging the effectiveness of our use of God's means of grace by how much new understanding we have. Of course, we want to grow in our knowledge and love of God, but that is often a deepening of what we already know or a new application of old truths rather than startling new discoveries. We all need to be reminded constantly of the most basic realities of our Christian experience, the foundations on which everything else depends, which explains the provision of the twelve stones at Gilgal and, for us, the institution of the Lord's Supper.

"Do this in remembrance of me" was Jesus' command to his disciples (Luke 22:19) as he gave them the ordinance of the broken bread and poured out wine as the sign of his atoning death, the inauguration of the new covenant. Here is a greater miracle than the crossing of the Jordan River. "The Son of God . . . loved me and gave himself for me" (Galatians 2:20). We need the visible, tangible reminder of what lies at the very heart of our salvation. We need to recall at what cost he opened the way into the land of promise for us, his redeemed people. We need to give ourselves to love and serve him forever.

And we also need to remember the great victory that Calvary accomplished over sin and evil and even death itself. Our slavery is ended, and we enjoy the freedom of the children of God, "blessed . . . in Christ with every spiritual blessing in the heavenly places" (Ephesians 1:3). While a cross may be a symbol of that reality, the Lord's Supper is a much more vivid reminder and memorial. At his table we actually take the elements, albeit only ordinary bread and wine, into ourselves and make them a part of us, so that we are not just recalling something that happened "out there" in history. Rather, in the words of the Prayer Book, we are to "feed on Christ in our hearts, by faith, with thanksgiving." So as we appropriate all that Jesus has accomplished for us in the atonement of his substitutionary death, we also remember personally and with renewed commitment to action what it means to be redeemed.

We need to revisit the goodness of God's grace and to recall to one another what the Lord has done for us—it helps us remember. That doesn't mean we have no other agenda for our church fellowship or family life, but it is an emaciated Christianity that cannot, or does not, share not only what the Lord has done for us on the cross of Calvary but also in the events of this current week. We need to be reminded, as an encouragement to one another, so that we realize again that God does not change and that all he has proved himself to be in the past, he will continue to be, now and forever. Parents have a special responsibility to pass on this body of truth in experience, with conviction, to the next generation. When they ask, "What do these stones mean?" (v. 6) let us tell them. The most effective communication is often in the family circle, where the questions arise naturally. Then is the time to tell our children the reality of our God, the certain fulfillment of his promises, and his dependable love and faithfulness. I remember in my own life what an anchor of my soul it was when I went off to university and faced all sorts of intellectual and other challenges to my faith, for which I had no immediate answer, to know the reality of my parents' faith and to have seen the unmistakable work of God in our family. By word and by example we need to tell the next generation that the Lord's hand is mighty, so that nothing is too hard for him. God speaks; we obey. God acts; we remember. "Bless the LORD, O my soul, and forget not all his benefits" (Psalm 103:2).

The more we recall his character, his goodness, and his grace, the more we shall make God the focus of our thinking and our trusting, whatever difficulties we may be facing. In John Newton's memorable words:

> His love in time past
> Forbids me to think
> He'll leave me at last
> In trouble to sink;
> Each sweet Ebenezer[5]
> I have in review
> Confirms his good pleasure
> To help me quite through.[6]

6

Essential Preparations

JOSHUA 5:2–15

SPEED IS ONE OF OUR unquestioned values that pervades so much of contemporary life. The more quickly a thing can be done, the better. The amazing capabilities of modern technology continue to develop at an exponential rate, so that what would once have taken long periods of time is now accomplished in seconds. Trying to keep up can leave us breathless! So with Israel now across the Jordan, rejoicing in God's miraculous intervention for them, and with Jericho just a few miles distant, all our modern instincts would be to push on as quickly as possible, while the people are still enthusiastic and motivated and while the citizens of Jericho are still panic-stricken and demoralized. Let's get straight into battle! But surprisingly in chapter 5 God slows the action down; indeed, he activates the pause button. Proceedings are halted.

We have already noted that 5:1 serves as a bridging verse. On the one hand, it is the fulfillment of God's promise, through Joshua, that "all the peoples of the earth" will know that he is "mighty" (4:24). That is already happening in 5:1, which is why it also has a forward perspective, since the paralyzing fear experienced by their enemies seems to point to a relatively easy conquest of the land. The Amorites were the tribal groups that inhabited the hill country with their fortress settlements, while the Canaanites were the traders on the plains, down to the Mediterranean coast. But whatever their location or cultures, they had never encountered a God like Yahweh, who could dry up a river in flood and then cause it to flow again. Wouldn't this then be the ideal time to make a sudden strike? Not in God's timing, because there are more important things for him to deal with first.

The pagan kings have no power against such a God. They can be blown aside in a moment and their fortresses reduced to rubble. That is not God's concern. His focus is on his own people, Israel, because there are essential preparations of trust and renewed obedience that need to be fulfilled if they are to continue to be rightly related to him, which is the prerequisite of victory. Essential preparations need to be made before Jericho can be targeted. From chapter 1 onward we have been taught that God's greatest concern is that his people faithfully observe all that he had commanded them through Moses—everything that is written in the book of the Law (the Pentateuch). One glaring omission from that obedience characterizes this whole generation of Israelites and must be remedied before the action can continue.

Renewing Covenant Obedience

It is striking that while the word "covenant" is not used in these verses, it is everywhere implicit. The glaring omission is the failure to circumcise the generation that was born after the exodus, to keep the terms of the covenant. The institution of circumcision as the covenant sign goes back to God's instructions to Abraham in Genesis 17:10–14. Although it was practiced in Egypt and by other people groups (see Jeremiah 9:25, 26), the rite had a unique significance for Israel, because God commanded it with the words, "This is my covenant, which you shall keep, between me and you and your offspring after you" (Genesis 17:10). Every male child was to be circumcised when eight days old as an indispensable requirement for membership in God's covenant community. "So shall my covenant be in your flesh an everlasting covenant" (Genesis 17:13). But this command had apparently been ignored or kept on hold for an entire generation. This is why God's command to Joshua in verse 2 speaks about being circumcised "a second time." It is as though the whole ordinance has to be renewed in a second giving of the covenant to the entire nation, since "all the people who were born on the way in the wilderness after they had come out of Egypt had not been circumcised" (v. 5). This act of obedience is essential if the people of Israel are to serve God's purposes and to know God's presence with them.

There is a parallel incident just before Moses encounters Pharaoh in Exodus 4:24–26. Traveling to Egypt to begin the work of the exodus, in obedience to God's command, Moses encounters the Lord at a lodging place on the way, and his life is in jeopardy because his own son was as yet uncircumcised. His wife, Zipporah, takes the necessary action, and Moses' life is spared. But the clear message is that if Moses is to do God's will as his devoted servant in Egypt before Pharaoh, he must be in a position of obedience within his own household. We cannot expect God's blessing to be seen in public obedience to his commands if there is hidden compromise in the private world of the self and the family. This deficient consecration and obedience to the instruction of God's grace is at root an unwillingness to receive the covenant promise that demands it. As J. A. Motyer puts it, "This relationship of circumcision to foregoing promise shows that the rite signifies the gracious movement of God to man, and only derivatively . . . the consecration of man to God."[1]

That is why verses 2–9 are essential preparation for the assault on Jericho. The seriousness of the issue is further underlined by the contrast between the two generations (vv. 6, 7). The reason the first generation had to delay entering the land for forty years involved waiting for the death of those who came out of Egypt, who "perished, because they did not obey the voice of the LORD" (v. 6). The irony is that while God has promised the land to their children, that new generation is in acute danger of making the same error in neglecting the covenant requirement of circumcision, an act of disobedience or even rebellion (v. 7). So Joshua obeys God's instruction. The whole nation is circumcised (v. 8), and of course in this, as in every other detail, God's timing is perfect. The healing referred to in verse 8 would take some time, during which Israel would be extremely vulnerable with all her fighting men out of action. But this is just the time at which their opponents are paralyzed with fear, so there is in fact no danger of an attack.

There are lessons of principle here for covenant people, within the new order as within the old. Obedient people who put themselves unreservedly into God's hands prove his promises and experience his protection, but it is only in the action that the proof is found. It always requires faith to obey, but we must never attempt to justify our disobedience by speculating about what the consequences might be. That is no way for a Christian to live. Sometimes it takes greater faith to trust God with the consequences of an act of obedience than to perform the original obedience, but either way we are never stronger than when we are dependent on and obedient to God's word. It is, however, important that Scripture is governing our actions, not some bright idea or spiritual notion that has just floated into our mind. But when Scripture is clear, we must trust and obey, confident that God can be depended on to look after the outcome. And verse 9 reveals what a glorious outcome it was in this instance. God had rolled away the reproach of Egypt, their cruel bondage, and their scorn in the forty years of wandering, and Gilgal is the location to be named for this reality. The Hebrew verb "*gâlal*," meaning "to roll," is clearly the root of the name given.

There is also a rather more specific relevance of this covenant renewal rite for us today as New Testament believers. In Colossians 2:11, 12, writing to a largely Gentile church as the apostle to the Gentiles, Paul affirms, "In [Christ] also you were circumcised with a circumcision made without hands, by putting off the body of the flesh, by the circumcision of Christ, having been buried with him in baptism, in which you were also raised with him through faith in the powerful working of God, who raised him from the dead." The covenant sign moves from circumcision to baptism in the new order, whereby the outward and visible sign speaks of an inward and spiritual grace. That grace means "putting off . . . the flesh," the old sinful, self-centered way of life. This is the spiritual reality of regeneration, accomplished in us by and through the saving work of Christ. The physical sign of circumcision was always intended to lead to a circumcised heart marked by obedience to God's Law. Now in the gospel the Law of God is written on the heart of the believer, and the power of the risen Christ transforms his people, liberating them from the downward pull of the sinful nature and empowering them to live in new-ness of life. The implications of this are further spelled out in Philippians 3:3, where the apostle tells his readers, "We are the circumcision, who worship by the Spirit of God and glory in Christ Jesus and put no confidence in the flesh." Instead the Christian's confidence and glory is in the Lord Jesus Christ whom he worships by the indwelling Spirit.

These then are the essential foundations on which we need to build if we are to enter into all that can potentially be ours through the gospel. If baptism is the outward sign of initiation into the Body of Christ, then such a person is one who has been crucified with Christ, who no longer relies on his own imagined righteousness and who no longer puts any confidence in himself. Yet Christians are confident people. We know our sin and guilt only too well, but we also know, by God's grace, that every sin and failure has been dealt with, once and for all, in the cross of Christ. As we put our faith in his finished work and draw upon his risen power through the indwelling Holy Spirit, we can begin to appropriate in our own lives the benefits of his victory over all the hostile powers.

Experiencing Covenant Blessings

Within the renewed relationship, expressed by their circumcision, the people of Israel are now able to keep the Passover (v. 10). Once again the emphasis seems to be on their attention to the detail of God's command. In Exodus 12:6 the Passover lamb was to be slaughtered on the fourteenth day of the first month "at twilight," and here the parallel is exact. The wording is probably designed to take our memories back to that first Passover in Egypt, although we know that it had been celebrated in the wilderness the following year

(Numbers 9:1–5) and presumably on other occasions. But this first Passover within the land is, of course, a unique celebration because the cycle is now complete. The same God who brought them out of Egypt through the blood of the Passover lamb has brought them into the land, just as he promised. Because they are now a circumcised people, the way is open for them to keep the feast.

Verses 11, 12 underline another great blessing of the covenant as the people eat the fruit of the land for the very first time. This is provided by God himself in fulfillment of his promise, and on that same day the manna, which had sustained them in the desert for so long, ceased. This is a further clear indication that their days of wilderness wanderings are truly over. The reference to "unleavened cakes" in verse 11 may indicate that they were celebrating the feast of unleavened bread, which began on the fifteenth day of the month and lasted for seven days (see Leviticus 23:6). There is no direct statement of this in the text, but it is a reasonable presumption. The first day was to be a "holy convocation" (Leviticus 23:7), a sabbath day, followed by the celebration of the firstfruits (Leviticus 23:9–14) when offerings were brought to the Lord first, in gratitude for the harvest, after which the harvest could begin to be eaten. It was certainly a momentous occasion for this generation who had been so dependent on the manna for such a long time. Three times in these two verses we are told that they ate of the produce of the land. God's promise has been fulfilled.

Meeting the Covenant Lord

The chapter ends with a magnificent paragraph that is rich in its significance and instruction. Here is the last piece of the jigsaw of necessary preparations before the conquest can begin. Verses 13–15 summarize and underscore the lessons we have been learning already, but they are also the secret of everything that is to follow in the next few chapters. We have noted parallels to Moses several times already in the book, and perhaps this is Joshua's "burning bush" experience. Certainly the language used in verse 15 is very similar to that in Exodus 3:5. Here is a personal interview with the covenant Lord, to prepare his servant for the challenges that lie ahead.

The shift of focus changes from Gilgal to Jericho and from the nation to one man. Joshua must have had an overwhelming sense of the huge responsibility he was facing. Undoubtedly he could look back with great thanksgiving to the river crossing and be encouraged and strengthened by the Passover and heartened by the news the spies had brought back from inside Jericho (2:24). But still Jericho stands before him unconquered. So it is likely that he has gone out on a secret reconnaissance mission to see for himself the state of affairs at Jericho and to plan his strategy for the attack. He wasn't inactive. He decided to do what he could to get a thorough look at the issues. It's a sensible move, but it has a most unexpected and dramatic outcome. Looking up, he encounters "a man . . . standing before him with his drawn sword in his hand" (v. 13). This impressive figure is ready for military action—his sword is drawn—but on whose side will he fight? Joshua's question to that effect ("Are you for us, or for our adversaries?") is entirely reasonable and to be expected. But it receives no direct answer ("No; but . . . ," v. 14) because it is the wrong question. The NIV translation "neither" could be taken to mean that he is not on Israel's side, though he clearly is. So the better translation is "No; but . . ." or "No; for . . ." In other words, "You have the question wrong, Joshua, because I am the commander of the army of the Lord" (v. 14). He has come not to take sides but to take charge.

Not only is the exact identity of this superior figure unclear, but also the army that he commands. It may refer to the fighting men of Israel as it does in its Exodus image, where "the hosts of the LORD" describes the ranks of the Israelites (Exodus 12:41). But the more common Old Testament phrase "the Lord of hosts" seems to indicate the angelic beings of a celestial army, of whom perhaps Joshua's visitor was the supreme leader. This focuses our attention upon his identity. What is clear is that the figure comes with the authority of God, presumably to govern and direct the tactics for taking Jericho. It may be that he gives the divine instructions that follow in 6:2–5, though there is no direct textual connection to this mysterious figure. However, there are clear evidences in Joshua's reaction that he knows he is at the very least in the presence of a divine messenger. He falls prostrate to the earth in worship (and is not rebuked). He humbly asks what message the commander has for Joshua, his servant. He is told that he is on holy ground, and so in reverence and obedience he takes off his sandals (v. 15). Suggesting that this all points to this figure being the commander of Yahweh's heavenly hosts, who are ready to fight in support of Israel, D. M. Howard comments, "There is no indication that the man Joshua met was taking personal command of Israel's army, displacing Joshua, and the language of verse 15 (concerning holy ground) strongly suggests that this is a divine being representing God and his hosts."[2]

Howard's commentary contains a helpful excursus on the "Identity of the Angel of the Lord," in which he suggests there are three possibilities, while recognizing that in view of the Scriptural silence on this detail we cannot be precise in our knowledge. In summary, the possibilities are: "(1) An angel with a special commission; (2) It may be a momentary descent of God himself into visibility; or (3) It may be the Logos himself (ie Christ)—a kind of temporary pre-incarnation of the second person of the trinity" (quoting J. M. Wilson).[3] Howard's own conclusion is that this was a self-revelation of Yahweh that communicated his immanence to Joshua and that "it certainly anticipated Christ in a typological way, even if it was not Christ himself."

What is clear and perhaps ultimately of greater significance to us is Joshua's reaction to the visitation. His actions and words indicate his total submission to the authority and direction of the commander. Joshua has all the responsibilities of the human leader, but the heavenly warrior has come precisely to direct operations. He is the one who will dictate the strategy, and he is the one who will deliver Jericho into his people's hands and give God's people the victory. Can we not perhaps imagine something of the joy, hope, and sheer relief that Joshua experienced as he lay on his face and worshipped? It wasn't until Joshua was in that position that the tactics for taking Jericho were revealed to him.

This God is our God. What an encouragement it is to see again how God takes the initiative! Joshua went to look at his problem and found himself meeting his God. So often we find the same mechanism at work. We go as it were to look at our problems, to think them through and express our needs to God in prayer, and suddenly there is fresh light. We see the issues more clearly. The Scriptures come alive in a new way. We are surprised by something we had not been aware of before, and suddenly we realize that God is with us in the complexity and confusion, calling on us to fall at his feet and find new assurance as we commit all our unknowns into his hands. At our precise moment of need the Lord reveals himself to the man or woman who walks with him in the darkness. He is the commander, the supreme strategist, and immediately the whole emphasis changes. The burdens are no longer carried by Joshua alone. The question is not whether the Lord is on our side or not, but whether we are submitted to his sovereign rule and authority because he is the Lord of earth and Heaven to whom all power belongs.

The essential preparation for the fall of Jericho is that the earthly leader falls flat on his face before God. That is the prerequisite for God's plans to be unveiled and God's purpose to be activated. And the same is true for the church of God today and for its individual members. It is when we live in glad submission to God's will, revealed in his Word, that he can lift us up and lead us on. We need to be much more concerned about his priorities than about our planning, our arranging of strategies, our ordering of scaling ladders or our building of battering rams. They may not even be needed. But what *is* needed is for us, as God's people, to recognize the commander of the Lord's army, worship him in his holiness and glory, and put ourselves unreservedly at his disposal. That is what changes things. Then we shall not think primarily about *our* church, *our* work, *our* service and become introverted and problem-oriented. Rather we will see that everything is in the commander's hands (including our little lives) and that the greatest wonder of all is that he deigns to take up and use a lump of unpromising clay like you and me.

Disposer supreme, and Judge of the earth,
Who choosest for Thine the weak and the poor;
To frail earthen vessels and things of no worth
Entrusting Thy riches which aye shall endure.

Those vessels soon fail, though full of Thy light,
And at Thy decree, are broken and gone;
Thence brightly appeareth Thy truth in its might,
As through the clouds riven the lightnings have shone.

Their sound goeth forth, "Christ Jesus the Lord";
Then Satan doth fear, his citadels fall;
As when the dread trumpets went forth at Thy Word,
And one long blast shattered the Canaanite's wall.

O loud be their trump, and stirring their sound,
To rouse us, O Lord, from slumber of sin;
The lights Thou hast kindled in darkness around,
O may they illumine our spirits within.[4]

7

The Battle That Wasn't

JOSHUA 6:1-27

JOSHUA FOUGHT THE BATTLE OF JERICHO, and the walls came tumbling down," so the old spiritual says. It's both right and wrong. The walls certainly collapsed upon themselves, and "everyone charged straight in, and they took the city" (v. 20 NIV), but there was no battle to be fought. God gave Jericho into Israel's hands, and the whole account of this dramatic sixth chapter centers on the gracious gift of the sovereign Lord. If ever there was a case study of the Lord as the hero of the narrative, it is this chapter.

We left Joshua prostrate in worship on the holy ground created by the manifestation of the Lord himself as the commander of his army (5:13–15). Joshua had gone out to survey his problem (Jericho) and found himself face-to-face with his commander. He had gone out most probably to think through the military strategy by which he might lay siege to this heavily reinforced guardian-city, and instead he discovered that God's plan was for him to take off his sandals and worship. It is a striking lesson. But it could easily be misinterpreted. This is not justification for inactivity. As we shall see, God's people had a large part to play in the conquest and destruction of the city of Jericho. It was not delivered to them on a plate, as it were, by overwhelming supernatural intervention that required them to do nothing. But the way in which the victory came was chosen by the Lord, so that it would be ingrained in their memory that this first victory was the gift of their gracious, sovereign commander. What happened at the beginning was to be the pattern for all their future advance into this land of promise and rest. Later our writer will reflect that "the LORD gave to Israel all the land that he swore to give to their fathers. . . . And the LORD gave them rest on every side" (21:43, 44). That is the principle of lasting validity we are being taught here. Obedient action in response to divinely-given promises is the channel by which the sovereign grace of their covenant Lord is experienced in the lives of his people.

The tactics vary from situation to situation, but the principle remains the same. The previous generation had been taught the same lessons when they first came out of Egypt. Led by God himself to their camp place, facing the sea, with an impassable barrier in front of them and Pharaoh's elite troops closing in on them from behind, Moses instructs them, "Fear not, stand firm [or still], and see the salvation of the LORD, which he will work for you today. . . . The LORD will fight for you, and you have only to be silent [or still]" (Exodus 14:13, 14). The sea parts, the people cross, and as the pursuing Egyptians are doomed, Israel knows that she has been delivered by supernatural power alone. But when, three chapters later, they are attacked by the Amalekites at Rephidim, Moses instructs Joshua, "Choose for us men, and go out and fight with Amalek," and the outcome is that "Joshua overwhelmed Amalek and his people with the sword" (Exodus 17:8–13). Of course, the divine element is not absent even if the human activity is far more dominant. The battle only flows Israel's way as Moses' hands are lifted up to Heaven, carrying the rod of God as a physical sign of their exclusive dependence on the power of the Lord to deliver his people from their enemies. The memory of this, written in a book and recited "in the ears of Joshua" (Exodus 17:14), would undoubtedly have had a profound influence on the military and spiritual education of this young warrior. And now, at Jericho, the lessons are indicative of exactly the same principle.

Verse 1 stands at the head of the narrative both as a blunt statement of fact—this is the reality of the situation—and also as a motivating explanation. Jericho is on an all-systems alert "because of the people of Israel," which is shorthand for all that God has done for his people in bringing them to this point. Jericho may know very little of Israel's God and want to give him even less credence, but they cannot ignore the multitudes who have crossed the Jordan, in flood, and who now threaten their citadel. Recent events give them no confidence that this conflict is avoidable. So they batten down the hatches. There is no way in and no way out. Jericho is a city under siege. By all the normal rules of human military engagement this stalemate situation will have to be resolved by an Israelite attack. But that is a daunting prospect for an under-equipped and inexperienced body of fighting men. It is every bit as impossible to think of them overcoming Jericho, a garrison city, as it was to think that they could cross the Jordan in flood. But God . . .

Divine Initiation

Verses 2–5 consist of Yahweh's instructions to Joshua, which are then passed on to the priests (v. 6) and to the people (v. 7). Here the tactics are revealed and the agenda is set for the rest of the account. This is the answer to Joshua's request, "What does my lord say to his servant?" (5:14), and it indicates that the chapter division does not serve us well here. These verses are the divine commander's strategies. As always, the commands are based upon the promises; the imperatives are possible only because of the indicatives. So verse 2 is a great statement of fact, though its experience is entirely future: "See, I have given Jericho into your hand." "See" draws Joshua's attention to this as the supreme revelation on which everything else hangs. Look, focus here, get your mind set on this. There is not a shred of doubt about the outcome. It is an echo of the promise back in 1:3, which came with the command to go over the Jordan: "Every place that the sole of your foot will tread upon I have given to you." It is not yet yours in experience, but the fact that it will be is so certain, in the providence of your sovereign, all-powerful God, that the future can be expressed by a tense of completed action ("I have given . . .").

On that basis, the command is given: "You shall march around the city . . ." (v. 3), and all the subsequent instructions then follow. For each of the next six days the whole army is to march around the city walls once. But the emphasis is not on the fighting men but on the ark of the covenant, the symbol of the divine presence. God is with his people, in their very midst, to accomplish his victory for them. He is not remote or at arm's length but is leading his people by his presence, just as he had done through all their wilderness years. That is why there is such an emphasis on the number "seven" in the text, occurring four times in just one verse (v. 4). Seven is the number of divine perfection or completeness, reflecting the seventh day of rest at the end of the six days of creation. So here the six days circling the city are to find their completion or culmination in the seventh day with its seven circuits around Jericho. The presence of the ark is heralded by seven priests each with a ram's horn trumpet, blown "continually" (v. 9), culminating in a long blast after the seventh circuit on the seventh day, which is the sign for a great shout from the people and the collapse of the city walls. The ESV footnote draws our attention to the literal translation both in verse 5 and verse 20: "the wall of the city will fall under itself"; that is, it will collapse as though from pressure from above rather than from outside.

I wonder what the reaction was when Joshua passed on this divine strategy to the priests and to the people (vv. 6, 7). From the human standpoint it seems a largely irrelevant and obviously ineffective plan; but these were people who had seen the Jordan parted and walked into the land on its bed. So the commands they were given were met with obedience, because the promises on which they were built were met with faith. This is how the New Testament teaches us to look at this extraordinary event. "By faith the walls of Jericho fell down after they had been encircled for seven days" (Hebrews 11:30). By God's sovereign will and his irresistible power, yes, but also in response to the faith of Israel, indicated by their obedience to his instruction. Woudstra comments, "The cities of Palestine in this period were not large. Jericho measured c. 225 by 80 metres and its circumference was 600 metres. The length of the column that marched around the city is not known. This would depend also on its depth. In view of the large numbers of marchers one must assume that the head of the column had long returned to the camp when the others were still marching."[1] This is a helpful comment, though it raises questions about the seven successive circuits on the seventh day. However, the narrative's emphasis is not so much on the detail of the arrangements but on the faith that unquestioningly put the plan into action.

Detailed Fulfillment

The focus of verses 8–14 is on the detailed execution of the commands in preparation for the fall of the city, which is then described in verses 15–21, in the context of further precise commands and instructions about how Israel is to proceed. Although these are placed at the climax of the narrative on the seventh day, to emphasize their importance and perhaps also to enhance the dramatic effect (verses 17–19), it is not unreasonable to suppose that they were given before the event rather than in the immediacy of the moment, since they govern what Israel's behavior is to be following the collapse of the walls.

Verses 8–11 provide us with a vivid word picture of the first day's encirclement. The army is divided into two parts, the first leading the procession (v. 9a), but the attention is on the trumpet-blowing priests, announcing the arrival of the center of the whole event, given its full title in verse 8b, "the ark of the covenant of the Lord." The rest of the army forms the rear guard (v. 9b). The purpose of the parade is to focus on the ark and therefore on the Lord, so that both Israel and Jericho will know who is responsible for what is about to happen. The only sound is the seven trumpets blown continually, but there is no shouting or even speech among the people on that first day or on any of the others, until the seventh day. The shout is to be reserved for the very end (v. 10b). All this helps increase the dramatic buildup of the narrative, as does the matter-of-fact report of verse 11 and the almost prosaic repetition of the detail in verses 12–14, describing the second day of identical activity. We, the readers, know what is to happen on the seventh day, but we are kept waiting for it (as they were), in our case by the tension-building device of repetition. A great storytelling technique is at work here.

And then we come to the seventh day (v. 15a), with a dawn start and seven circuits to be completed. No additional description of the marching is given until the command to shout is fulfilled (v. 20), but in between what might seem to be something of an anticlimax is the detailed instruction given about what is to be done with the city and its people, including Rahab. However, the positioning here is highly significant. At the level of narrative coherence we need the information of verses 18, 19 in order to understand what is going to happen in chapter 7. So there is an important link here to the ongoing story line. But at the spiritual level what happens here is the central lesson of the victory of Jericho, and thus it occupies center stage because this is the most important perspective of the narrative. It is there to teach Israel essential principles that are to govern the further conquest and possession of the land. Perhaps the tense of completed action in verse 16 is better rendered "Joshua *had* said," though the actual command "Shout" is clearly given at this precise moment.

With the exception of Rahab and all who are gathered in her house, marked out by the scarlet cord and by their faith in God's promise through the spies (2:14–21), "the city and all that is within it shall be devoted to the LORD for destruction" (6:17). When God's wrath falls, it is only by faith in any provision of his grace, which he offers, that sinners can be rescued. Israel learned that lesson on Passover night in Egypt (Exodus 12:13), and it is being taught again here. Rahab's faith, expressed in her works, is the means by which she is justified and rescued from the judgment of Jericho (see James 2:24–26). The rest of the city and its treasures are to be destroyed, as God had previously commanded through Moses (Deuteronomy 7:1–5; 20:16–18).

We need to pause here to explore what is a strange concept to modern ears, and to many an objectionable and unacceptable one. This is the first occurrence in the Joshua narrative of the concept of "devoted things," described in the ESV footnote as "set apart (devoted) as an offering to the Lord (for destruction)." The NIV footnote elaborates further: "The Hebrew term refers to the irrevocable giving over of things or persons to the Lord, often by totally destroying them." The noun is *hèrem*, and its verbal root (*hàram*) means to set apart, or devote, with the object of what is set apart belonging to the Lord for him to determine absolutely its use or destruction. It is entirely and irrevocably his property. Now, of course, in the most foundational sense that is true of every being and thing within the created order of the universe.

God owns everything, because he has created everything. Even human artifacts are entirely dependent on the raw materials that God has made. *De facto*, he has the right to dispose of anything within the created order according to his sovereign will. This Biblical theme reaches its New Testament development in Romans 9:21, 22, where the Apostle Paul writes, "Has the potter no right over the clay, to make out of the same lump one vessel for honorable use and another for dishonorable use? What if God, desiring to show his wrath and to make known his power, has endured with much patience vessels of wrath prepared for destruction?" As he has said earlier, we have no right to answer back to the Creator (Romans 9:20) or to question his wisdom. So there can be no question about the justice of God's judgment against Jericho.

Actually the divine justice of the Canaanite conquest is a strong theme in the Old Testament. When God promises the land to Abraham's descendants in Genesis 15:16, he also states that it will be several generations before the promise is realized, "for the iniquity of the Amorites is not yet complete." But now the time had come when it might be. Moses taught the people in Deuteronomy 9:5, "Not because of your righteousness or the uprightness of your heart are you going in to possess their land, but because of the wickedness of these nations the LORD your God is driving them out from before you, and that he may confirm the word that the LORD swore to your fathers, to Abraham, to Isaac, and to Jacob." Judgment is always God's final resort, and in this case it came after generations of provocation. That wickedness or uncleanness is graphically described in Leviticus 18, with its focus on sexual perversions, child sacrifice, and other "abominations" to the Creator: "For by all these [things] the nations I am driving out before you have become unclean, and the land became unclean, so that I punished its iniquity, and the land vomited out its inhabitants" (Leviticus 18:24, 25). By recognizing the devotion of these things to Yahweh to destroy them, Israel was in effect being set apart, not as *hèrem* and not according to their record, which was also sinful, but as the chosen people of their rescuing covenant Lord, redeemed from slavery to be God's special possession, his treasure chest, his exclusive property. And their purpose is therefore to be set apart for holiness and for life rather than for judgment and destruction. "Every devoted thing is most holy to the LORD" (Leviticus 27:28). All that has been discovered about Canaanite paganism only serves to confirm the gross and barbaric manifestations of evil that were endemic in their idolatrous culture. So there can be no accusation of injustice against the Creator God of perfect righteousness and justice.

Nor can it be claimed that the nations in the promised land were not culpable because they had not received the Mosaic Law. Again the New

Testament helps us to be perfectly clear about this, and it is a major principle of Biblical interpretation that later revelation provides the interpretative key to a right understanding and application to the former. Speaking of God's wrath being revealed against all human ungodliness and unrighteousness, Paul sees the whole race as morally culpable before God for the suppression of the truth that has been revealed. "For what can be known about God is plain to them, because God has shown it to them. For his invisible attributes, namely, his eternal power and divine nature, have been clearly perceived, ever since the creation of the world, in the things that have been made. So they are without excuse" (Romans 1:19, 20; cf. Romans 1:18). That is why Hebrews 11:31 can affirm that "by faith Rahab the prostitute did not perish with those who were disobedient, because she had given a friendly welcome to the spies." The citizens of Jericho were disobedient. They were not without the knowledge of God, both through his general revelation and through the residue of the image of God within every created human being, however rebellious and depraved. Moreover, they received the specific revelation of God's redemptive deliverance of his people from Egypt and had themselves witnessed the miraculous crossing of the Jordan. They were not without evidence, but unlike Rahab they chose to be disobedient. So after generations of escalating rebellion and a refusal to believe, the judgment of a just Creator had irrevocably to fall. Charges by "the new atheism" that the judgments of the conquest are xenophobic ethnic cleansing chime in well with the hostility of a God-rejecting contemporary culture, but these are very wide of the mark in terms of the self-testimony of Scripture as the word of God himself.[2]

The text in Joshua itself highlights the hardening of the Canaanites' hearts against God and his purposes and their refusal to sue for terms of peace. Indeed 11:19, 20 underlines that, as with Pharaoh in Exodus, this hardening of the heart was also an act of God's judgment. They knew well enough about the powerful victories that Yahweh had won for his people, but they refused to bow the knee. If Rahab was willing to change, others could have done so too. If the Gibeonites (chapter 9) were willing to sue for peace, albeit by deception, others might have made similar approaches. Instead they chose to resist Israel's God, and they bore the consequences. As David Howard comments, "We should note that the instructions to Israel to annihilate the Canaanites were specific in time, intent, and geography. That is, Israel was not given a blanket permission to do the same to any peoples they encountered, at any time or in any place. It was limited to the crucial time when Israel was just establishing itself as a theocracy under God, to protect Israel's worship, as well as to punish these specific peoples."[3]

Returning now to the text at 6:18, 19, we see how the principle of the *hèrem* worked out. If everything in Jericho belonged to God, then to keep any of these things, such as the silver and gold, the bronze and iron vessels, or the valuable garments, for oneself would be to ally oneself with that which had to be destroyed. The camp of Israel would then itself be liable to destruction, not just because of stealing from Yahweh what was rightfully his, but because appropriating devoted things would make oneself liable to destruction as their human "owner."

The actual fall of Jericho is recorded with a minimal description in verse 20 as the trumpets blow and the people shout, probably both as a war cry and also as a victory celebration, since the destruction was so instantaneous. The obedience is detailed and the destruction terrifying (v. 21).

Promised Deliverance

With the scarlet cord in the window, Rahab's house would have been easily recognizable, but now that the walls have collapsed it is presumably more so in that her house is still standing. Whatever the detail, the two spies now return to the story, and with specific obedience to a direct command from Joshua they go into Rahab's house and bring her out, along with all her family, rescued by Israel's faithfulness to the promise made and because of her faithfulness to them. Because of her faith in Yahweh as the true and living God, she and all who belonged to her are "saved alive" (v. 25). Although the verse adds, "she has lived in Israel to this day," that does not necessarily mean that the book was written soon after the event. The use of a proper name such as Abraham or David can sometimes stand for their descendants, and that may be the case here. But dating the text is not the purpose for this statement. Rather it is one of those notes of long-term effects. God's promises have lasting value. He will not go back on his word, and there in the midst of Israel is the living proof. Rahab and her family began outside the camp of Israel (v. 23b), but soon they were living among the people, and eventually she finds her true place in the genealogy of Christ in Matthew 1:5. Acts of faith have long-lasting effects.

But so can curses against evil. Because Jericho was the first city of the conquest, overcome solely by the power of God, and because it belonged exclusively to him, any act of rebuilding would be seen as an act of rebellion "before the Lord," equivalent to the arrogant defiance that first brought his judgment on the original city. Verse 26 makes the terms crystal-clear, and 1 Kings 16:34 shows its outworking many generations later. By contrast the summary in verse 27 reaffirms the growing refrain of the book. Joshua continues to grow in stature, not only among the Israelites, but "in all the land" because the Lord is with him. No other explanation is possible, and none is needed. As the word of God is believed and obeyed, so the God of the word is with his people to give them all the blessings of his covenant faithfulness. Everything seems set fair after this first great victory, but sadly the story now takes a turn for the worse.

So where does this leave us as twenty-first-century Christian believers, knowing that Joshua's God is our God too, the God and Father of our Lord Jesus Christ? Firstly, it is important to underline that the church is not to apply the principles of the devoted things to our very different location in space and time. Evil is still rampant in our world, and perhaps the mark of how much we are truly God's people is how deeply we first share his hatred of sin in our own hearts and then how determinedly we turn from it. That is the place to start before we imagine we can sit in judgment on others. Wherever we see manifestations of evil, we are to oppose it vigorously and purposefully, but using the weapons God has provided for this cosmic spiritual warfare. There are several ways in which the New Testament will help us apply Joshua 6 rightly.

Writing to the Corinthians, Paul states, "For though we walk in the flesh, we are not waging war according to the flesh. For the weapons of our warfare are not of the flesh but have divine power to destroy strongholds. We destroy arguments and every lofty opinion raised against the knowledge of God, and take every thought captive to obey Christ" (2 Corinthians 10:3–5). This warfare is for the minds and hearts of men and women, to liberate them from the chains of the world, the flesh, and the devil through the proclamation and application of the gospel of God's grace. Further, "we do not wrestle against flesh and blood, but against the rulers, against the authorities, against the cosmic powers over this present darkness, against the spiritual forces of evil in the heavenly places. Therefore take up the whole armor of God, that you may be able to withstand in the evil day, and having done all, to stand firm" (Ephesians 6:12, 13). Far from Christians engaging in some form of holy war against other human beings, we are to concentrate on the ground that Christ has already won for us in his great redemptive work and to fight the spiritual battle against the onslaughts of the devil "in the heavenly places." That is why truth, righteousness, the gospel of peace, faith, salvation, and the word of God are the vital weapons of this spiritual battle (Ephesians 6:14–17). It is not jihad but Jesus who wins the victory for the people of God. If we are to see the Jerichos of our contemporary world collapse before the gospel of God's grace, it will be on the terms of the commander of the Lord's army and by his life-giving power alone. And he says to his kingdom citizens, "Love your enemies and pray for those who persecute you, so that you may be sons of your Father who is in heaven" (Matthew 5:44, 45).

This New Testament perspective lifts the battle beyond the time perspective of this world to the eternal realities of the heavenly kingdom and the life of the world to come. Christians are not fighting individuals, nor even other erroneous belief or religious systems. The Lord's army is set to fight the world and the flesh, the pressures of evil outside and within us, and behind both, manipulating them for the destruction of Christ and his church, the devil himself. That is where the battle is to be joined—in the heavenlies. But if the enemy can get us to fight earthly battles with human weapons, nothing will please him more, and especially when those battles are between believers in church. Jericho principles still apply. (1) We need to search out, listen to, accept, and adopt the divine strategy for victory, revealed in all the Scriptures, the living and enduring Word of God. (2) Because Christ is the Commander, our job is to trust him, believing his wonderful promises, and to obey him with detailed, meticulous attention. We don't have to know always why we are called to a certain course of action, but just that if God's Word says it, we need to obey it. (3) The battle belongs to the Lord. He knows the end from the beginning, and he knows exactly how he will bring us there. Nothing is ever outside his sovereign control, and "we know that for those who love God all things work together for good, for those who are called according to his purpose" (Romans 8:28). As Charles Spurgeon observed, "If everything works together for our good, then nothing is left to work for our ill." (4) We are not to waste time or energy speculating or trying to imagine how God might achieve what seems to us to be frankly impossible. No one would have thought of God's Jericho strategy in a million years. Joshua did not have to engineer the victory; God gave it. Our problem is that so often we substitute our plans for God's priorities, and we foolishly convince ourselves that our ingenuity can be a replacement for our obedience. But Jericho will not yield to any power except the sovereign authority of the Lord, appropriated by us, his people, in our march of obedience and our shout of faith.

> O Church arise and put your armour on;
> Hear the call of Christ our Captain;
> For now the weak can say that they are strong
> In the strength that God has given.
> With shield of faith and belt of truth
> We'll stand against the devil's lies;
> An army bold whose battle-cry is "Love!"
> Reaching out to those in darkness.[4]

8

Tragedy Strikes

JOSHUA 7:1–26

SUDDEN REVERSAL is a common element of our human experience. How often a soccer team is cruising complacently, a goal up on its opponents, only to be eclipsed by two quick goals in the last five minutes! The mark of a great tennis champion is the ability to climb back from being two sets down to an opponent and eventually win in five. We have an ironic description of this when we talk about snatching defeat from the jaws of victory! That is certainly what seems to be happening here in Joshua 7. The preceding chapter ends on such a high note, with Jericho's city walls reduced to piles of rubble, that one might imagine Israel to be on the crest of a wave, about to enjoy an uninterrupted set of easy victories as they occupy the land. But the opposite is in fact the case, and here in chapter 7 tragedy strikes.

The first word of the first verse strikes an ominous note—"But . . ." In fact, as with 6:1, the whole of the first verse sets up the situation of which the rest of the narrative is the explanation and exposure. The walls of Jericho fell flat because of Israel's mighty God, who gave the city into his people's hands. Israel did not have to overcome her enemies by force of arms or military prowess. Yet there was a battle raging as Jericho fell that day, a battle within the hearts of the Israelites themselves, a battle to keep trusting God and observing his instructions in detailed, disciplined obedience. It was a battle that Achan spectacularly lost. The army kept rank in its obedient circuiting of the walls, but at the moment of victory Achan, son of Carmi, "broke faith in regard to the devoted things." Woudstra points out the significance of the verb's literal meaning, frequently translated "trespass." It "means 'to act under cover,'" hence "'treacherously,' 'secretly.' It indicates a breach of trust (Leviticus 5:15), generally against the Lord, as here, by purloining or withholding what was sanctified to him."[1] Moreover, the whole nation was implicated in this act of covenant unfaithfulness, for Achan's theft caused the whole nation to experience the fierce anger of the Lord burning against them (v. 1).

We are told about what has happened right at the beginning of the chapter so we can make spiritual sense of everything that follows. But, of course, Joshua did not know about it until halfway through the narrative, nor did the nation as a whole, and doubtless Achan imagined he had gotten away with it. However, the whole idea of the "devoted things" was designed to teach Israel lessons of holiness and separation, which had been on God's agenda ever since he met Moses in the burning bush at Sinai and commanded him to take off his sandals since he was standing on holy ground. We tend to think of holiness in somewhat limited ethical terms as the word that describes God's perfect moral righteousness. Certainly it does that, but in doing so it becomes a key word that distinguishes God from his creation. Holiness speaks of his sheer "otherness," not only in moral perfection, but in all the divine attributes that separate the Creator from the creature. It is the word that describes the very Godness of God. So to be allied with this supreme divine being demands of his people a set-apartness or separation that reflects their otherness as distinct from an unbelieving and rebellious world. Where that rebellion is relentlessly pursued, as in Canaanite paganism, it must eventually be set apart for destruction. But where the redeemed community of sinners, who have been redeemed by the blood of God's appointed sacrifice, are concerned, they are to be set apart as the Lord's own special possession, to live as reflections of his perfect holiness among "a crooked and twisted generation" (Philippians 2:15). That is our calling too, as Paul is making clear, as the new covenant community.

Many times in Israel's national history, although only some forty years old at this point, the judgment of God has fallen against those who rebel against him and wilfully break covenant. Ethical righteousness can only be made possible by covenant trust and obedience. Israel had to keep herself holy, pure, and undefiled from all the contamination of pagan idolatry that surrounded her. That is why we have the record of Korah's rebellion in Numbers 16, when the Lord "creates something new" (Numbers 16:30) as "the ground opens its mouth and swallows them up." That is why we are told of the plague of snakes in Numbers 21:4–9 as the Lord's response to impatience and ungrateful grumbling. That is why Numbers 25 recounts that when the people of Israel indulged in sexual relations with the people of Moab and "bowed down to their gods . . . Israel yoked himself to Baal of Peor. And the anger of the Lord was kindled against Israel" (Numbers 25:2, 3), and 24,000 died from the resulting plague of God's judgment. God is not open to the charge of double standards with regard to his treatment of Israel and the Canaanites. Joshua is not a narrative of ethnic cleansing; God does not indulge Israel and arrange more favorable terms for them. If the Canaanites are to be judged for their sin and destroyed by God's righteous wrath, so will Israel if she adopts the same disloyalty, idolatry, and impurity. If Achan decides to ally himself with that which is devoted to destruction by taking what belongs exclusively to God and appropriating it for himself, then that destruction will certainly fall upon him, and his Israelite ethnicity will be no defense against God's judgment. Indeed, covenant privileges serve to deepen covenant obligations. As a later prophet would one day declare as the Lord's word, "O people of Israel . . . You only have I known of all the families of the earth; therefore I will punish you for all your iniquities" (Amos 3:1, 2). That is why one man's actions could have such a devastating effect. The camp had become unclean in God's eyes due to Achan's disobedience, and the Lord would therefore no longer go out with them in their battles, until the matter had been settled. However, at this stage no one else is aware of it.

Defeat

This is the unhappy heading for verses 2–5, where sadly everything seems to be going wrong. What we must realize is that the sequence of events is the outcome of the Lord's anger burning against them. This is what Israel will be like if God is no longer with them—very human and very vulnerable. Throughout the narrative there are valid parallels with what happens to the new covenant community, the church, when God's truth is compromised by human rebellion against his divine word. If our message is progressively disregarded or trashed by the prevailing cultural ethos, so that the church becomes known for its ineffectiveness and its capitulation to the enemies of truth, should we not ask ourselves whether this represents a withdrawal of God's presence in blessing because of our compromise and sometimes outright rejection of his word?

Ai is the next city to be dealt with if they are to continue to press further into the land. So they do the sensible human thing, which any responsible commander would order—they send some spies to assess what is required. On this occasion there are no divine tactics given, nor apparently were any sought, though the text does not draw any attention to that fact. The report back has more than a whiff of complacency about it. Ai is not much of a place, and about 2,000 or 3,000 men will easily be able to deal with it, they decide. "Do not make the whole people toil up there, for they are few" (v. 3b). But there were quite enough to cause a major reversal! Perhaps the complacency was bred of overconfidence following the Jericho victory. That was far less arduous than they had expected, and now a smaller and less significant city could surely be accounted for quite speedily. So only 3,000 men go up to fight; but thirty-six do not return. The rest turn tail and run. The first Israelite victims of the conflict lie dead outside Ai, and defeat is staring Joshua and the people in the face. The Jericho shout must have seemed a long time ago.

The comment of verse 5 that "the hearts of the people melted and became as water" is a poignant, ironic echo of Rahab's comment in 2:11 ("our hearts melted, and there was no spirit left in any man because of you") or the narrator's comment in 5:1 that when the kings of the Amorites and the Canaanites "heard that the LORD had dried up the waters of the Jordan for the people of Israel until they had crossed over, their hearts melted and there was no longer any spirit in them because of the people of Israel." Now the boot is on the other foot. Now it is Israel's turn to feel the helplessness and then the panic bred by defeat. There is not a Christian who has not been there, when our disobedience or unfaithfulness to God's word has brought about a total lack of confidence and coherence in our spiritual lives, and our hearts melted with fear. But that is where we will always be as sinful people living in a fallen world if God's gospel smile is turned away because of our unconfessed sin. Then even our prayer mocks us because, as the psalmist testifies, "If I had cherished iniquity in my heart, the Lord would not have listened" (Psalm 66:18). The only way through such despair is the guilty person's cry for grace, "God, be merciful to me, a sinner!" (Luke 18:13). The only way to be justified is to turn from our sin and failure and cast ourselves upon God's mercy.

Dismay

Verses 6–9 describe how Joshua and the elders reacted to this devastating news. Their instinct is right, but their thinking is all over the place. The torn clothes and the dust on their heads are an expression of grief and mourning, but not necessarily of repentance. Indeed, at this stage Joshua does not know that any repentance is needed. So he and the elders go to God—he is "on his face before the ark of the LORD until the evening" (v. 6). But when he speaks, Joshua reveals how flawed his view of what has just happened really is. In many ways it is a rerun or an echo of numerous speeches God had endured from Israel during their forty years in the wilderness. The content is instructive. (1) Why have you let this happen? (2) We would be better off where we were. (3) Now we are disgraced. (4) Our enemies will build on this to destroy us completely. (5) And then what will happen to your great name and reputation? It is a mixture of grief and petulance, perplexity and accusation. It is a powerful reflection of our human hearts and the default position to which we so often return when things are not going our way.

We need to remember that this is the first generation that has to live by the book, without the channel of direct fresh revelation, which Moses had given in the past. As Joshua was meditating on the books of Moses, he might have recalled the promise in which God spoke of his angel in whom is his name, who would go before his people to bring them into the land: "If you carefully obey his voice and do all that I say, then I will be an enemy to your enemies and an adversary to your adversaries" (Exodus 23:22). Clearly the corollary is happening because God's word has either not been heeded or not obeyed. More instructive still is the speed with which Joshua forgets all the guarantees of God's great promises that he will certainly bring them into the land and the confirmations he has just witnessed in the crossing of the Jordan and the fall of Jericho. Of course, Yahweh will not allow the Amorites and Canaanites to destroy his people. Of course, he will not go back on what he promised long ago to Abraham. These are the words of a man in despair, fed by panic. What began as a flawed assessment of Ai based on complacency and trust in human agency has now morphed into a flawed interpretation of God's great salvation purposes, based on just one reversal. Yet Joshua's instinct to pour it all out before the Lord is right and good, because when we are flat on our face before him there is always a way forward. So whenever we find our prayers are peppered with "Ah, Lord, why?" and "if only" and "what can I say" and "what are you going to do about it?" we need to learn from Joshua that it is time to seek and listen to the Lord's directive. Sin always blurs our vision and distorts our view of God, so that we become aggrieved and peevish. Defeat shows us that we are not strong in and of ourselves, and like Joshua we imagine that our enemies are stronger than they are, so strong that even God will not be able to defend his name against them. What rubbish! But how incredibly true to our experience in the paralysis and paranoia that swiftly follow when our whole world seems to come crashing down around us.

Joshua did the right thing with his despair—he took it to God. He didn't say the right words, he didn't have the right diagnosis, but he began to open up the situation to the Lord, and then things begin to change. So whatever our acts of foolish disobedience or overconfident complacency may have produced, perhaps leaving us paralyzed by our helplessness, we need to tell God all about it. We may get it all wrong. That doesn't matter—tell God anyway. It was when Joshua lay before the Lord and laid out his problem that God began to put things right.

Diagnosis

God's diagnostic response (vv. 10–13) begins with a blunt rebuke. It seems that the Lord has little patience with Joshua's prostration, perhaps because the self-pitying, remorseful prayer of his servant is so disregarding of God's faithful promises. The corrective God employs says in effect, "The trouble does not lie with me or any mistakes or volatility of which you may accuse me. The problem is Israel, and the trouble is sin." That is what has caused God's anger, and until that issue is dealt with, relations between the Lord and his people will be strained. The explanation that follows is clear, concise, and instructive, and we should be thankful that the Holy Spirit has caused these verses to be written for our learning.

First, we are told that the essence of the sin, its true nature, is covenant transgression (v. 11). This is expressed by disobedience, but it has deeper significance than that since it affects the very heart of Israel's relationship with Yahweh. The actions are detailed as the verse unfolds—"they have taken . . . they have stolen and lied . . ."—but these are the symptoms of the underlying disease, which is an attack on the relationship of trust and obedience that lies at the heart of the covenant. In order to put things right, the problem has first to be diagnosed. "But God does not merely address the actions of theft, deceit and selfishness."[2] What they represent is an attack on his covenant faithfulness and a rejection of holiness. "Therefore the people of Israel cannot stand before their enemies" (v. 12a). Their sin is the one reason for their defeat and ensuing disgrace at Ai.

Next, God explains the logic of the spiritual mechanism that is at work in this situation. Because Israel has appropriated the devoted things and not offered them to the Lord, to whom they belong, they are now devoted to destruction themselves (v. 12b), and that is why their enemies have prevailed. If you join the side of opposition to Yahweh and rejection of his covenant terms, you make yourself liable to his judgments, as do all his enemies. Worst of all, you divorce yourself from his presence—"I will be with you no more" (v. 12c)—so that the blessings of the covenant can no longer be yours. "Unless"—that is the word of hope in verse 12—"unless you destroy the devoted things from among you." There is a way forward. It involves the renunciation of the sin, which is the essence of repentance, and an act of reconsecration to the service of the covenant Lord. Once again the stress is put upon holiness as the prerequisite for the enjoyment of the covenant relationship. Again the books of Moses teach the principle: "For I am the LORD your God. Consecrate yourselves therefore, and be holy, for I am holy" (Leviticus

11:44). So the restoration process is beginning. The "get up" is repeated (Joshua 7:10, 13a). There is work to be done. The nation has to be assembled and purified ritually in order to be able to appear before the Lord, and he will then deal with the sin that is polluting his people.

Disclosure

The section from verses 14–21 divides into two parts. First, God gives instructions about how the matter is to be resolved (vv. 14, 15), and then we see the familiar pattern of Joshua's detailed obedience, rising early in the morning as he did when Jericho was encircled, as an indication of his readiness to do everything that he is commanded. The process decreed by God is duly worked through, and Achan is disclosed as the offender, to which he confesses (vv. 16–21). Of course, from the very beginning the Lord knows both the offense and the offender, so why does he not reveal the name to Joshua directly? Why this long process?

The answer lies in the fact that the whole nation is implicated in the one man's sin, and although Achan and his family alone will bear the punishment, God deals with the whole nation since they are all the object of his anger. So first all the twelve tribes are to be gathered, since all are infected by the sin. From the twelve, the Lord takes the tribe of Judah, then the clan of the Zerahites, then the household of Zabdi, and lastly the man Achan. All this is determined by lot, to indicate the supremacy of the Lord's will and his sovereign overruling in all the affairs of his people. The process does not depend on human knowledge, wisdom, or choice but entirely on the authority of God. It cannot be engineered or contrived by Joshua or any other human being. As at Jericho, so here Yahweh alone is in sovereign control.

There is a strong, dramatic grip to the narrative as we see God's net closing in on the guilty man, and one can only imagine what that must have meant for Achan. He saw the inevitability of the process and certainly knew his guilt (v. 20), and yet there is no confession until it is wrung out of him and no apparent evidence of remorse, let alone repentance. Either he is paralyzed by the process or stubbornly hardened in his rebellion, but as the text stands, Achan comes out with his hands up (he hasn't gotten away with it), but this is an admission of guilt and nothing more. This seems to be the point of verse 19 where Joshua speaks to Achan personally, almost sympathetically, as a father to a son, exhorting him to give glory and praise to the Lord God of Israel. Is this perhaps an appeal, even at this last moment, not only to confess his sin rather than deny it but also to cast himself on God's mercy? The public confession is important so that God's justice is glorified, but also so that the whole nation is aware of what the sin was and why it was heinous, for the whole nation had been infected by it, and thirty-six men had lost their lives as a result.

Achan's response (vv. 20, 21) is straightforward, almost matter-of-fact in its wording, but it is very instructive for us. His sin is against the Lord, even though its consequences have been grievous for his countrymen. So he does not just say what he did, but he defines his actions as sin and accepts the full responsibility for them ("this is what I did"). Then look at the sequence of verbs in verse 21. "I saw . . . I coveted . . . [I] took . . . they are hidden." Here is exactly the same anatomy of temptation and sin that we witnessed in mankind's first great disobedience in the fall. "When the woman saw that the tree . . . was a delight to the eyes, and that the tree was to be desired to make one wise, she took of its fruit and ate, and she also gave some to her husband who was with her, and he ate . . . and the man and his wife hid themselves from the presence of the LORD God" (Genesis 3:6–8). John puts the same insight into New Testament terms in his first letter. "Do not love the world or the things in the world. If anyone loves the world, the love of the Father is not in him. For all that is of the world—the desires of the flesh and the desires of the eyes and pride of life—is not from the Father but is from the world. And the world is passing away along with its desires, but whoever does the will of God abides forever" (1 John 2:15–17).

Covetousness is the root of the problem. The eighth commandment was broken by Achan because he had already broken the tenth. We constantly face the same pressures. What happens when God's command says "no" and my heart says "but I want it"? Such desires are in direct conflict with God's Law. No wonder that Paul uses this commandment as the great example of the tyranny of sin in our lives. "I would not have known what it is to covet if the law had not said, 'You shall not covet.' But sin, seizing an opportunity through the commandment, produced in me all kinds of covetousness" (Romans 7:7, 8). This is where the battle is joined against the world, the flesh, and the devil every day. It is what I see and desire that will determine what I do, and where that is contrary to God's revealed will in Scripture the Achan issue becomes our issue. Are we prepared to let God be God at this precise point in our lives? For Achan the answer was no. A Babylonian robe, silver, and gold mattered more to him than the word of God and the glory of God. These were the objects of his desire, the idols of his heart—personal grandeur and wealth—and these are the things that he buried in his tent. What idol shrines would God find buried deep within us? We cannot point the finger of righteous superiority at Achan if we know the struggles of our own hearts and the various God-substitutes to which we bow in worship in our tents. If it is true that no one has less of God than he truly desires, then what is it that we still cling to as a rival to his rule deep within our hearts? When we think that something else can take God's place, can earn our trust and devotion, the consequences will always spell disaster.

Destruction

Verses 22–26 bring the whole sorry story to its conclusion. The stolen goods are discovered in Achan's tent, his confession is verified, and the judicial sentence is carried out on everything that Achan has, starting with the silver and gold but including his family and livestock. All are devoted to destruction in the Valley of Achor by stoning and burning. The trouble Achan has caused Israel is now visited upon him, and his line is blotted out from Israel. Here are the terrifying consequences of sin, and a great heap of stones is piled up over those who have been destroyed as a constant reminder and memorial to Israel of sin's outcome. It was only then that the Lord turned from his fierce anger (v. 26).

The message of the final paragraphs concerns the ruthlessness with which sin has to be rooted out and punished. The details are horrifying to us on a purely human level, but they should be felt much more acutely as a spiritual warning. We dare not make God in our own image or downplay his holiness. Achan was not a poor man—he had oxen, donkeys, and sheep. But he was a greedy man, and that poison was his undoing. It had to be ruthlessly exterminated from Israel. Yet that is true of all human sin, for the wage it pays is always death. If we are troubled by Achan's death and the destruction of all that he had, we need to remember what our sin did to our Lord and Savior, Jesus Christ. "He himself bore our sins in his body on the tree, that we might die to sin and live to righteousness. By his wounds you have been healed" (1 Peter 2:24).

For us, the story of Achan should end with the glory of the gospel. We travel back to Calvary and see the spotless, sinless Son of God nailed to a Roman cross because of our iniquities, dying in our place as our representative and substitute so that we might not have to suffer the destruction Achan knew, but instead be forgiven and restored. If it depends on our record, we deserve to be under a pile of stones in the Valley of Achor, or even more terrifying, to be in the eternal punishment that the Scriptures call Hell. "But God, being rich in mercy, because of the great love with which he loved us, even when we were dead in our trespasses, made us alive together with Christ—by grace you have been saved—and raised us up with him and seated us with him in the heavenly places in Christ Jesus" (Ephesians 2:4–6). Hallelujah! What a great Savior! This is the true grace of God, freely given to all who turn to him and trust him, and it is greater than our greatest offenses. But let us not forget that God is ruthless about sin, and let us worship in awe and holy reverence as we see his wrath falling on his own beloved Son to secure our soul's redemption. And let us seek his continuing grace and the power of the indwelling Spirit to enable us to fight the good fight of faith. We need to be ruthless with our greed and envy, our complacency and self-indulgence, our deceit and disobedience. The Lord Jesus paid the price through his death on the cross, and God has buried our sins in the depth of the sea; so let us be done with them and get rid of them and not bury them in our tents. Rather, with Charles Wesley let us praise our rescuing God.

> Plenteous grace with thee is found,
> Grace to cover all my sin;
> Let the healing stream abound;
> Make and keep me pure within.
> Just and holy is thy name,
> I am all unrighteousness;
> False and full of sin I am;
> Thou art full of truth and grace.[3]

9

Conquest Resumed

JOSHUA 8:1–29

ALTHOUGH WE ARE TREATING CHAPTER 8 as a separate unit, it is, of course, totally integrated with chapter 7, and many scholars suggest that we should see no break in thought between them. In his introduction to the whole unit David M. Howard draws attention to the parallels that exist between the Rahab narrative in chapter 2 and the Achan narrative here.

> Rahab, a believing Canaanite, acted faithfully and, as a result, was promised deliverance from destruction. In effect, she became an Israelite. In Joshua 7, Achan, a disbelieving Israelite, acted faithlessly and, as a result, was not delivered but destroyed. In effect, he became a Canaanite. Achan thus stands as a foil to Rahab, and the two characters embody striking contrasts.[1]

Everything depends upon trust in and obedience to the word of the Lord, alongside which ethnicity, gender, or privilege are irrelevant.

In chapter 8 we are back in Rahab territory so to speak as the Lord's anger is turned away from his people and he begins to show his grace in the specific instructions he gives to Joshua, in order to turn the tragedy of defeat at Ai into a glorious victory. Like Rahab, God's people need to put their entire confidence in him and carry out his instructions in detail, which will mean unswerving loyalty to Joshua's leadership. The end result will be a great victory and the progress of the conquest getting back on track.

Divine Initiative

Verses 1, 2 are wonderfully encouraging in a variety of ways. Restoration is often a costly and time-consuming business, not least in the area of broken relationships. So we would not be surprised if Israel felt at some distance from God following the Achan incident and if the business of the conquest was kept on hold for a period of time. But nothing could be further from the reality here. As soon as the sin is dealt with, God's anger is removed, and he takes the initiative in coming to Joshua with words of great encouragement and fresh direction. What God is teaching us about himself in these opening verses is what David was later to affirm in Psalm 23:3—"He restores my soul." He is a great restorer, and he does that with great sensitivity and appropriateness throughout this chapter—in the exhortation of verse 1, the affirmations of verse 2, and the battle plans of verses 8, 18. The word of God is once again in the driver's seat; so the promises of God will certainly be fulfilled. God's restoration deals first with the inward need of the soul, which is then translated into the outward circumstances of life.

God's gracious encouragement to Joshua in verse 1 is, "Do not fear and do not be dismayed." Clearly in chapter 8, as on previous occasions in his life, Joshua is inclined to do and be both. Here are two internal, psychological reasons that could threaten to become roadblocks to the whole process of restoration—fear and discouragement. Both can have a paralyzing effect. Also, we have already seen in chapter 1 that Joshua was naturally prone to both, since he had often to be reminded why he should not succumb to either (1:6, 7). It may be that his basic temperament was inclined to be pessimistic, as is the case with many Christian believers, and that was unlikely to change at a fundamental level. Here God comes in a gentle, strengthening way to unveil his strategy to Joshua and so provide him with the divinely-given assurance of his word as a remedy and corrective to both his adverse circumstances and his possible temperamental weakness. We are not Joshua, and we do not have to try to identify ourselves with his character in order to benefit from this Biblical account. But Joshua's God is our God too, and we can be reassured that his loving care of each of us will be tailored exactly to the situation of our needs, whether the challenges we face are internal, external, or both.

For Joshua, the turning point is the promise of victory (v. 1) because God has "given" Ai into his hand (the past tense is used to express certainty of fulfillment). This is to be a victory as total and irrevocable as that at Jericho. But this time the spoil and livestock can be taken as plunder by the Israelites. If only Achan had been prepared to wait for God's timing! The tactics are simple, although later verses unpack more of the detail. Ai is to be conquered by a strategy of ambush (v. 2b). Again, it is important to see that although the defeated city will be God's gift, there has to be a full utilization of the resources God has given ("take all the fighting men," v. 1), not just the 2,000 to 3,000 of 7:3, 4. There has to be maximum effort, founded on maximum trust ("I have given [Ai] into your hand"). The way to strengthen melting hearts is to go forward in faith, not lamenting the past or wishing that things were other than they are, but rather building on the promises of God and putting our maximum effort into obedience to his commands.

It is worth pausing here to recall how the New Testament reinforces and develops these priorities with regard to our own progress as Christian believers. God's sovereignty and our responsibility are not polar opposites between which we oscillate, but different sides of the same spiritual reality. As has sometimes been stated, our responsibility is our response to his ability, a response of faith and obedience. The two belong together. That was the testimony of the Apostle Paul. "For this [to present everyone mature in Christ] I toil, struggling with all his energy that he powerfully works within me" (Colossians 1:29). The energy and ability, toil and struggle in Christian life and service come from God alone, but we still have to do the work, to utilize what God has given. This was also the advice Paul gave to Timothy. "Think over what I say, for the Lord will give you understanding in everything" (2 Timothy 2:7). You do the thinking, Timothy, and God will grant the understanding, but the one will not come without the other. Supremely, Jude teaches the same principle with great clarity when he exhorts his readers to "keep yourselves in the love of God" (Jude 21) on the grounds that he "is able to keep you from stumbling and to present you blameless before the presence of his glory with great joy" (Jude 24). The two belong together. Many preachers have used a story about a man who wanted to know greater victory in his Christian walk and who was told that he must let God do it for him. So he cut out the six letters L-E-T-G-O-D and fixed them on the wall of his room. When he came home that night the last letter had fallen off, and the message read L-E-T-G-O. So he concluded that the only way to "let God" was to "let go," to cease the struggle, no longer to wrestle and strive, but to rest effortlessly in Christ. This is what J. I. Packer has called "hot tub religion,"[2] a Jacuzzi Christianity. There is a truth in this—we do have to let God be God—but it is a half-truth and a distortion if it leads us to imagine that we do not need to "be all the more diligent to confirm [our] calling and election" (2 Peter 1:10).

Battle Preparations

From verses 3–13 we are given a window into the strategy and its application by which Ai is to be overcome. But we do have some textual difficulties here. Are there 30,000 mighty men of valor involved (v. 3) or only 5,000 (v. 12)?

What is the relationship between verses 3 and 10, both of which describe Joshua and the army (or part of it) rising to go up against Ai? Were there two different actions, or are we looking at one event from different perspectives? There are full discussions of the possibilities in the commentaries, but the difficulty is, I think, superficial and largely due to the narrative method we have already seen operating in chapters 3, 4 with the account of the Jordan crossing and in chapter 6 with the fall of Jericho. Our writer likes to unpack more of the detail of the situation as his narrative progresses, which can sometimes look like repetition or even contradiction. Here, for example, Joshua is simply told in verse 2, "Lay an ambush against the city, behind it." But that is not everything God said because his explanation of how that is to work, in verses 4–8, indicates that all this is "according to the word of the LORD" (v. 8b). The details of the ambush strategy seem to be equally divine in origin. So this section explains the tactics that are to be used, of which the whole force of 30,000 is made aware and is potentially involved. But it is not activated until the next day, when 5,000 of them are chosen by Joshua to carry out the attack (v. 12) and to camp to the west of the city. That would seem to make more sense numerically if the total population of Ai was only 12,000 (v. 25). Also an attack force of 5,000 would be easier to conceal than the whole force of 30,000, who are, however, ready to be engaged, waiting to the north.

The bulk of the army, therefore, marches from Gilgal and is stationed to the north of Ai, across a ravine, but not far away so they can be ready to invade the city (v. 4, activated in v. 11). Joshua and the 5,000 position themselves to the west of Ai, on the way to Bethel, as the attack force (v. 5a, activated in v. 12). Sight of this will bring the people of Ai out to chase off the Israelites as previously, and Joshua will appear to flee with his army as before (v. 6). Then the large ambush to the north will appear, seize the city, and set it on fire, so that the men of Ai, pursuing Joshua, will see their city on fire and become sandwiched between the Israelite ambush and Joshua's attack force (vv. 7, 8). It is because "the LORD your God will give it into your hand" (v. 7) that "you shall do according to the word of the LORD" (v. 8). The details are revealed, the plan is activated, and by verse 13 the two groups are bedded down for the night, north and west of Ai, ready for the battle the next day.

Battle Joined

Suddenly the narrative speeds up at verse 14, and in the section that runs to verse 23 we have the historical record of how Ai came to be defeated. The plans work out perfectly because, as with Jericho, Yahweh is the commander, and he is giving Ai to his people. The king of Ai, seeing the 5,000 camped to the west, thinks this is an acceptable number to engage in conflict. It is somewhat larger than the last force, but the men of Ai already have a record of victory. Accordingly he marches out to a suitable location at which to engage the enemy in order to obviate a siege and to settle the matter a second time, but more decisively (v. 14). The drama is brilliantly written. "But he did not know that there was an ambush against him behind the city" (v. 14b). The ruse works as Joshua and his troops pretend to flee (v. 15), which draws out all the remaining forces inside Ai to join in the pursuit and share the victory laurels. The tactic is disastrous, of course, because "they left the city open" in order to pursue the Israelites (v. 17b).

At this point there is a renewed divine intervention as Joshua is commanded at that moment to lift his javelin against Ai, which seems to have been the signal for the ambush north of the city quickly to enter Ai and set it on fire (vv. 18, 19). The pall of smoke rising from the city can mean only one thing for the pursuing army from Ai, and that is the signal for Joshua and his troops to stop their simulated flight, turn around, and begin to destroy the beleaguered forces, trapped between the Israelites in the field and the Israelites within the city, some of whom came out to join in the slaughter. The consequent annihilation of Ai is total (vv. 22, 25).

Mission Accomplished

The king of Ai is now captured and brought before Joshua (v. 23), though he no longer has a city or population over which to rule. They have been devoted to destruction, as the Lord commanded. Woudstra comments, "As another Moses, Joshua continues to stretch out his hand, holding the javelin until the ban (the *hèrem*) is executed fully upon Ai. Since it was the Lord who originally ordered the extending of this weapon (v18), the narrative means to say that the ban was carried out at the Lord's behest."[3] This is an important point for us, since it reminds us again of the judicial and moral nature of the cleansing of the land of Canaan and exonerates the Israelites from the charge that they were merely pursuing an ethnically-based policy of liquidation.

It also helps us to see the relevance of passages like this to the church today. God's wrath against sin is a facet of the perfect righteousness of his judgment, which requires the punishment of all evil that opposes itself to the holiness of the Creator of all. But there is more to it than that. If God's kingly rule is to be exercised throughout eternity, there is also a necessity that his enemies should not just be defeated but ultimately destroyed by what the book of Revelation calls "the second death" (Revelation 2:11; 20:6; 20:14; 21:8). Joshua 8 therefore carries its own eschatological significance as a precursor of that great and final judgment at the end of time when the devil and all his hosts will be thrown into the lake of fire, along with Death and Hades. "This is the second death, the lake of fire" (see Revelation 20:10–15).

The Old Testament foreshadowing is seen supremely in the prophecy of Isaiah, written as an extended answer to the question posed in his opening chapter. How can the faithless city (Jerusalem) become the faithful city (the new Jerusalem)? Or to put it in more universal terms, how is the sinful human race ever to be rescued, redeemed, and restored to the image of God in which we were created? Isaiah's answer is given in the three portraits of the Messiah as the incarnate Son, God with us, Emmanuel (Isaiah 1—39), the suffering servant (Isaiah 40—55), and the warrior king or the anointed conqueror (Isaiah 56—66). The last of the three figures is especially significant here. In Isaiah 63:1–6 the portrait is drawn of a mysterious figure clothed in splendid apparel, but his garments are red-stained not with the vintage of the trodden grapes but with the lifeblood of the nations, trampled in his wrath. This is "the day of vengeance of our God" (Isaiah 61:2). If there is no ultimate destruction of all God's enemies, there can be no guarantee of the ultimate inviolability of his eternal kingdom of love, joy, and peace.[4] The opposition has to be vanquished and removed if the kingdom of God is to rule as the new creation. So the picture of the king of Ai hanging on a tree until evening (v. 29), gruesome as it is, conveys the reminder that the same destruction ultimately awaits all God's enemies, "for our God is a consuming fire" (Hebrews 12:29). Or in Paul's words, "Then comes the end, when [Christ] delivers the kingdom to God the Father after destroying every rule and every authority and power. For he must reign until he has put all his enemies under his feet. The last enemy to be destroyed is death" (1 Corinthians 15:24–26). This is the logical necessity if there is to be an everlasting kingdom, a holy city, the new Jerusalem, where death shall be no more and where there will be no mourning or crying or pain or tears (see Revelation 21:1–4).

In Joshua 8 the narrative concludes with another memorial pile of stones, heaped up at the gate of Ai over the corpse of its erstwhile king and visible "to this day" (v. 29). It is another permanent reminder that there is but one true and living God who will indefatigably work out his purposes in his world. Psalm 2 summarizes the message of Ai's defeat so memorably. "Now therefore, O kings, be wise; be warned, O rulers of the earth. Serve the LORD with fear, and rejoice with trembling. Kiss the Son, lest he be angry, and you perish in the way, for his wrath is quickly kindled. Blessed are all who take refuge in him" (Psalm 2:10–12). The glorious reality is that we *can* take refuge in him because he hung on a tree for us, outside the city walls, that Good Friday afternoon, and because he took our place, atoned for our sins, and carried our guilt we will not face the fate of the king of Ai, which is what we deserve.

> But we never can prove the delights of his love
> Until all on the altar we lay;
> For the favor he shows, for the joy he bestows,
> Are for them who will trust and obey.[5]

10

Covenant Renewed

JOSHUA 8:30-35

WHERE NEXT? That must have been the question uppermost in the minds of the people of Israel as they concluded the business of the conquest of Ai and began to look for the next steps of advance into the land. But for Joshua there is not a flicker of doubt about what comes next. He has the guidebook. My wife and I enjoy following planned walks of a recreational or historical nature, which can introduce you to all sorts of byways and hidden treasures you might otherwise miss. You are in the hands of the expert, who provides the script, and there is great satisfaction in following the instructions and benefiting from the expertise. That is always supposing that the script is both accurate and clearly expressed; otherwise confusion and frustration can quickly take over!

Follow the Script

But for Joshua there is no such problem. He has the script. "This Book of the Law shall not depart from your mouth, but you shall meditate on it day and night, so that you may be careful to do according to all that is written in it" (1:8). And in Joshua's instructed mind there is no doubt what must come next. Deuteronomy 27:1–8 make the procedure very clear in the words that God gave through Moses and the elders to the whole nation. After the crossing of the Jordan, they are to make their way to Mount Ebal where all the words of God's Law are to be written on large stones coated with plaster. An altar of uncut stones is to be built for the presentation of burnt offerings and fellowship offerings to the Lord. But there is more to follow. Deuteronomy 27:9ff. instructs the nation to assemble there, six tribes on Mount Gerizim and six tribes on Mount Ebal, where the blessings and curses of the covenant are to be recited by the

Levites to all the people. This is clearly the script that Joshua is now carrying out in meticulous detail. He is being careful to do everything as prescribed by God through Moses. This is the clear message of our opening verse (8:30), which sets the scene, and is followed in verse 31 by the reminder that this is "as it is written in the Book of the Law of Moses."

"Follow the script" is clearly the first message of this unit, as it is so frequently throughout this whole book. Mount Ebal and Mount Gerizim stand opposite each other, Ebal to the north and Gerizim to the south, with the settlement of Shechem between them. After the victory at Ai, the nation made a journey of about twenty miles, through occupied territory, to the beautiful valley of Shechem, which is about two miles wide. It was clearly something of an amphitheatre, where the natural acoustics would facilitate the ceremony that our passage describes. Again the location was prescribed even earlier by Moses in Deuteronomy 11:29, 30: "And when the LORD your God brings you into the land that you are entering to take possession of it, you shall set the blessing on Mount Gerizim and the curse on Mount Ebal. Are they not beyond the Jordan, west of the road, toward the going down of the sun, in the land of the Canaanites who live in the Arabah, opposite Gilgal, beside the oak of Moreh?" To the north, Mount Ebal was barren and rocky, which is where they found the uncut stones to build the altar and from where the covenant curses were to be proclaimed. To the south, Mount Gerizim was wooded and fruitful, and from here the blessings were to be recited. Even the natural characteristics of the landscape would serve to reinforce the spiritual message of the Law and would proclaim that there are only two ways to live, and they carry profoundly different consequences. This message still needs to be preached today.

Renew the Relationship

Although there is no doubt that God commanded, through Moses, that this event should take place soon after the crossing of the Jordan, the first necessity was to take Jericho and then Ai as these garrison towns barred the way north to the Shechem valley. The defeat at Ai had added to the time delay. But it had also served to alienate the Lord from his people, since as God said to Joshua, "Israel has sinned; they have transgressed my covenant that I commanded them" (7:11). So before there can be any further forward movement, this relationship had to be renewed. This was begun with the exposure and judgment of Achan, but there needed now to be a national recommitment ceremony. It is easy to read this section as simply a breathing space after the two initial victories, but it has much greater spiritual significance. Not only does the nation need consciously to renew its relationship with the covenant

Lord, on whom all their prosperity depends, but also, as always, God is moving in grace toward his people by consolidating their victories in terms of their relationship of dependence on him.

The order is significant. First come the sacrificial offerings (v. 31b), followed by the public copying of the Law on to the plastered stones (v. 32). Then the people assembled for the reading of the Law, with its blessings and curses, and the whole nation ("assembly") was gathered together under its authoritative truth (v. 35). We have become used to the idea of physical markers of great events in the progressive fulfilment of God's purposes for Israel in the book of Joshua, such as the twelve stones at Gilgal (4:20–24) or the judgment piles over Achan (7:26) and the king of Ai (8:29). Here the permanence of the Law in visible, written form is an important marker, enabling what Joshua had until now retained as his personal possession, probably handed down from Moses (v. 32), to become the property of the whole nation. There is also a sense in which its public reading within the land is a proclamation that the land belongs to God and that these are the only terms on which it can be possessed and enjoyed. How the inhabitants of Shechem reacted to this we are not told, but it is likely that the defeat of Ai renewed their fear of Israel and her God, and certainly this covenant reading served as something of an eviction notice on all who refused to submit to the Lord's rule.

There is, however, a further level of significance here. Genesis 12:7, 8 records that after God had given his great covenant promises to Abram, Abram "moved to the hill country on the east of Bethel. . . . And there he built an altar to the LORD and called upon the name of the LORD." When he later separated from Lot and went to live at Hebron, again "he built an altar to the LORD" (Genesis 13:18). Woudstra helpfully comments, "Altar building, during the patriarchal period, often had accompanied theophanies in the land of Canaan. These altars were an expression of the symbolical claim which the patriarchs, themselves 'strangers and sojourners' in the land of promise, were laying to the land of Canaan which had been given to them."[1] As this altar was built on Mount Ebal it was a visible demonstration that the divine promises had indeed been fulfilled. Abraham's descendants are indeed being given the land, and here is another tangible confirmation of Yahweh's utterly dependable faithfulness.

The offerings have their own deep significance. First, the altar is built at the place where the curses are to be pronounced. That is why the burnt offerings are mentioned first (v. 31). When the sacrificial system was first instituted, the burnt offering stood at the head of the list. Leviticus 1:4 tells us that the worshipper is to "lay his hand on the head of the burnt offering, and it shall be accepted for him to make atonement for him." That is why the animal is to be "without blemish" and the whole of it is to be consumed by fire, as "a pleasing aroma to the LORD" (Leviticus 1:10, 13). Clearly these offerings come first to deal with the residual effects of Israel's covenant-breaking sin at Ai. The atoning sacrifice removes all guilt and reestablishes the proper relationship between a repentant nation and her covenant Lord.

Only then is the way open to sacrifice fellowship offerings, often called "peace offerings" (v. 31). The same requirements, that the animal be without defect and that the offerer lay his hand upon its head, pertain (Leviticus 3:1, 2), but this voluntary act of worship is a celebratory thanksgiving for restored fellowship with God and with others. Thus it included a communal meal in which parts of the sacrificed animals could be eaten by the participants. First comes the establishment of righteousness and then the enjoyment of peace. Indeed this principle that there can be no peace except on a basis of righteousness is woven throughout the Old Testament witness. Even that mysterious figure Melchizedek, the priest-king from the patriarchal period, is used to teach the point. As Hebrews 7:2 points out, "He is first, by translation of his name, king of righteousness, and then he is also king of Salem, that is, king of peace." The principle is equally clear and unchanging throughout the apostolic teaching.[2] So as New Testament believers there are principles here that we really need to embrace and hold firmly.

Commit to the Covenant

This event is in itself a witness to the covenant faithfulness of Yahweh to keep the promises he has made. Its geographical location (inside the promised land) and its spiritual purpose (opening the way to renewed fellowship with God and the subsequent enjoyment of all his promised blessings) both testify eloquently to the fact that God is on target with his purposes to multiply and bless his people. The obvious corollary to this is that Israel must, in her turn, recommit herself to the covenant obligations, on which the covenant privileges all hang.

All the potential is there, waiting to be realized. The ark of the covenant, the visible representation of the presence of God, is present in the very midst of his people (v. 33). His people are assembled all around him, with the Lord himself at the center of their national life. The very fact that this great multitude is there is testimony to the promise fulfilled to bless Abram and make of him a great nation (Genesis 12:2). The fact that they are gathered here, in this place, in the heart of the land is testimony to the promise fulfilled to give to Abraham's offspring a land of their own, this very land, to take possession of it (Genesis 15:7). In this rehearsing of the covenant there is, therefore, a strong element of thanksgiving and joy, expressed by the fellowship offerings, at the very heart of which is the recognition that all this has not only been promised but accomplished by the Lord's mighty power. The initial victories are strong reinforcement of the dependability of covenant promises for coming hostilities. Their conquering Lord has given them this land since it is his own, and his altar established and his Law read are proclamations of his sovereignty over these massive historical developments.

Everybody needs to hear the repeated revelation of the mind and will of God—men, women, children, the resident aliens including proselytes like Rahab (v. 35b). And they need to hear "all the words of the law" (v. 34). Every individual has a personal responsibility to be obedient to the terms of the covenant, and neither gender nor age nor ethnic origin is a cause for exception. There is never to be another Achan. We are not told specifically about the people's response, for only God knows the heart, but certainly no one was left in any doubt as to what the Lord required of them and how to live so as to be pleasing to him. However, the predominant note is that of blessing the people of Israel (v. 33b). Yes, the curses will have to be read and heeded, since they are the obverse side of the covenant relationship when unfaithfulness occurs; but they are not the main emphasis, nor is their avoidance the major motivation. It is the rehearsal of the blessings that is designed to win the people's gratitude and affections, so that obedience becomes the natural response of thankfulness. "Just look what can be yours if you will love the Lord your God with all your being, expressed by trust and obedience." That is the emphasis.

This is helpful as we come to see how these principles relate to us in our own day. We live in a culture that wants to be self-sufficient. We don't want to have to trust or be dependent on anybody; we want to run our own lives in our own way. We are adept at creating and worshipping any number of idols as substitutes for God, but behind them all stands the great idol of self—governing our lives with all the false confidence of creaturely pride in rebellion against the Creator. Obedience then becomes a hateful concept, since we have come to believe that no one (not even God if he exists) has the right to tell us what or what not to do. One of the most recorded popular songs in recent decades is "My Way," with its recurring line "I did it my way." So when someone is converted to Christ, a great deal of reprogramming is needed. The most fundamental Christian creed is, "Jesus Christ is Lord," which is why he can be the Savior. Yet so much contemporary evangelism either plays down or even ignores this central reality. Thus we have many who would claim Jesus as Savior and expect to enjoy all the blessings of forgiveness and peace, but who clearly are not living their daily lives with Jesus as Lord. Biblically this is not just inconsistent but ultimately impossible, since there cannot be a rescue without coming under the rescuer's rule.

The problem is that we do not think in covenant terms. We are so individualistic that we imagine Christ's work is primarily to bless me personally, to tolerate my continuing sins, and even to be grateful for my allegiance to his cause. In this view all the benefits of the new covenant flow one way, from Christ's work on the cross into my life, without there being any ongoing demands on me of covenant loyalty, expressed by faith and obedience. When the alternative view is presented and the glorious blessings of the new covenant are shown to be only experienced through faith that submits in loving obedience to Jesus as Lord, it is frequently labeled as legalistic. We have been redeemed from the curse of the Law; so we are not to go back to the bondage of its rules and regulations. That is the way to tie ourselves up again in works religion instead of enjoying the free gift of God's grace in Jesus Christ.

Of course, there are grave distortions that devalue grace and drive many back to a religion of performance, as though we could attempt to justify ourselves by our keeping of the Law. This leads either to ignorant pride or abject despair. We need to guard against this default position of the human heart, both in our own lives and in our teaching of others. We are all works religionists by nature, and the last thing our sinful, self-justifying hearts want to do is to cast ourselves on God's mercy and be totally dependent on his grace. But there is an equivalent danger of forgetting that the blood of the new covenant not only seals our pardon, in the unbreakable guarantees of God's justifying grace, but also seals our ownership. Having been redeemed "with the precious blood of Christ, like that of a lamb without blemish or spot" (1 Peter 1:19), we belong to the one who has paid the purchase price to liberate us from our slavery to sin. As Ephesians 1:13, 14 teaches us, believers have been marked with a seal of divine ownership, in the gift of the Holy Spirit as a down payment and guarantee of the full redemption and total transformation that will one day be ours. In the same vein Paul asks the Corinthians, "Do you not know that your body is a temple of the Holy Spirit within you, whom you have from God? You are not your own, for you were bought with a price. So glorify God in your body" (1 Corinthians 6:19, 20). We do not seek to obey the Lord in order to obtain either his forgiveness or his covenant blessings. Rather, it is because we have already received these gifts by grace that we seek to show our love and gratitude in and through our obedience. Listen to Jesus himself. "Whoever has my commandments and keeps them, he it is who loves me" (John 14:21). "If anyone loves me, he will keep my word" (John 14:23). "If you keep my commandments, you will abide in my love, just as I have kept my Father's commandments and abide in his love" (John 15:10). "You are my friends if you do what I command you" (John 15:14).

The pattern is inescapable, and Joshua 8:30–35 is one of its strongest Old Testament expressions. But it was there from the very beginning of Israel's covenant history. The crossing of the Red Sea launched them on the path that led directly to Sinai, where the Law was given to redeemed people so that they might know how to live in right relationship with their Redeemer. It was not given as a means of rescue but as a means of grace for the already rescued. The preface to the Ten Commandments could not be clearer—"I am the LORD your God, who brought you out of the land of Egypt, out of the house of slavery" (Exodus 20:2)—and then the commandments immediately follow. The God who has carried them on eagles' wings to himself is the one who has the right to say, "Now you are to obey me fully and keep my covenant" (see Exodus 19:4, 5). The crossing of the Jordan has launched them on a path that leads them to Mount Gerizim and Mount Ebal and to the reaffirmation of both God's covenant mercy and his covenant requirements as the whole nation is committed once again to his sovereign rule through rescue. Obedience, then, is not the price that God demands in order to dispense blessings from his otherwise reluctant grasp. Rather it is the means by which the channels of overflowing grace are kept open, so that all the blessings of the covenant faithfulness of Yahweh can be experienced by a dependent people who trust and obey.

For us, the fact that covenant privileges require covenant obligations is fulfilled corporately every time we come to the Lord's Table as his redeemed people, to eat the bread and drink the wine, in remembrance that every good we have is entirely the gift of his grace. As we feed on Christ in our hearts, by faith, with thanksgiving, we are expressing that indissoluble union with our Lord, which means that, because we are in him and he in us, we are committing ourselves again to be holy, because he is holy. But we do not have to wait for a Communion service celebration. Our altar is the wooden cross of Calvary, where the sin offering was made for us, once for all and where fellowship is established between God and man. We can, and should, be there every day of our lives in our personal devotional time with the Lord, reclaiming his forgiveness and reaffirming our own trust in his promises of grace and renewing our commitment to obey his commands.

This, then, was how God consolidated the victory over Ai. The place of sacrifice became the place of covenant commitment. It is one thing to win a victory, but another to consolidate it by a renewed commitment to God. Many of us in the very ecstasy of victory begin to drift from our total dependence on the Lord. We need to have the insistence of Psalm 44 ringing in our ears: "You with your own hand drove out the nations, but them [Israel] you planted . . . for not by their own sword did they win the land, nor did their own arm save them, but your right hand and your arm, and the light of your face, for you delighted in them" (Psalm 44:2, 3). That is why their security was total as long as they obeyed; but it also explains why any rebellion against God's commands could only spell disaster, as it still does. Being a Christian is not about playing spiritual games or having a spare-time religious interest. It demands the whole of our being, since spiritual neutrality is impossible. We cannot worship truly at the cross, our altar, and then go on living in disobedience, because the two attitudes are mutually exclusive. But if we seek to live in obedience, although we will often fail and fall, if our lives are characterized by repentance and faith, God is with us. He is committed to those who trust him, and his victories will become ours.

> When I survey the wondrous cross
> On which the Prince of Glory died,
> My richest gain I count but loss
> And pour contempt on all my pride.
>
> Were the whole realm of nature mine,
> That were an offering far too small;
> Love so amazing, so divine,
> Demands my soul, my life, my all.[1]

11

Flattering to Deceive

JOSHUA 9:1–26

WHOEVER LONGS FOR A QUIET LIFE has been born in the wrong generation." These words are attributed to Trotsky, as the Russian revolution appeared to sweep everything away before its advance. But has there ever been
a generation that has not known conflict as a given of everyday life? Certainly no Christian can expect to be immune from the conflict "against the
rulers, against the authorities, against the cosmic powers over this present
darkness, against the spiritual forces of evil in the heavenly places," all of
which are "the schemes of the devil" (Ephesians 6:11, 12). That is why the
Prince of Peace told his disciples, "Do not think I have come to bring peace
to the earth. I have not come to bring peace, but a sword" (Matthew 10:34).
There is no easy ride for the people of God in this fallen world, for it lies
in the powerful grip of the evil one (1 John 5:19). Realism recognizes that
conflict is endemic to human life and unavoidable for a Christian disciple.

One fruitful way of reading the Old Testament is to trace the devil's
constant resistance to the purposes of God as he does everything possible to
prevent the coming of the offspring of the woman who will crush the serpent's
head (Genesis 3:15). Now as the promise of the land begins to be realized
in Israel's experience, it is not surprising that the opposition increases in its
size and intensity. At one level it could be argued that the Canaanite kings
mentioned in Joshua 9:1, 2 are simply human leaders trying to preserve
their inheritance against invaders. But the perspective of the book of Joshua,
reflecting the insights of the whole Bible, teaches us to see these events as
part of that cosmic spiritual conflict of which Joshua's conquest is the earthly
outworking. After all, this part of the world had long been under the devil's
control, and over centuries the sins of the Amorites had multiplied, and now

the pot was overflowing with wickedness, all of which constituted an assault upon the righteous character of their Creator. The conquest is a divine initiative to cleanse the land of its iniquity. So it is not going to happen without diabolic resistance, which means conflict.

For Israel, this means that at this stage they have to focus on their one supremely important task and commission—often to fight, always to pray, and above all to be obedient to everything God commands them. He is giving them the land, but it is not presented on a plate. This in itself is a depiction of the Christian life in our still fallen world, where there are no spiritual advances, personally or corporately, without challenge and conflict. But the great lesson is that the outcome is not in the balance at all. As the opening chapters of Job reveal, the devil is real and implacably opposed to God and his people; but as a creature he is ultimately subservient to God's will, under God's judgment, and facing God's eternal condemnation. The perspective of the Bible is that whatever rope he may be allowed is only given so that the greater purposes of God may be fulfilled, to the greater praise of the glory of God's grace. This means that while the alliance of Canaanite kings at the start of chapter 9 is powerful and daunting in human terms, and the devil would love to have Israel tremble before them, we need to read all that is happening here in the light of 11:20: "For it was the Lord's doing to harden their hearts that they should come against Israel in battle, in order that they should be devoted to destruction and should receive no mercy but be destroyed, just as the LORD commanded Moses." It brings great glory to God when the overweening arrogance of evil is temporarily allowed to demonstrate itself in what turns out to be its own destruction. That is what divine sovereignty is all about.

Before we look at this chapter in detail, it will be helpful to take a step back and remind ourselves of the structure of the book as a whole and to take note of where we are, since chapter 9 is clearly designed to begin a new section. As David M. Howard points out, 9:1 is an almost exact repeat of the formula that we saw in 5:1.[1] There the verse served to introduce the second main section of the book, which runs to the end of chapter 8. So in broad terms chapters 1—4 detail the preparations for the conquest culminating in the miraculous crossing of the Jordan, and chapters 5—8 record the initial victories, starting with the consecration of the nation, the miraculous fall of Jericho, the victory at Ai, and the covenant renewal at Mount Ebal. Now we launch into the third section (chapters 9—12), which takes us further into the conquest and culminates in the list of defeated kings in chapter 12. The unit deals in detail with the Gibeonite deception, Israel's victory in the battle at Gibeon, and the later victory at the waters of Merom, with many other references to cities and kings that fell before the Israelite advance. Joshua 9:1, 2 and 12:7–24 act as the bookends of the unit, detailing first the kings who set themselves "to fight against Joshua and Israel" and then, at the end, "what became of them."[2] This section is the major bulk of the conquest narrative, and many spiritual lessons can be learned from it.

Determined Opposition

Although the wording of 9:1 begins with an almost exact replica of 5:1, the outcome is very different. In chapter 5, the kings' "hearts melted and there was no longer any spirit in them because of the people of Israel." But now "they gathered together as one to fight against Joshua and Israel" (9:2). What has made the difference is surely Ai. The miraculous Jordan crossing and Jericho's extraordinary collapse terrified these kings. Perhaps the Israelites and their God, Yahweh, really were invincible. But the defeat at Ai also put new heart into them. They would need the greatest strength they could muster, hence the coalition of verse 1; but now they are confident enough to take the fight to the Israelites. Reversals and defeat always empower the enemy, which is why the people of God can never become blasé about their total dependence upon him. There will be more coalitions of opposition throughout this section. Joshua 10:3 draws our attention to the southern coalition of five kings under Adoni-zedek, king of Jerusalem, while 11:1, 2 details the northern coalition under Jabin, king of Hazor. The opposition is increasingly determined and organized. Indeed, the extent of it from the hill country through the western foothills to the coastal plain as far north as Lebanon (v. 1) seems deliberately recorded so that the reader grasps just how widespread and potentially devastating this opposition now is. The whole country is in arms against Israel.

But fighting is not the only way to oppose God's purposes, and though we might expect the rest of the chapter to detail a great battle between the alliance and the Israelites, nothing of the sort seems to have happened. We hear no more of the Canaanite kings until chapter 10, when the alignment is rather different. So although the intended threat is daunting, at this point it does not materialize. Instead our attention is directed to a totally different but no less determined attempt to oppose and subvert God's purposes. The rest of the chapter is the narrative of the Gibeonite deception. Joshua 9:24 provides the key: "Because it was told to your servants for a certainty that the LORD your God had commanded his servant Moses to give you all the land and to destroy all the inhabitants of the land from before you—so we feared greatly for our lives because of you and did this thing." Instead of coming out to fight, although "Gibeon was a great city . . . and all its men were warriors" (10:2), they decided to risk a more subtle, manipulative, and deceptive approach to save their own skins and to forestall the conquest of their city. "They on their part acted with cunning" (9:4a).

Deception and Disguise

This different tactic is surprising and totally unexpected. Verses 3–15 tell the story very effectively, at times almost humorously, as we watch the Israelites swallowing the Gibeonite bait. All too easily they are caught in the trap. The Gibeonites are reacting to exactly the same news about Jericho and Ai that all the other city-states had heard, but their response is ingenious, to say the least. Gibeon was an important city with a number of other small and probably dependent towns clustered around it. It could have defended itself as well as any other city, but their thinking is outside the Canaanite box. Why walk into conflict and potential destruction when you might be able to negotiate your way around it? What about a covenant, a binding agreement, to assure peace without capitulation? Certainly it must be worth a try, but there has to be a carefully prepared deception if they are to have a chance.

The book of Joshua frequently reminds us that one primary means of advance in the conquest is the word of truth about Israel's God and what he has done getting into the Canaanite cities and into the hearts of the leaders. The Gibeonites know that the fall of Jericho and Ai are just stage one in the process by which God will give the land to the Israelites and destroy its inhabitants (v. 24). Did they also know the details of what God had commanded in Deuteronomy 20:10–18? Probably so. In a nutshell there is a divine provision for the Israelites to offer terms of peace to a city before attacking it, provided it is a city "very far from you" and not a city "of the nations here" (Deuteronomy 20:15). Those close by are to be destroyed. A peaceful surrender leading to servitude is an option for the more distant cities, which explains why the Gibeonites claim, "We have come from a distant country" (Joshua 9:6) and then produce their evidence to prove it.

The ruse is well-prepared and confidently executed. Worn-out sacks, wine skins, sandals, and clothing along with "dry and crumbly" provisions (v. 5) all seem to add weight to their story. They arrive at Gilgal, which is still the headquarters of operations for Joshua (v. 6), and make their request for a covenant directly to him. Here, however, the narrator, with the benefit of hindsight, inserts a warning note by identifying them as "Hivites" for the benefit of us, the readers (v. 7). There is an irony in the objection of the men of Israel that perhaps they live nearby. In fact, Gibeon is less than twenty miles away and should certainly be devoted to destruction. But the ruse of disguise is now followed up by flattery. Twice they tell Joshua they are his "servants" (vv. 8, 9), that they are submissive to him. Furthermore, it is the fame of Yahweh that has brought them such a long way to make an alliance with him (vv. 9, 10). The reports of what God has done to his enemies brings them to sue for peace. It is all very convincing. Nothing is said about the recent victories over Jericho or Ai because they have been traveling while all this was happening, from very far away, they claim. They hadn't caught up with the news bulletins yet. It all fitted the story, and the dry, crumbly food seemed undeniable corroboration.

What will Joshua and Israel decide to do? That is the issue poised at the end of verse 13. Will they go on the evidence of what they see and what they hear, what their senses and logical deduction seem to tell them? Or will they follow what the Law given to Moses prescribed? Numbers 27:21 is very specific in the instructions directly to Joshua about what he is to do when the Book of the Law does not cover the detail of a particular circumstance. "He [Joshua] shall stand before Eleazar the priest, who shall inquire for him by the judgment of the Urim before the LORD." That will provide the authoritative direction. But verse 14 of our text is the sad reality and constitutes the turning-point in the story. The men "sampled" (NIV) some of the provisions, "but did not ask counsel from the LORD." Here they walk by sight and not by faith, as we so frequently do ourselves.

Nobody asks God what they should do—that is the tragedy of the situation. If the enemy cannot batter down the front door, he will slip in by a side entrance in order to compromise God's people in their fulfillment of God's will. Notice that all the leaders are implicated in this, although Joshua is the one who draws up the binding agreement "to let them live" (v. 15). They moved forward entirely depending on their own senses and logic, their own wisdom, but they did not follow the Lord's word and ask the Lord's counsel. They did not pray (v. 14). Instead they entered into a covenant sealed with a solemn oath, the most serious commitment it was possible to make. The applications to our own faithlessness and folly are many and obvious. A challenging statement in James 4:17 says, "So whoever knows the right thing to do and fails to do it, for him it is sin." The context is a false self-confidence about our future rather than a daily submission of every part of our lives to the will of God. We are all guilty of many sins of omission. How often the Lord is waiting for us to seek him, to pray that he will direct our steps and govern our decision-making through the light of his Word and the grace of his providence. Yet how often we snatch our lives back into our own control. We sample the moldy bread, and we act foolishly because we have been deceived by what we see and what people say, by flattery and pride.

Disguise and flattery are still among the enemy's most often used and frequently successful weapons to bring about compromise on God's revealed will and required standards in our lives as his redeemed people. In our personal relationships, in our church life, in our homes and families, as well as in our business and professional life, we are constantly under pressure not to follow God's Word in complete dependence and obedience, but to make alliances with people who may seem impressive and charming, yet will lead us further and further away from doing the will of God. We are not to be ignorant of the devil's devices. We must never forget that appearances can be deceptive; indeed they very often are.

Remorse and Resolution

When we drift into making our decisions on the basis of moldy bread, rather than inquiring of the Lord, we are bound to face a rude awakening. And here it comes with great rapidity in verse 16. Suddenly the horror of the reality hits them. The Gibeonites are in fact their neighbors, living among them. In fact, verse 17 indicates there was a larger federation of cities, of which Gibeon was probably the chief, which the Israelites visited to ascertain the truth but did not attack. It seems there was some impetus among the people to do just that, because they complain strongly against the compromise into which Joshua and the leaders have led them (v. 18), but the oath prevents them. The leaders rightly assume responsibility for what has happened (v. 19); to add a further wrong by breaking the solemn oath they have sworn "by the LORD, the God of Israel" would not make things right. This is the first act of wisdom in the chapter. As verse 20 makes clear, if they were to break the terms of their promise they would themselves become liable to God's wrath since his name has been involved in the process.

The honor of Yahweh is at stake, and his very name implies that he is the God who faithfully keeps every one of his promises. To turn upon the Gibeonites would be to infer that Yahweh's word is unreliable, that his character is capricious and his actions unpredictable. His name is not to be trodden underfoot because of his people's foolish mistakes. However remorseful they may feel and however inconvenient it may prove to be, there is no alternative for Israel. For the Gibeonites, it meant their lives were spared, but their future was one of servitude (v. 21). In making them "cutters of wood and drawers of water," the Israelites are reverting to the script of the Law of Moses (Deuteronomy 20:10, 11) and to the practice that seems already to have been active regarding the aliens within the community of Israel (Deuteronomy 29:11). As Joshua makes clear (vv. 22, 23), this is a punishment for their deception. The primary need for wood and water was for the ministry of the tabernacle, but verse 27 indicates that the servant role was to be wider than that. The Gibeonites became a subservient people within Israel.

That is expressed by their reaction to Joshua's interrogation, recorded in verses 24, 25. They are perfectly straightforward in their response to his question, "Why did you deceive us?" (v. 22). They have heard that in giving the land to the Israelites, "the LORD your God" had commanded Moses to destroy the inhabitants; so they were motivated by two fears. The first was common human fear for one's life in the face of a powerful enemy. But the second was the fear of Israel's God, brought out in the phrase "for a certainty" (v. 24). Although their knowledge of Yahweh is minimal at this point, their awe for what he had already accomplished led them to sue for terms of peace. They are content to put themselves and their future into his hands by submitting to Joshua. "Whatever seems good and right in your sight to do to us, do it" (v. 25b). This is a great statement of submission, which illustrates that the fear of the Lord is indeed the beginning of wisdom (Proverbs 1:7).

The note at the end of verse 27 that the Gibeonites continued in Israel "to this day" is a significant pointer to the future. Promises made in the name of Yahweh are never to be broken, as Israel's first king, Saul, was to demonstrate. In 2 Samuel 21:1, 2, King David, suffering from three years of famine in Israel, discovers that this is "bloodguilt on Saul and on his house, because he put the Gibeonites to death" (v. 1b). In his zeal for his country, Saul attempted to remove them and so to break the oath sworn by Joshua. But an oath sworn in the name of Yahweh can never be broken, not even by an anointed king. The Gibeonites continued in Israel through the generations, even beyond the Babylonian exile, so that when the walls of Jerusalem were being rebuilt centuries later under Nehemiah, we find among the list of the builders "Melatiah the Gibeonite and . . . the men of Gibeon" (Nehemiah 3:7).

As we reflect on this curious incident, we can make several general observations. One unwise decision and commitment had continuing repercussions for both peoples down the years. We should be particularly cautious about trusting our own judgment, since appearances can be deceptive and our own perspectives are partial and limited. That is one reason why the Bible tells us not to judge people by what we see. Only the Lord can know the heart. This narrative becomes, then, a negative example by which we can better understand and reinforce the positives of Proverbs 3:5–6: "Trust in the LORD with all your heart, and do not lean on your own understanding. In all your ways acknowledge him, and he will make straight your paths." All these inferences are valid and useful, but the danger is that we forget that God is always the hero of the Old Testament narratives, and thus we become confined to the human sphere in terms of application, ending up with a few pieces of good advice and a moralizing tone.

What is God teaching us about himself in this story? Surely we are meant to see his overruling, sovereign hand in everything that happened and through that his total rule and ingenious redirections both of the devil's attacks and of his people's weakness and fallibility. This incident is clearly a different sort of satanic attack on God and his purposes—much more cunning and subtle than outright hostile aggression—but it is nonetheless real. The Gibeonite deception has all the marks of the devil's lies throughout. So it seems likely that this incident represents an attempt to destroy Israel from within, bringing Canaanite idolatry and immorality into the very heart of the nation, and so threatening the worship of the living God and the fulfillment of his stated purposes. How does God deal with the devil's devices? He uses human agents to keep the altar fires in the temple burning and to keep the water well supplied for the cleansing rituals, so as to continue, increase, and extend Israel's worship of their living God. The very thing the enemy planned to destroy is preserved and enhanced by God's overruling providence. This does not provide an easy excuse for our failure and sinful self-confidence, but it gives wonderful hope to those of us who are only too conscious of our past mistakes and weaknesses. And in the ingenious wisdom that belongs to God alone, he even causes the Gibeonites, the agents of deception, to be rescued. It was their temporal blessing that their lives were spared, but their eternal blessing that they were made members of the community of Yahweh and Israel, albeit as woodcutters and water carriers.

This is the glory of Yahweh. He cannot be outmaneuvered by human cunning or hindered by human fallibility. That glory is shown in the grace that can turn a curse into a blessing, that can use our mistakes and foolishness to bind us more closely than ever to him, that can reveal where we went wrong and make it become the means by which we can begin to go right. Think of those ninety-five sons of Gibeon rebuilding the walls of Jerusalem (Nehemiah 7:25). What privileges came their way because their lives were refocused on the tabernacle, the place of sacrifice and communion with God, the manifestation of his living presence among his people! In David Howard's words, "They appear to have been fully assimilated among the Jews, as much believers in Israel's God as was Rahab and other foreign 'converts' and as much recipients of God's grace."[3] Neither the Gibeonites nor the Israelites came out of the story untainted, but the grace of God superabounds over all human sin and failure. He is the hero of the story.

   And that grace leads us directly to the cross, where we see in the clearest possible way that "the free gift is not like the trespass. For if many died
through one man's trespass, much more have the grace of God and the free
gift by the grace of that one man Jesus Christ abounded for many . . . so that,
as sin reigned in death, grace also might reign through righteousness leading
to eternal life through Jesus Christ our Lord" (Romans 5:15, 21).

12

No Day Like It

JOSHUA 10:1-15

SOME DAYS IN OUR personal experience and as a nation are so extraordinary that we say we will never forget them as long as we live. They are usually days of remarkable achievement or unexpected deliverance, often in a context of conflict. I think of the Battle of Britain, fought in the skies above the English Channel coast, where I am now sitting in my peaceful study writing these words. Or the evacuation from Dunkirk or the Normandy landings, both of which were turning points in World War II. Just two days ago, as I write, with the Olympics in London in full swing, the team from Great Britain achieved three gold medals in the space of two hours in track and field events, making it a night for British sport like no other. That was a celebration of human strength and skill on a massive scale for our nation. But chapter 10 of the book of Joshua celebrates a divine intervention unparalleled in world history. There was "no day like it" (v. 14).

Our study of this unique account raises two key questions that are simple to ask but difficult to answer. The first is, what actually happened? The second is, what are we to learn from it? In dealing with this we shall need to keep the focus fairly and squarely on what the Bible says and on its own intended emphases, for make no mistake, this chapter has become a celebrated battleground between atheistic materialists and Bible-believing Christians. The new atheists (like the old ones before them) are drawn like moths to the flame of verse 13: "The sun stopped in the midst of heaven and did not hurry to set for about a whole day." Completely impossible, literally incredible—these are the accusations of the critics who would reduce the whole corpus of Old Testament history to the status of myth. That's understandable at the level of human experience and reason, isn't it? So we need to use this chapter as a test case on how to deal with the attitude toward the Scriptures that claims that they have been "disproved" by science and are therefore to be rejected by intelligent, modern minds.

First we shall need to establish exactly what the text actually says and set it in its Joshua context in order to understand its own significance. Then we shall have to face up to the challenges it presents and the possible resolutions of the apparent conflict between science and faith. But, thirdly, because the Bible is never merely intellectual, we shall also need to understand and appropriate the message of this narrative for our lives today in what is still God's created order, his world.

What the Text Says

John C. Lennox, professor of mathematics at the University of Oxford, warns us that in the dialogue between the Bible and science two extremes must be avoided. The first is that of tying interpretation of the Bible too closely to the current scientific orthodoxy, while the second and opposite is to ignore science altogether.[1] "The Bible says it, so I will believe it, whatever evidence you may produce"—that is the latter line. That sounds commendable and reveals an instinct to trust God's Word against all comers, which is admirable. But it can too easily degenerate into the response of the elderly minister who, accused of extremist views on the authority of Scripture, reacted, "Extremist? Well, perhaps I am an extremist, but that's because I'm extremely right and you're extremely wrong!" We need to do better than that if we are not to bring the Bible and the gospel into disrepute.

Lennox has as his main focus, in the book quoted above, the dialogue between Genesis and science about the beginning of all things, and he uses the example of Galileo as a template for a way forward. For us, in Joshua 10, this is of paramount relevance. Copernicus had advanced the "heretical" view that the earth and the other planets in our solar system orbit the sun in his work "On the Revolutions of the Celestial Orbs" (1543). Quoting from Martin Luther's "Table Talk" (1539), Lennox points out that even before the book's publication Luther is recorded as saying, "The fool wants to turn the whole art of astronomy upside-down. However, as Holy Scripture tells us, so did Joshua bid the sun to stand still and not the earth."[2] When Galileo popularized and developed this understanding of a sun-centered universe, he was opposed by the Christian orthodoxy of the day, although his motivation was not at all atheistic. Yet today we, as Christians, readily accept that Copernicus and Galileo were right. Their explanation accords with reality. It is not that we have subordinated Scripture to science, but that we have come to understand what Scripture means when it declares that the world "shall never be moved" (Psalm 93:1; 104:5) or that the sun "runs its course with joy" (Psalm 19:5). In a helpful and extended discussion of the issues, John Lennox points out that there can be more than one natural reading of a word or phrase and that when we assign a metaphorical reading of its truth (as when Jesus says, "I am the door" in John 10:9) we do so because of our experience of the world. This helps us decide at what level a particular text should be read. "We take the natural, primary meaning; and if that doesn't make sense, we go for the next level."[3]

The natural, primary level of the behavior of King Adoni-zedek is not at all hard to understand (vv. 1, 2). Already greatly afraid because of what has happened to Jericho and Ai, the Gibeonites' contract with Israel only serves to make matters worse and stirs him to preemptive action. At this point in the drama Israel stands poised on the highlands, ready to fan out to the south and the north as they sweep westward across the Shephalah, the fertile plain, toward the Mediterranean Sea. There are many more cities to conquer and vast areas of territory to be possessed, but at this critical stage the battle is about to be joined with an alliance of five Amorite kings from Jerusalem and the area immediately to the southwest. They were surprised that Gibeon, a well-fortified city with a defense force noted for its mighty men, decided to seek peace with Israel. Presumably Adoni-zedek thought that if as great and well-endowed a city as Gibeon was looking for peace, his own chances of success against Israel were minimal. That is why the alliance is formed (vv. 3–5) and why they decide to seize the initiative and take the war to the invaders. The strategy of going to attack Gibeon has perhaps a double-pronged significance. First, it is an act of revenge against Gibeon for their betrayal of the Canaanite cause and subsequent provision of a potential base for the Israelites within their own area. But secondly, it will test the quality of the Israelites' alliance with Gibeon and either draw them both into the conflict, so the alliance can kill the two birds with one stone or demonstrate that the Israelites' promises are worthless.

The tactics work (v. 6), and the Gibeonites, under threat, activate the terms of their agreement with Israel and send an urgent call for help against the alliance of the hill-country kings. There seems to be no hesitation at all on Joshua's part as he moves his army from Gilgal to Gibeon to fulfill the treaty they had so recently made with the Gibeonites. Verse 8, however, is crucial to everything that follows. There is divine intervention with a word from God of direct encouragement and promise to Joshua: "Do not fear them, for I have given them into your hands." The words recall and underline God's unchanging commitment to his servant, as in 1:5, 9. Joshua may have felt that this battle was being forced on him as a result of his foolish mistake, but God is able to turn the defense of Gibeon into the conquest of five enemy cities, all in the space of one day's engagement. The urgency of Gibeon's plight prompts a night-long march from Gilgal to Gibeon, just over twenty miles, involving a climb to higher terrain, which enabled a sudden attack on the alliance, probably very early in the morning. The element of surprise obviously helped spread confusion among the Amorites, and the Israelite army clearly has a key role to play in the outcome, but the emphasis in the brief account of the battle (vv. 10, 11) is on divine intervention. "And the LORD threw them into a panic" (v. 10). "The LORD threw down large stones from heaven" (v. 11). But Israel also had her part to play. They "struck them with a great blow at Gibeon and chased them . . . and struck them . . . as they fled before Israel" (vv. 10, 11). Yet the summary of the action makes abundantly clear the balance between God's activity and that of his people, so as to stress where the initiative and the ultimate victory actually lay. "There were more who died because of the hailstones than the sons of Israel killed with the sword" (v. 11b).

That same note is dominant in the explanatory paragraph in verses 12–14; but the text, as it stands, is not without difficulties. Clearly Joshua's prayer played a highly significant role in God's victory for Israel. In stark contrast to 9:14, where Israel did not inquire of God, Joshua now speaks directly to the Lord. We are not told in verse 12 at what time of day Joshua spoke these words to God. Was it when he arrived, before the battle was joined, before the hailstones fell, or later in the day as the pursuit intensified? It seems to have been a public occasion ("he said in the sight of Israel," v. 12), presumably so the people would have no illusions as to the source of their victory. For all their future history they would know that the Lord, the Creator, used his sovereign rule over his created order to accomplish his purposes for his people. Whatever we may be unsure of regarding the detail of these verses, this is the big picture, the overarching reality to which we must give pride of place in the narrative. Within the paragraph itself, the climax is clearly intended to be in verse 14: "the LORD heeded the voice of a man." This is the essential uniqueness of the occasion. "The two previous miracles on Israel's behalf—the stopping of the waters of the Jordan and the victory over Jericho—had been at God's initiative; this time, it was in response to one man's petition. This fact again highlights Joshua's importance in the book, and it also underscores God's faithfulness to his people."[4]

But what precisely Joshua said and where exactly the quotation from the Book of Jashar begins and ends is much more problematic. Some scholars suggest that the text does not indicate a quotation at all, but is merely a reference to a parallel historical source, outside of the Scriptures. Mentioned again in 2 Samuel 1:18, "the work appears to have been a collection of odes in praise of certain heroes of the theocracy, interwoven with historical notices of their achievements."[5] Others suggest that the "he" who spoke to the sun and moon in verse 12 is the Lord, who should be the antecedent rather than Joshua earlier in the verse. Howard favors this view for its consistency. On this reading Joshua appeals to the Lord for help, and we are told not what he prayed but how God responds. He speaks to the sun and moon, ordering them to "stand still" (v. 12) until the destruction of the Amorite alliance is complete. The amazing fact then is that this disruption in the created order is the result of the request of one man.[6] This also gives due weight to the concluding observation of verse 14 that "the LORD fought for Israel."

This does not, however, end the speculation about what actually happened on that unique day. Did the sun stand still? Did God actually halt the rotation of the earth for twenty-four hours, which would have had catastrophic implications for the planet and everything held on its surface by the force of gravity? This is not a question of whether God could do such a thing, but what he actually did. It is not a matter of belittling in any way the extraordinary and unique thing that God did, but rather of trying to understand better how he did it. For Hugh J. Blair in *The New Bible Commentary* (1970 edition), Joshua's request made in the early morning, with the sun just rising over Gibeon to the east and the moon over the Valley of Aijalon to the west, arriving after his night-long march, was not for the longest day but for a lengthening of the darkness, augmented by the hailstorm. His arguments are textual, translating "stand still" (v. 12) as "be silent, cease, or lay off" and "stopped" (v. 13) having the sense of "cease" and "for about a whole day" being better rendered as "when day is done." His suggested translation then becomes, "The sun ceased shining in the midst of the sky, and did not hasten to come, [so that it was] as when day is done." Blair comments, "And so in the darkness of the storm the defeat of the enemy was complete. It should be noted that one is not disparaging the miraculous nature of the occurrence by suggesting that there was a less spectacular divine intervention than is postulated by the more customary interpretation, which takes it that the day was lengthened. It was still God who lengthened the night by a miraculous intervention on behalf of his people."[7] A similar interpretation is offered by Dale Ralph Davis in his exposition of Joshua, *No Falling Words*.[8]

What the Test Signifies

Whatever we may conclude about the details of the text, the clear message is that there was some supernatural upheaval in the normal order of things, by which the created order was used by its Creator to win a great victory for his people. At root this means both that God is and that he is able to intervene in his creation, culminating in the supreme intervention in the incarnation of our Lord Jesus Christ. We do not have to know how God did what he did in order to defend the basic reality of the passage that Israel's victory was dependent upon divine intervention in response to human prayer. Objections come from both atheistic and theistic thinking.

Although science is not opposed to Scripture (consider the large number of academic scientists who are Christian believers), current scientific orthodoxy tends to think in terms of evolutionary development, which can have no place for what is sometimes called catastrophism—the idea of God intervening in his world. That is seen as too naive a view of the world. It is often misrepresented and ridiculed as a wooden literalism regarding the Bible text, which is seen as belonging to a primitive worldview that has been gradually displaced by the fruit of scientific advances. God is then reduced to the gaps in our scientific understanding, which are rapidly disappearing, so that his own existence is the ultimate casualty. In all such discussions it is important to distinguish between factual evidence and philosophical presuppositions. To use the uniqueness of an event (and therefore its implied unlikelihood) to support a destructive, atheistic view is to argue from presupposition and to make unfounded assertions that are ultimately statements of faith, not fact.

Similarly, theistic objections reflect the deist view of God as a noninterventionist. Like a watchmaker who constructs and activates a watch, but then leaves it to run itself, so, in this view, God is remote from what he has made and leaves the world to run on its own. To intervene would be contrary to his nature. Again this is presuppositional, and we need to draw attention to its irrationality in the light of the total witness of Scripture. Since all truth is God's truth, we have nothing to fear from scientific investigation and discovery, but we do have to distinguish between the ability of science to answer some of the "how" questions about life on Planet Earth and its inappropriate philosophical speculation about the "why" questions.

For those who wish to delve deeper into these issues, I commend the detailed discussion of possibilities as to what actually happened at the battle of Gibeon by David M. Howard in his commentary. Each of the major lines of interpretation is reviewed and evaluated and his own most plausible solution presented.[9] The five main approaches are: the earth stopped rotating, the sun's light lingered, the sun's light was blocked, a special sign was involved, and lastly the passage is figurative. Howard's own position is to favor the figurative option, seeing the unique day's existence "not because of some extraordinary astronomical phenomenon but because the Lord listened to the voice of a man and fought for Israel."[10] Alternative explanations abound, such as a solar eclipse on September 30, 1131 b.c. or the passage of the planet Mars within about 70,000 miles of earth around 1404 b.c., which is nearer the right date for Joshua. There will always be fascinating and ingenious arguments put forward to explain what might have been going on. But what we need to develop most clearly is the practical value for us today as God's people in God's world.

What the Text Teaches

First, this passage brings home to us most forcefully the sovereignty of God in every situation. He is the Creator and controller of everything that exists. As New Testament Christians we can rejoice in this wonderful reality about the Lord Jesus, our rescuer. "All things were made through him, and without him was not any thing made that was made" (John 1:3). "For by him all things were created, in heaven and on earth, visible and invisible, whether thrones or dominions or rulers or authorities—all things were created through him and for him. And he is before all things and in him all things hold together" (Colossians 1:16, 17). The physical laws of the universe, which we observe as uniform and on which our whole experience of life is based, are God's gifts to us. He wants us to live in the security of his sovereign rule. This is not a world that he has wound up and left; it is a world in which he is intimately and constantly involved. He is in control of all the circumstances that his people face and of all the outcomes of their actions.

The narrative is full of this. The promise of victory given to Joshua in verse 8 is an implicit statement that God rules in the affairs of men, since the Amorite kings would have undoubtedly assumed they were free agents. When they set out to attack Gibeon, they thought they were carrying out their best plans to head off the Israelite invasion. They did not guess that they were in fact under the sovereign hand of their Creator and totally his agents. The Lord is in control all the way through, even in the details of the events described. One evidence of this is seen in the fact that the huge hailstones were directed upon the enemy and not on the Israelites who were pursuing them. We need to constantly relearn that lesson in our lives, whenever we face situations of danger, difficulty, or complexity. God's back is never turned. Nothing can slip into your life without his knowledge. Nothing can happen to you with his eyes closed. "Behold, he who keeps Israel will neither slumber nor sleep" (Psalm 121:4). We can sleep because he never does. Divine sovereignty embraces a wisdom that is infinite, a power that is total, and a rule that is absolute. One of the great foundations of our faith is that we know that nothing occurs outside the sovereign will of God, who works all things together for the good of his people (Romans 8:28). What look like impossible circumstances to us are within his knowledge and control; in fact he is actively working out his good and perfect will through them.

Second, we must learn the importance of prayer in every situation. Whatever his exact words, verse 12 makes it plain that Joshua asked God for a miracle, and verse 14 underlines that what happened was due to the prayer of this man. It was a day like no other, and not simply because he heard his people's prayer. He does that every time we bring our requests to him in penitence and faith. The striking verb in verse 14 is that the Lord "heeded" the voice of a man, just as the sun and moon obeyed him. This is a most wonderful encouragement for our prayers and for our persistence in them. It is of huge practical benefit to realize that this is the God with whom we have to do. But there is also a caution here. We must remember that Joshua's request is totally in line with God's stated purposes for Israel and God's promise already given in verse 8. We are not to take a verse like this and use it as an excuse to play King Canute who ordered the sea waves not to encroach on his throne sitting on the beach. Like Canute, we have no power to stop the incoming tide, however much we may psych ourselves into imagining this to be God's will. God is not committed to my bright ideas; he is not a supernatural slot machine, programmed to produce.

Joshua could never have prayed like this had he not been well-instructed in God's will revealed in his already-given Word. But when we are aware of what God's purposes and promises are, when through study of the Bible we realize to what God is committed, then we should appeal to him for his will to be accomplished, with just this sort of buoyant confidence. The uniqueness of verse 14 is not designed to discourage us because it is so unusual. Rather, it shows us the extremes to which God is prepared to go in answering his people's prayers of faith, in accordance with his promises. He will bend his omnipotence to fight for his own when they are in his will, doing his work, and seeking his greater glory, however strong the opposition may be and however extraordinary the exercise of his providence may need to be. That is why we "ought always to pray and not lose heart" (Luke 18:1).

Finally, as we move to the next part of the narrative, we are to remember that God's priority is always the destruction of evil, embodied in those who rebel against his will. Recall that what happened at Gibeon is part of Yahweh's ruthless rooting out of all the evil of the land, which has been so abused by human sin. The iniquity of the Amorites has now reached its full measure (cf. Genesis 15:16), and he is dealing with it. Again we need to be cautious. This does not give us carte blanche to launch into a holy war or any violent crusade against the enemies of Christ and his cross. Instead we are meant to apply it to our own lives and to the evil within us, so that we are ruthless with our own sin and rebellion. It is a wonderful thing to know that the blood of Jesus goes on cleansing us and that there is no condemnation for those who are in Christ (1 John 1:7; Romans 8:1). If we are living close to the Lord we will be aware of the evil that still lurks in the hidden places of our lives, which we have allowed to live on unchallenged. If God was prepared to overrule the created order so that his land might be purged of evil and his people be kept pure, and if his only beloved Son died an agonizing death for our sins, how can we lightly tolerate the evil in our own lives? The victory can be ours through that death on the cross, when even the sun hid in darkness at noonday. He wants us to trust his sovereignty in every situation. He wants us to pray for the demonstration of his mighty power in rescuing grace. He wants us to live totally committed lives as he fights for us and gives us the victory. There was "no day like it" (v. 14), but its lessons are for every day of our earthly pilgrimage, until at last we reach our promised rest.

Alas! And did my Saviour bleed?
And did my Sovereign die?
Would he devote that sacred head
For such a worm as I?

Well might the sun in darkness hide
And shut his glories in,
When Christ, the mighty Maker died,
For man the creature's sin.

But drops of grief can ne'er repay
The debt of love I owe:
Here, Lord, I give my self away
'Tis all that I can do.[11]

13

The Southern Conquest

JOSHUA 10:16–43

IN OUR DIVISION OF JOSHUA 10 we have been able to concentrate on the challenges and lessons of the text describing the progress of the battle at Gibeon (vv. 1–15) and to explore some of the issues it raises with the contemporary reader. Now we move on to the outcome of the battle, which serves as a prelude to the description of the comparatively rapid conquest of the remaining Canaanite cities in the southern part of the land. An interesting connection is made by the repetition of verse 15 at verse 43. In strictly chronological terms, it seems likely that verse 15 is misplaced. Would Joshua have gone back to Gilgal before he knew what had happened to the five kings who opposed him? It is possible, I suppose, but unlikely, especially in light of verse 19. This has led to speculation about the corruption of the text, but I think there is a more than adequate explanation in seeing verse 15 not as a separate sentence-paragraph but as the conclusion of the quotation from the Book of Jashar that began in verse 13b. It forms a satisfying conclusion to the statements about the miraculous nature of the victory Israel enjoyed and represents the facts, which find their chronological position at verse 43.

Dealing with the Five Kings

As the narrative began with the formation of the alliance as a preemptive strike against Joshua, so it ends with the fate of the main protagonists. Their armies routed, with many slaughtered, they make their escape to a cave in Makkedah (v. 16), now called "the cave" because of its fame due to what is about to happen there. What they hoped would be their refuge in reality will become their tomb. First Joshua traps them by sealing the entrance to the cave with large stones and posting a guard, while the rest of his forces continue the pursuit of the fleeing armies to prevent them from returning to their cities (vv. 18, 19). This is the human agency in the story, at full stretch fulfilling the divine imperatives through Joshua—pursue, attack, prevent. Again Joshua rallies his troops with the assurance that the victory they are about to pursue is the Lord's gift (v. 19b), as indeed it proves to be (v. 20). But it is also significant to note that this verse informs us that although many were killed, some escaped and "entered into the fortified cities" (v. 20), which explains why those cities had to be besieged and attacked later (vv. 31–37).

In passing, it is worth noting that although the victories of the book of Joshua are often expressed in sweeping terms that might be taken to indicate the annihilation of everyone ("striking them with a great blow until they were wiped out," v. 20), later indications in Joshua reveal that there were pockets of resistance in many areas. The conquest was always incomplete in that sense, and we shall note as we progress through the book how often our attention is drawn to that fact. It is a major ingredient of Joshua's parting addresses in chapters 23, 24, and by Judges 2:1–5 it is declared by God to be the major cause of the increasing problems they are facing in the land. Here we have a first hint of that developing theme.

With the result of the battle secured, Joshua orders the opening of the cave, from which the five kings are brought out (vv. 22, 23). What follows is of symbolic significance to Israel's military leaders. Putting their feet on their enemies' necks (v. 24) is the most powerful demonstration of their total victory and their enemies' utter subjection. To make your enemies your footstool is a sign of complete conquest, attributed to the Lord's anointed in Psalm 110:1, and so to the Lord Jesus Christ in 1 Corinthians 15:24–28. Joshua now uses this physical manifestation of victory to nerve his commanders for what is yet to come. Repeating the words often spoken to him personally, he now exhorts his leaders to be fearless and strong, "for thus the LORD will do to all your enemies against whom you fight" (v. 25b). This was a common custom for victorious armies in the ancient world, and far worse. In fact the subsequent death of the kings and their exposure as a public spectacle, hung on trees (v. 26), is dealt with in a summary way, with the minimum attention to detail. However, the narrator takes time to tell us that they were taken down at sunset (v. 27), as Deuteronomy 21:22, 23 prescribed. Even in the flush of victory, Joshua is careful to obey all that God had commanded through Moses (see Joshua 1:7), and the kings are buried in the cave at Makkedah. Here is another stone memorial, remaining "to this very day" (10:27) our writer tells us, as an indication of the final obliteration of all God's enemies. Just as the stones from the Jordan were an eloquent reminder of the powerful grace that rescues and preserves (4:21–24) and the stones that buried Achan and his family were a permanent memorial to God's righteous wrath (7:26), so the cave at Makkedah spells out what will happen to all who set themselves against God and his purposes.

Advancing the Conquest

There now follows a list of the cities that were conquered in what has become known as the southern campaign. Beginning at Makkedah (v. 28), Joshua and his forces move on to Libnah (vv. 29, 30) and then to Lachish (vv. 31, 32), where Horam king of Gezer unsuccessfully comes to the aid of his ally (v. 33). From Lachish they move on to Eglon (vv. 34, 35), then to Hebron (vv. 36, 37), and finally to Debir (vv. 38, 39). Howard observes a chiastic structure to the unit, centered on the intervention of Horam probably in stark contrast, due to its ignominious failure, to the intervention of Joshua and the Israelite forces in support of their allies, the Gibeonites. The fact that there are seven cities speaks of the completeness of the campaign but also "suggests that this may be a summarizing account, showing the destructions of representative cities and not intended to be comprehensive."[1] It is also significant that Lachish, Eglon, and Hebron feature here, since each was one of the cities of the Amorite alliance formed by Adoni-zedek (10:3). Not only their kings but the cities themselves have fallen to Joshua's sword.

None of the accounts of the fall of the seven cities exactly replicates another, but there are strong similarities all the way through. Sometimes there is a siege, as at Lachish and Eglon, sometimes not; but the outcome is always the same—a total victory for Israel and the apparent annihilation of all her enemies. It is worth noting that in the first and last accounts (Makkedah and Debir), as well as in two intervening ones (Eglon and Hebron), we come across the phrase that we saw earlier in the account of Jericho (6:17)—Joshua "devoted to . . . destruction" the entire population of the city.

Verses 40–43 provide the concluding summary for this unit. The geographical precision of verse 40 indicates that having entered the land at Jericho, which is around the middle of the land viewed from north to south, and then having pressed westward, Israel now sweeps south and succeeds in subjugating and "devoting to destruction" the whole territory. These verses provide the termination of the section that began back in 9:1, when the kings beyond the Jordan gathered together to fight against Israel. This passage shows that both the land and its Canaanite rulers were conquered and after describing the events provides the explanation, "because the LORD God of Israel fought for Israel" (v. 42b). It is easy to read this account and to assume that it all happened at great speed and with consummate ease, but of course it was not like that. The outcome was never in doubt, because of God's commitment to his word of promise, but there was much blood, toil, sweat, and tears along the way. When we read the conclusion, it is easy to underestimate or even forget the process.

Understanding the Implications

God had always told his people that the conquest would be gradual (cf. Exodus 23:29, 30), and many times during the course of this book there are reminders that there is much more to be done and they can never sit back and rest on their laurels. Though verse 42 says this part of the conquest happened "at one time," this does not indicate that it was rapid. Rather it was viewed as an entire campaign to deal with the opposition in the south. But how extensive were the victories and the subsequent destruction?

Drawing on 11:22, 13:2, 3, and 15:63, Woudstra points out that while the conquest of this area was not yet fully complete, "the author of this section is at pains to draw a provisional conclusion which indicates that enough had been accomplished to pause and reflect on the very substantial progress that had been made toward subjugation of the land."[2] In a similar vein, Howard suggests that this is a "stylized summary" that from a more general perspective indicates that "No significant opposition remained; the power of the Canaanite was broken and their land effectively belonged now to Israel."[3] He goes on to draw an analogy with the German occupation of France in World War II, when the country was under the invaders' authority, but only temporarily and with many pockets of resistance.

This thinking is more developed by Paul Copan, writing on what he calls "Ancient Near Eastern Exaggeration Rhetoric."[4] Setting Joshua within his geographical and historical contexts, Copan argues that the book of Joshua uses "the language of conventional warfare rhetoric." To our minds it may sound overly inflated and exaggerated, but Joshua is neither making mistakes nor deliberately misleading. "He was speaking the language that everyone in his day would have understood. Rather than trying to deceive, Joshua was just saying he had fairly well trounced the enemy." Copan draws the analogy with contemporary rhetorical ways of describing sporting victories in terms of "slaughtering" or "annihilating" the opponents. The thesis is supported by several quotations from ancient Near-Eastern texts outside of Israel.

Perhaps the most telling point of his argument occurs in the use of Deuteronomy 7:2–5, where the tension is recognized between the command regarding the Canaanites that "when the LORD your God gives them over to you, and you defeat them, then you must devote them to complete destruction" (Deuteronomy 7:2) and the following prohibitions of intermarriage and idolatry (Deuteronomy 7:3–5). Copan asks, "If the Canaanites were to be completely obliterated, why this discussion about intermarriage or treaties?" His answer is that the devotion to destruction was not primarily directed to the Canaanite people but to the Canaanites' religion (e.g., Deuteronomy 12:2, 3). The land had to be purged of its false gods since "failure to remove the idolatry would put Israel in the position of the Canaanites and their idols before God. Israel would risk being consecrated to destruction."

Against this it might be argued that the provisions of verses 3–5 in Deuteronomy 7 are made precisely because God knows that Israel's obedience to the commands of verse 2 will be less than complete. Rather than qualifying the command, they may be construed as a second line of action to which Israel must return in the light of failure to fulfill verse 2.

However, this raises a larger issue as to what exactly was required by the concept of the *"hèrem,"* the curse that required its objects to be devoted to destruction. Discussion was given to this in chapter 7 of this book when we were dealing with the Lord's instructions to Joshua regarding Jericho (6:16–19) and does not need repetition here. But whatever may have been the intended parameters of the destruction, there can be little doubt about either its moral purpose or its judicial validity. Viewed Biblically, the destruction was entirely righteous, for it is true of the whole human race that our sinful rebellion renders each one liable to the wrath of God "revealed from heaven against all ungodliness and unrighteousness of men" (Romans 1:18). If we are to ask for justice for the Canaanites, living in Yahweh's world and created by him in his image, then destruction is the only proper outcome. "It is of the LORD's mercies that we are not consumed" (Lamentations 3:22 KJV). What our sinful humanity cries out for is mercy, not justice. Yet there can be no true mercy if justice remains unsatisfied, which leads us to the cross, where "steadfast love and faithfulness meet" and where "righteousness and peace kiss each other" (Psalm 85:10). There, as the Lord Jesus was "devoted" to the destruction we deserve, as he carried the weight of human sin and guilt in his own body on the tree, there and there alone can the curse be lifted and mercy triumph over wrath.

It is not surprising, then, that a rebellious world will seize upon these issues as a *cause célèbre* in its ongoing war against the Creator. Atheistic critic Richard Dawkins may label the conquest as genocide or ethnic cleansing and distort the Biblical account in his claims of "bloodthirsty massacres" carried out with "xenophobic relish."[5] But at least part of the animus behind that view is an unwillingness to allow any authority to sit in judgment on the sovereign self. It is a denial that there is a Creator and we are his created beings, a resistance to the basic Biblical reality that the life we have is not ours to exercise in proud independence but is the gift of God, to whom we shall each give account. The judgments on Canaan are precursors and foreshadowings, terrible though they were, of the ultimate judgment that awaits the whole creation at the last day.

> Then I saw a great white throne and him who was seated on it. From his presence earth and sky fled away, and no place was found for them. And I saw the dead, great and small, standing before the throne, and books were opened. Then another book was opened, which is the book of life. And the dead were judged by what was written in the books, according to what they had done. . . . And if anyone's name was not found written in the book of life, he was thrown into the lake of fire. (Revelation 20:11–15)

It is that reality, here in embryonic form, that the atheist must at all costs deny or denigrate. That is why the Lord Jesus himself warned us to fear the greater judgment and to live now in the light of eternity. "I will warn you whom to fear: fear him who, after he has killed, has authority to cast into hell. Yes, I tell you, fear him!" (Luke 12:5).

> Fear him, you saints, and you will then
> Have nothing else to fear;
> Make you his service your delight;
> Your wants shall be his care.[6]

14

The Northern Conquest

JOSHUA 11:1–23

AS THE CONQUEST PROCEEDS, Joshua now directs his attention to the north country. The parallels between this account and that of the southern campaign in chapter 10 are striking and deliberately drawn. In each case the conflict is precipitated by a king who gathers a coalition of other leaders to join him in the fight against the Israelite advance. Here it is Jabin, king of Hazor (v. 1). The success of such an appeal and the strength of such an alliance is noted, but the test of both comes in a pitched battle with Israel at Gibeon in chapter 10 and here "by the waters of Merom" (11:7). In each battle Israel is given specific encouragement and instruction directly from the Lord that enables God's people to inflict a crushing blow against her foes. This initial victory supplies the people of God with a more secure footing in that part of the land, from which they are able to subdue and conquer all the remaining city-states in that area, until 11:23 is able to record, "So Joshua took the whole land, according to all that the LORD had spoken to Moses." This statement is the conclusion toward which this part of the book has been moving since chapter 9 and is followed by what we might call an appendix in chapter 12 that lists each and every one of the conquered kings, first under Moses and then under Joshua.

The Victory at Merom

Chapters 9, 10, and 11 all begin with an identical formula. The enemies of Israel hear of the great victories that Yahweh has won for his people and immediately lay plans to resist their further advance. The main point of verses 11:1–5 seems to be to stress the strength and geographical range of the northern alliance that Jabin is able to muster. Many kings are alluded to in verses 1, 2 and no less than six people groups that inhabited the northern sector of the land in verse 3. This is a powerful and daunting force to be overcome, "a great horde, in number like the sand that is on the seashore" (v. 4a). But it is not only geographical spread and numbers that make this so impressive. They are also equipped with the latest in military hardware and weapons technology—"very many horses and chariots" (v. 4b). Hazor was clearly an important city with great clout in the area, and its readiness for war seems to have been parallel to that of the Egyptians forty years earlier when the Israelites first left the land of slavery. Those advanced "weapons" along with Pharaoh's elite troops found themselves at the bottom of the Red Sea, and within a few verses this impressive alliance will also find itself disarmed (v. 9). But at this point they are determined to bring the attack to Israel, choosing the waters of Merom as the location at which to base their camp (v. 5), a site that has not been identified.

In accordance with the pattern of the book of Joshua, at this point, with the enemy encamped and ready to fight, the commander of the Lord's army (cf. 5:13–15) seizes the initiative with a direct word of revelation to the human leader, Joshua. In spite of the enemies' numbers and impressive array, Israel is not to "be afraid" (v. 6a). This command can only be fulfilled by faith in the promise that accompanies it: "I will give over all of them, slain, to Israel." The battle will be done and finished in a day, and the military capability of the opposition will be neutralized. "You shall hamstring their horses and burn their chariots with fire" (v. 6b). In this case there would be no directly visible divine intervention to bring victory to Israel. They would have to fight for it; but there is no doubt as to why they would be so comprehensively victorious. Once again the battle is the Lord's, and all the glory and the praise belong to him.

There are no battle details, apart from the surprise attack generated by the Israelites (v. 7) and the fact that its success was the Lord's work (v. 8a). The sovereign God who controls the whole of his creation "gave them into the hand of Israel." As in chapter 10, the alliance breaks up, and the warriors scatter, fleeing to their own cities with the Israelites in hot pursuit. Again the scale of the victory is emphasized as the opposition disintegrates to the west and east, only to fall into the hands of their pursuers and to see the weaponry they had left behind destroyed (vv. 8, 9). Joshua has believed the promise and obeyed the command to the letter, and the Lord has kept his word. There is no hope of a regrouping or a counterattack. The defeat is total.

The Conquest Pursued

The failure of the coalition armies in the battle has disastrous repercussions for their home city-states that they had set out to defend. Joshua is now at liberty to execute God's justice (*hèrem*) on the whole land. He begins with Hazor, the most powerful city of the area and the generator of the alliance, whose king and citizens are destroyed, and the city itself is burned (vv. 10, 11). Besides Hazor this fate was reserved only for Jericho and Ai, since God had promised his people that they would be brought into the land, which would first mean living in "great and good cities you did not build" (Deuteronomy 6:10). These cities were to be resettled by the Israelites in due course, but the three that were burned were perhaps representative of the strongest and most determined opposition to God's purposes.

Once again the text emphasizes Joshua's detailed obedience to all that God had commanded Moses and was written in the book of the Law (v. 12). The physical cities are not destroyed, but the spoil and the livestock are taken as plunder by the Israelites, and the Canaanite population is decimated (vv. 13–15). This strict conformity to the written, recorded instructions of Yahweh mark Joshua out as a second Moses, equally obedient and equally deserving of the title "the servant of the Lord." Quoting T. C. Butler, David Howard underlines the effect that this detailed obedience to the word already given was intended to have on future generations in Israel and on the readers of this book. This narrative stands "as a monument to the great faithfulness of Joshua to the Mosaic law. It [his faithfulness] thus stands as a goal for all future leaders of Israel. Rather than being lawmakers, the kings of Israel are law takers and law keepers."[1] The need for the same detailed obedience to the Scriptures should not be lost on the contemporary leadership of our churches today.

Verses 16–23 conclude the unit with a summary of the northern conquest that matches that concerning the south in 10:40–43. The land that has now been taken is extensive in its scope. We are being reminded of just what great territories God had purposed to give his people back in 1:4. The detailed geography (vv. 16, 17) is covered in all the major commentaries, but the unusual note here is the historical one that "Joshua made war a long time" (v. 18). Unfortunately we cannot know precisely just how long this took, though the best suggestion is seven years. This is based on the fact that Caleb was forty years old when Moses sent him (and Joshua) to spy out the land (14:7), and Deuteronomy 2:14 tells us that from that time to the entry of the land was thirty-eight years, making Caleb seventy-eight at the start of the conquest and eighty-five when he later claimed his inheritance (14:10). So the period in view here would be seven years.[2] Just as Rahab is the only example of an individual Canaanite's repentance, so the Gibeonites are the only example of a people who sought a peace treaty with Israel. All the other cities were taken (v. 19). However, the emphasis here is on the divine purpose overruling the actions of men (v. 20).

"It was the LORD's doing to harden their hearts" (v. 20), just as in the generation before he had hardened Pharaoh's heart to resist the exodus in spite of and perhaps because of the plagues. Woudstra comments, "The stubborn heart is due to God's hardening process . . . but this in no way exonerates the Canaanites. The other way was open, as is shown by what the Gibeonites did." In a footnote he adds, "God gives up to their own wickedness those who have shown that they prefer the lie to the truth. Nevertheless, the sovereignty and majesty of the divine counsel is not limited by the will of man."[3] This helps us understand why the Canaanite resistance was so determined in spite of all the evidence that Israel was assisted by supernatural power. Of Pharaoh in Exodus 9:34—10:1 we read that first he hardened his heart, so that it became hardened, a decision confirmed by the Lord, so that there could be no going back. This seems to be how the wickedness of the Canaanites in the end brought about their own destruction. As Christopher Marlowe has his central tragic hero Dr. Faustus declare in his Elizabethan drama, after selling his soul to the devil, "My heart's so hardened I cannot repent." That possibility seems to have become an immovable reality for the Canaanites, whose wickedness must come under the judgment of their righteous Creator.

The note about Joshua's victory over the Anakim (v. 21) might strike us as odd and somewhat out of place, were we not to remember that these were the very people who had terrified the ten spies and moved them to present their bad report when Moses sent them out with Joshua and Caleb from Kadesh-barnea. It was because of these imposing giants that the rebellion occurred and the forty years in the wilderness resulted. And now they too have been cut off (uprooted and exterminated), their only refuge being in Philistine territory (v. 22b). This is a fitting climax to the long narrative, which stretches back to the original spies forty-five years ago, and to this section of the book that brings the account of the entry and conquest of the land to its culmination. Verse 23a puts it all in one glorious sentence: "So Joshua took the whole land, according to all that the LORD had spoken to Moses." That is chapters 1—11. Then the verse looks forward to the second half of the book and the allotment of the land as Israel's inheritance. That will be chapters 13—19. For the moment there is "rest from war," but there will be much more land to be possessed and a greater rest for the people of God to enjoy in the future.

The Gospel Implications

This is an appropriate place for us to step back from the unfolding narrative, the halfway point in the book of Joshua, and to reconsider its wider application to us as Christian believers today. Hebrews 4 provides us with the key

New Testament text for a Biblically authorized interpretation of the Joshua narrative. Building on an extended quotation from the closing verses of Psalm 95 concerning the danger of a hardening heart through unbelief, the writer exhorts his readers not to fail to reach the promise of entering God's "rest" (Hebrews 4:1). The "rest" theme comes from Psalm 95:11, quoted in Hebrews 3:11, where God says, "I swore in my wrath, 'They [the exodus generation] shall not enter my rest.'" Immediately the writer warns his readers to "take care . . . lest there be in any of you an evil, unbelieving heart, leading you to fall away from the living God" (Hebrews 3:12). For them that was the fruit of their "unbelief" (Hebrews 3:19), and the same danger is a present reality for the author's readers. For us this promise of entering God's rest has been conveyed in the gospel and its promises. For the Israelites it was the promise of entering the land that God was giving to them where they would experience his rest; but this would only happen if the promises were met with a living faith expressing itself in obedient action. Joshua and Caleb had the faith to believe, but the majority did not. They discounted God's promises in favor of what they saw and what they feared.

But the writer moves on to explain that when David wrote Psalm 95 the land had long been in Israel's possession. So the concept must have a greater and richer fulfillment than the literal conquest of the land under Joshua. "For if Joshua had given them rest, God would not have spoken of another day later on" (Hebrews 4:8). David had a rest beyond the physical in view, an ultimate "rest" that Joshua, for all his godly leadership, was not able to provide. "So then, there remains a sabbath rest for the people of God" (Hebrews 4:9). We know from the argument of the whole letter that this "rest" equates with the eternal kingdom, the heavenly country, the city that is to come, which is the inheritance of all who believe the gospel. At one level it is already ours, entered into by repentance and faith in the Lord Jesus Christ as rescuer and ruler. But at another level it is not yet ours in all its fullness of experience and enjoyment. What we have already is real and a wonderful down payment, guaranteeing the rest that will one day be ours in its totality. "For now we see in a mirror dimly, but then face to face. Now I know in part; then I shall know fully, even as I have been fully known" (1 Corinthians 13:12).

The "rest" referred to at the end of Joshua 11 is therefore a prototype or foreshadowing of the rest that remains for the New Testament people of God. Joshua could only replicate in the physical, temporal sphere what Jesus has won for his people in his spiritual and eternal kingly rule. That is God's gracious intention for his people. "Let us therefore strive to enter that rest, so that no one may fall by the same sort of disobedience" (Hebrews 4:11), namely the fruit of unbelief. Real faith shows itself in obedience, and while that faith is never a work by which we earn our salvation, it is the means by which we receive and appropriate the promises of the gospel, made real for us in the person and work of our Savior, Jesus Christ. So Joshua points us to his infinitely greater namesake and to the liberation from our works into the rest that is the new birthright of everyone who turns and trusts in him. "Today if you hear his voice, do not harden your hearts" (Hebrews 3:7, 8).

In the Hebrews context, those addressed were in danger of being tempted back to Judaism with its visible, tangible realities of the temple and its sacrifices, the Law and the offerings, the priests and their ministries. But the writer insists that there is nothing to which to go back. All that was prefigured in the Old Testament era has been fulfilled in Christ. So "let us run with endurance the race that is set before us, looking to Jesus, the founder and perfecter of our faith, who for the joy that was set before him endured the cross" (Hebrews 12:1, 2). So whenever we are tempted to give up the race, to go back to our Egypt or our wilderness years, let us take heart from Joshua and grasp more firmly the eternal realities, of which Joshua's earthly triumphs and their consequent "rest" could only be the palest foreshadowing.

That incentive to keep on keeping on seems also to be the purpose of chapter 12 of Joshua, which to our eyes and ears may at first seem a somewhat tedious list. But in the context of what we have already seen in Joshua, it is in fact a glorious celebration. Verses 1–6 speak of the conquest and settlement of the land east of the Jordan, which had happened under Moses, while verses 7–24 list the thirty-one kings that fell to Joshua from Jericho onward. Some of them we have seen briefly in the dramas of the book's first half, while others have been unknown until now. But as each one is delineated, with the repeated "one" tolling like a bell, they represent the removal of those impossibly strong opposition forces at the hand of the living God and his limitless, sovereign power. "Not to us, O LORD, not to us, but to your name give glory, for the sake of your steadfast love and your faithfulness" (Psalm 115:1). Whatever spiritual blessings we enjoy, whatever victories are won, whatever experience of God's rest is currently ours, it is not due to us but to our great God and Savior Jesus Christ, who has rescued us from the domain of darkness and transferred us to his eternal kingdom (Colossians 1:13). To him be the glory forever and ever!

15

Receiving the Inheritance

JOSHUA 13:1—14:5

MANY COMMENTATORS POINT OUT that at 13:1 the second half of the book of Joshua begins. So before we launch into a more detailed exploration of the text, this would seem to be a good moment to stand back and do some big-picture thinking about the book as a whole.

The division of Biblical texts is a helpful analytical tool, but one that can owe a great deal to the subjective assessment of the analyst. We are not looking for right or wrong answers so much as helpful guides to the internal categories that became the building-blocks of the writer's work. Such careful observation work will greatly deepen and enrich our exposition of the text.

In any historical book like this the most basic division is into two parts, since there is usually a pivotal point on which the narrative turns. Think of Exodus for example, where the giving of the Law on Mount Sinai is the pivot that divides the book into its pre- and post-Sinai halves. Similarly, here in Joshua we have reached a pivot point with the summary of 11:23. The first half of the book is about the conquest of the land, and the second half will be about its allocation to the twelve tribes. We move from vivid dramatic narratives to lists of places and people. As Howard observes, "The sedentary pace, relaxed tone, and relative lack of action contrast dramatically with the first half."[1]

Once the major division has been noted, subdivisions become much clearer. Chapters 1—12 can be divided into two major sections, as we have seen. The first five chapters are largely preparatory for the actual conquest, which is then dealt with in detail in chapters 6—12. Here there are four key battles or narratives of conquest—Jericho, Ai, Gibeon, and the waters of Merom. There are also two major reversals caused by Achan's sin and the

Gibeonite deception; yet both are overruled by God for the ultimate deepening of his people's trust and the development of his sovereign purposes. Similarly, we shall discover within the second half of the book a major subdivision. Chapters 13—21 deal with the distribution of the land as God's gracious inheritance to his people, Israel. Within that section there is a clear ordering and balancing of the material around a chiastic structure, with the establishment of the tabernacle at Shiloh and the writing of a description of the land in 18:1–10 as the central point. Based on the work of H. J. Koorevaar, this is now accepted by many scholars as its basic construction.[2] This leaves chapters 22—24 as the concluding section of the book, with the return of the two and a half tribes east of the Jordan and Joshua's farewell addresses to the leaders and to the nation.

As we come, then, to the section comprised of chapters 13—21, which forms a substantial proportion of the book's whole content, we are entering what has been called the book's center of gravity because of its historical and ultimately theological significance. But we have to admit that to us, as twenty-first-century Christian readers, it does not really grab our attention and involvement. After the excitement of the battles and the celebrations of the Lord's great victories on behalf of his people, we might be forgiven for regarding these nine chapters as something of an anticlimax and very hard work. What is a preacher to do with them? He would be an unusual pastor who felt justified in spending a series of Sunday mornings plowing through the geography of the land and the history of the tribal divisions, even with the help of PowerPoint presentations! Yet "all Scripture is . . . profitable" (2 Timothy 3:16), and this is part of God's Word. So what are we to make of it? Even the great John Calvin, whose commentaries often provide just the help needed to understand the Scriptures five hundred years after he wrote them, tells his readers that he "would not be very exact in delineating the site of places, and in discussing names, partly because I admit that I am not well acquainted with topographical or chorographic science, and partly because great labor would produce little fruit to the reader; nay, perhaps the greater part of readers would toil and perplex themselves without receiving any benefit."[3] With grateful thanks to John Calvin, we should perhaps be prepared to follow in his steps!

My plan, over the next few chapters, will not be a detailed exposition of places and people but rather, using the tools of Biblical theology and practical application, to draw out the principles that are still salient for us today in our own battles to possess our spiritual possessions in Christ and to enter more fully into God's rest, both here and in eternity. But before we do that we need to take a moment to recognize that our position in relation to this material is so different from that of the book's first readers. For us in the western world the title deeds to the property we own or the lease agreement on the home we rent are hugely important legal items. They may make for mundane and rather boring reading, but we make sure that they are carefully stored and preserved as indisputable proof of what is rightly ours. That gives us some perspective on why these chapters mattered so much to Israel and to each tribe, clan, and family group. Here are the title deeds to the family inheritance, written down and authorized by their appearance in the Holy Scriptures, the reference point of indisputable authority for any controversies that might occur in the generations to come. This matters as a document of practical importance, but of course it also underlines for every successive generation that the Lord gave Israel the land and that these arrangements were disposed and enjoyed under the authority of their sovereign Yahweh, on whom they are dependent for all things.

The Importance of Joshua

Verses 1–7 provide an important control on our understanding of everything that follows. Joshua's old age (v. 1) is presented as the trigger for the command to him to divide the land for an inheritance now (v. 7). Joshua's own role in the process is vitally important. We have been watching his stature with God and with the people grow during the first half of the book, so that, as God had promised, he is now exalted in the sight of all Israel (3:7; 4:14). No one has the authority and leadership that Joshua exercises. When he dies, he will leave behind him a vacuum of immense proportions for which there is no hint that any successor is being provided. Indeed this will become the tragedy of the book of Judges, leading eventually to the demand for and the establishment of the monarchy. So although "there remains yet very much land to possess" (v. 1), the allocation and distribution of it among the tribes must be carried out by Joshua, under God, while he is still alive and active.

Of course, the fact that large swaths of the land are not yet under Israelite control will be a stimulus to faith and action among the people in order to make secure in reality what God has assigned to them by promise. If you know that something to be prized is within your grasp and that it will be indisputably yours when it is secured, the motivation to press on and make it your own is huge. This provides us with a parallel analogy to our Christian experience, backed up by Paul in Philippians who, speaking of the resurrection, writes, "Not that I have already obtained this or am already perfect, but I press on to make it my own, because Christ Jesus has made me his own" (Philippians 3:12). There is the stimulus of what is already one's own, by

God's decree, becoming increasingly the warp and woof of one's life in practice by pressing on. Paul continues, "Brothers, I do not consider that I have made it my own. But one thing I do: forgetting what lies behind and straining forward to what lies ahead, I press toward the goal for the prize of the upward call of God in Christ Jesus" (Philippians 3:13, 14). To have a settled faith that the promised blessings of the gospel are ours now in a measure and will be ours increasingly—that will change our whole perspective on how we live our lives in the present. So much of our Christian experience is the practice of what John Stott described as "making patent what is latent." Rightly applied, these chapters of Joshua can have a very beneficial effect on our own discipleship. Think of what God has promised you, and go for it!

The Extent of the Task

Verses 2–6 give the full dimensions of the land that has yet to be won, and they are considerable, beginning in the west on the Mediterranean coast, from the Shihor, the Nile, east of Egypt in the south, all the way to Ekron in the north (vv. 2, 3). Although settled by the Philistines, who probably came originally from Crete, it is "counted as Canaanite" (v. 3) geographically, if not ethnically, and therefore is part of the promised inheritance. The five principal cities are then named and with them the Avvim, who are thought to be the original Canaanite inhabitants, now squeezed to the south (v. 4a). Turning north, the whole land of the Canaanites extends to the Sidonians and the Amorites, probably equivalent to modern Lebanon, as verse 5 indicates. Looking east, there is still work to be done in the hill country, though the emphasis in the paragraph is on the needed push west, into the plains. "These comments show that Israel carved out its territory in the mountains of Palestine while the native populations remained in the plains, because they intimidated Israel with their iron chariots (see 17:16; Jdg 1:19)."[4]

This is the challenge that the Lord lays before Joshua and the people. It is a large geographical area with many key cities and large people groups, well-armed and resourced. But it is "the land that yet remains" (v. 2). That is to say, Israel has more than a toehold in the land. She is in control of much of the eastern half of the country, and that is only because of the Lord's fulfillment of his promise. As they survey the long to-do list facing them, all that has so far happened is meant to be an enormous encouragement for all that is yet to be. In this context the Lord graciously reaffirms his promises: "I myself will drive them out from before the people of Israel" (v. 6b). That is the confidence, appropriated by faith, that the allocation of the land is not an empty action of wishful thinking. Rather it is obedience to God's instruction generated by an unshakable confidence in the promises. To trust is to obey. What Joshua has to do is crystal clear (v. 7).

The Eastern Inheritance

From verse 8 to verse 33 we see again what God had already promised to the tribes of Reuben, Gad, and half of Manasseh as their inheritance east of the Jordan, back in the days of Moses. The story of what happened has already been revisited in 12:1–6. It is probably repeated here to stress the unity of the nation. That is, the inheritance east of the river was as much God's gift to the two and a half tribes as the land to the west, which they had joined with their brothers to conquer. This underlines that what is happening in the allocation of the land throughout these chapters has the quality of a legal transaction as God gives the land, which is his by creative right, to his people in trust for their possession and enjoyment. They are now to make it their own, to settle, govern, and use it in accordance with God's instructions. The conquest is only the first step (and that is, as yet, far from complete) on a road that is intended to stretch down the centuries to come as Israel serves Yahweh by her faithful tenancy of the property, the land.

The survey begins with the territories of Sihon, king of the Amorites, and Og, king of Bashan, whom "Moses had struck and driven out" (v. 12), all the area east of the Jordan already distributed (vv. 8–12). However, there are warning notes in verse 13. From his own historical perspective, the narrator records Israel's failure to deal with Geshur and Maacath "to this day." There is a helpful spiritual lesson here. It is not just that the truth must be told, however embarrassing it may be. The Lord's promise of verse 6 ("I myself will drive them out") was conditional upon Israel's willingness to act on the command. There was no conditionality within the will and purpose of God, but there was nothing automatic about the fulfillment of the promise if Israel failed to activate it by faith and action. The parallels to the New Testament believer are clear and exact. In the gospel of Christ God has "granted to us his precious and very great promises, so that through them you may become partakers of the divine nature" (2 Peter 1:4), but those promises have to be believed and acted on in obedience. Electricity flows through the national grid, but until an appliance is plugged in and switched on, none of its potential can be realized. Another significant point here is that Geshur and Maacath were mentioned back in 12:5 as defeated by Moses, but clearly that did not imply complete annihilation. There is always more to be done, and in spiritual affairs, as in political, the price of freedom is eternal vigilance.

Verse 14 singles out Levi as the only tribe without title deeds to a portion of the physical land. They reappear at verse 33 where the same comment is made. Putting the two verses together, we are told that "the offerings by fire to the LORD God of Israel" (v. 14) and to "the LORD God of Israel" himself (v. 33) constitute their inheritance. Cities would be provided in other tribal areas in which they were to live, but their special calling and privilege, in the service of the tabernacle, marked them out as distinct. The tithes and offerings would be the means of their support.

Reuben's allocation follows in verses 15–23, in the south of the country, consisting mainly of the area formerly ruled over by Sihon from his capital, Heshbon (v. 17a). The focus is on twelve captured cities in the tableland (vv. 17–21), some of which were featured in Numbers and Deuteronomy. Reference is also made to Balaam (v. 22), hired by King Balak to curse the Israelites, which God turned into blessing (Numbers 22—24). His death is recorded as evidence of God's sovereignty over all who conspire against him and his purposes.

Verses 24–28 continue the story with the inheritance to Gad, like Reuben bordered by the Jordan on the west, occupying the central region of the country, which verses 26, 27 describe from Heshbon in the south to Debir in the north, all the way to the lower (southern) end of the Sea of Chinnereth (Galilee). Again cities and villages are mentioned, the former usually walled and the latter unprotected settlements scattered around the cities, dependent on them and supplying produce to them.

Finally, in verses 29–31, the inheritance of the half-tribe of Manasseh is briefly outlined, in large part the previous territory of Og, king of Bashan. This is the area further to the north, on the plateau beyond Gilead, north and east of Galilee. The allocation of these areas, already determined by Moses, relied largely on the conquests carried out by the forebears of these tribes, which accounts for who received what. The rest of the allocations will be by lot, but these have already been determined, and the purpose of the statements here seems to underline the settlements' authenticity and to keep the tribes east of the Jordan firmly anchored to the unified entity that is the emergent nation.

The Western Inheritance

The first five verses of chapter 14 now serve to balance up the allocation of the land east of the Jordan with that across the river, on the west side all the way to the coast. They also serve as an introduction to the long account of the distribution to the nine and a half remaining tribes, excluding Levi, which will bring us eventually to the end of chapter 19. Almost in the form of a legal document it begins with the establishment of the authority by which the process was carried through. The mention of Eleazar, the son and successor of Aaron as high priest, indicates that this is a process of religious significance. He was involved in Joshua's commissioning, and now he stands with the military and political leader along with all the leaders of the tribes. But neither of them decides the details of the inheritance. There is no governing committee, no inner circle of influence. "Their inheritance was by lot" (v. 2a). God had instructed Moses that this was to be the method (Numbers 26:52–56), and once again Joshua is careful to do according to the Law. Provision has been made for larger groups to have larger areas, so that there is a proportional element to the settling of the land, but no human being determines its location.

The other side of that reality, of course, is the sovereignty of God over this as in every other situation. The theology behind this method of discerning God's will in matters where there is no clear word of revelation to determine the right course of action is succinctly expressed in Proverbs 16:33: "The lot is cast into the lap, but its every decision is from the LORD." It has been remarked that about a third of all the references to casting lots in the Old Testament occur in the book of Joshua. Clearly it was the most important ingredient in the allocation of the land. See for further examples 15:1; 16:1; 17:1; 18:6, 8, 10. This was the clearest way in which the will of God could be made known, and even as late as Acts 1:24–26 we find the practice in use, to select Matthias to replace Judas Iscariot. This was done in the context of prayer, but the prayer presupposes that God will control the outcome of the lot-casting and specifically asks God to show which of the two candidates he has chosen for this ministry. Clearly the expectation is that in the right context of prayer and dependence on God, the Lord will reveal his will through the lots. However, after the gift of the Holy Spirit to indwell all of God's believing people (Acts 2:38, 39), we hear no more of casting lots but rather seeking the inner work of the Spirit to give wisdom and guide God's people into his will. Of course, with the completion of the canon of Scripture in the New Testament we have a far richer and more detailed resource of revealed truth on which to base our decision-making. Commenting on the Acts incident, F. F. Bruce observed that "it belongs, significantly enough, to the period between the ascension and Pentecost; Jesus had gone and the Holy Spirit had not yet come. But if there are better ways of appointing the right man to ecclesiastical responsibility, there are also worse ways."[5] Of these we could all, no doubt, think of several!

Of all the commentators, Calvin makes clearest the details of how the process actually worked out. He points out that the men delineated in verse 1 "were not selected simply to divide the land by lot, but also afterwards to enlarge or restrict the boundaries of the tribes by giving to each its due proportion."[6] This demanded more than a simple casting of lots. We shall discover more about how the process worked out when we come to chapter 18, but before we get there, the tribes of Judah, Ephraim, and the half-tribe of Manasseh (the sons of Joseph) are singled out for their allocation, presumably on the ground of their already established importance within the twelve, as seen in earlier Old Testament narratives. Think for example of Jacob's blessing of his sons in Genesis 49. "Judah, your brothers shall praise you . . . your father's sons shall bow down before you" (v. 8). "Joseph is a fruitful bough, a fruitful bough by a spring; his branches run over the wall . . . by the God of your father who will help you, by the Almighty who will bless you. . . . May they [God's blessings] be on the head of Joseph, and on the brow of him who was set apart from his brothers" (vv. 22–26). With these blessings already in place, it is not surprising that Judah comes first in the list of allocations, and chief among them one of the greatest heroes of the Old Testament story, Caleb, the son of Jephunneh. It is his story that now takes center stage.

16

Wholehearted Following

JOSHUA 14:6–15; 15:13–19

Joshua, the son of Nun, and Caleb, the son of Jephunneh,
Were the only two, who ever got through
To the land of milk and honey.

The old Sunday-school doggerel explains to us why Caleb now appears, to take center stage. He and Joshua are not just the oldest men left in the nation, they are also unique in their record of faithful devotion and service to the Lord. Before the allocation of land can be made to Judah, Caleb steps forward, because there is a prior promise that Yahweh had made and that now has to be fulfilled. The scene backtracks forty-five years to Kadesh-barnea when Caleb, a comparatively young man of forty, is chosen to be the representative of his tribe of Judah, along with Joshua from the tribe of Benjamin and ten others, to spy out the land of Canaan. The details of the story are recorded in Numbers 13, 14, and that passage helps fill in the background to Caleb's summary statement in verses 7, 8.

At that time Israel had been out of Egypt for about one year. Having experienced God's saving power from Pharaoh's tyranny in the exodus, they also knew what it meant to be rescued from the righteous wrath of God through the provision of the Passover lamb. In the year that followed, they had seen the pursuing elite Egyptian troops drowned in the Red Sea, had experienced God's provision of water and daily manna, had won a great victory over the Amalekites, and had been brought to meet with God at Sinai, where they received the Law. Now they had traveled on to Kadesh-barnea, to the very edge of the land that God had promised to give to them. It was a year of astonishing progress, but mixed with unbelief, discontent, and grumbling as many of them often looked back over their shoulders, wistful for what they had known in Egypt. They soon forgot the slavery and the cruel burdens, and they began to put on rose-tinted spectacles when they recalled the food supplies and the relative stability of their life in subjection. But now they are on the edge of the land, and surely it will prove to have been worth all the privations and testings.

The twelve spies are sent to reconnoiter the situation in Canaan. They are away for six weeks, and at the end they return to present a majority report to Moses. "We came to the land to which you sent us. It flows with milk and honey, and this is its fruit. However, the people who dwell in the land are strong, and the cities are fortified and very large. And besides, we saw the descendants of Anak there. . . . We are not able to go up against the people, for they are stronger than we are" (Numbers 13:27, 28, 31). That was the majority conclusion signed by ten of the spies. But alongside it was a contradictory minority view, signed only by Caleb and Joshua. "Let us go up at once and occupy it, for we are well able to overcome it" (Numbers 13:30). The majority fight back, multiplying the difficulties and magnifying the horrors—the land will devour us; all its inhabitants are of great height, and we are like grasshoppers. This sets the people weeping and grumbling, longing for Egypt, but Joshua and Caleb are undaunted. They repeat and develop their case with very careful reasoning. The land is "exceedingly good," it indeed flows with milk and honey, and God will bring them in (Numbers 14:6–9). "Only do not rebel against the LORD. And do not fear the people of the land, for they are bread for us. Their protection is removed from them, and the LORD is with us; do not fear them" (Numbers 14:9). But the reaction of the crowd is to pick up stones to stone them. As a result God's judgment falls as he pronounces that none of this unbelieving generation will see or enter the land because they have despised his word of promise and his faithful character. "But my servant Caleb, because he has a different spirit and has followed me fully, I will bring into the land into which he went, and his descendants shall possess it" (Numbers 14:24).

And now, at last, the time for the fulfillment of God's promise to Caleb has come, forty-five years later, the vast majority of which he spent in the wilderness with a frequently rebellious people who were kept from entering God's rest through their unbelief. Their eyes were on the giants, but Caleb's eyes were on the Lord. He treasured God's promise, knowing that it would most certainly be fulfilled, and that is what kept his faith fresh and alive and his heart united in its dependence on the Lord. That is the refrain that recurs three times in Joshua 14 (vv. 8, 9, 14): Caleb "wholly ["wholeheartedly" NIV] followed the Lord." That is the secret to everything that follows.

Caleb's Vision

His vision is not some mystical projection of his own wishful thinking, much less a creation of his own imagination. Spiritual vision means being able to see a situation from God's perspective, based on his self-revelation, and so to be able to go forward into that situation confident that God's purposes will indeed be fulfilled, trusting him and expecting him to work. Such a vision of spiritual reality is as desperately needed in the church today as it was in Israel in the days of Caleb. It means seeing the invisible God, in the sense of reckoning on his secret power and sovereign will to do things that no one otherwise would begin to guess could happen.

The first characteristic of true spiritual vision, which Caleb exemplifies, is realism. Vision is a great quality. It is always needed in Christian ministry and personal discipleship, but it is often in short supply. When it is absent, other alternatives move in, falsely bearing the same name. Vision is not pretending things are other than they are. Vision is not psyching ourselves up to believe that God has said what he has not said or is committed to do what he has not promised to do. Vision is not seeing in my mind's eye what I would like to do and trying to "believe" hard enough to make it happen. Caleb followed the Lord "wholeheartedly." Vision starts with the heart, which in Biblical thinking is the control center of the personality where we decide on choices in life and formulate our decisions. That consistent Godwardness of his innermost being kept Caleb constant when everyone around him was losing their way and turning aside into the most appalling faithlessness. The ten spies would doubtless have defended themselves by claiming that they were only being realistic, but their hearts were not fixed on Yahweh. Their perspective was distorted because their hearts were divided. Caleb was the true realist. He and Joshua saw exactly the same challenges as the others, but they saw them through the lens of faith in the promises of God, a great God committed to his people, to whom giants are as nothing. But they only maintained that faith because their hearts were wholly committed to the Lord. No wonder the psalmist prayed, "Unite my heart to fear your name" (Psalm 86:11), or as the NIV renders it, "Give me an undivided heart, that I may fear your name."

We can make a good deal of pertinent application for our situation in the contemporary church. Conquering Canaan was an impossibility in human terms, but the spies were unrealistic when they left God out of the reckoning. So often the church today is committing exactly the same error. Realism recognizes that we live in a world of cause and effect, in which as people turn their backs on God there will inevitably be negative effects in society that will prove very hard to change. Humanly speaking Western culture is not going to be won back for the gospel easily, because the drift has been going on so long and the erosion has been deeply penetrating in so many areas of life. The capital of our past Christian commitment has largely disappeared, and we have to be realists about that. Sin pays a wage, and its degenerative power is not going to be removed at the clap of our hands or the whisper of a prayer. Giants of evil all around us have grown strong and have become entrenched over many years of moral collapse caused by sheer unbelief. Yet for the ten spies factual accuracy was matched by spiritual bankruptcy, as it often is today. The issue is whether we measure the giants by our strength or by God's promises, and the results are polar opposites. The undivided heart is totally realistic about the dimensions of the challenges and problems, but its focus is on the dynamic power of the gospel to transform human lives and turn around whole communities.

In eighteenth-century England, when evil was rampant and the church moribund, trapped in its unbelief, when it could be said that the population could be drunk for a penny and dead drunk for tuppence, when it seemed that the cause of the gospel had all but expired, God moved. He awoke a sleeping, comatose church as the Spirit raised up George Whitefield and John Wesley and many others to understand and proclaim the gospel with life-giving power. The Great Awakening that brought multitudes to faith on both sides of the Atlantic was a mighty intervention of God in a situation that realistically looked impossible and impenetrable. There is no diminution in God's power or grace today, but there are few Calebs who see beyond the problems to the promises and claim a mighty work of God in faith. Why? Because there are so few undivided hearts.

A second aspect of Caleb's vision is his humility, which is again a very rare quality among us. C. S. Lewis says that the first step on the path to humility is to realize that we do not have it, and that is too big a step for most of us. With Christian bookstores full of paperbacks with titles along the lines of *Humility and How I Achieved It*, there would seem to be little hope. But for Caleb this was an essential ingredient of his undivided heart. "If the Lord delights in us, he will bring us into this land," he said on that day at Kadesh-barnea (Numbers 14:8). Vision is not dictating to God what he is to do or how he is to do it, under the delusion that this is evidence of great faith. It is not. The wholehearted believer knows the greatness of God's infinite wisdom and inexhaustible power and submits himself unreservedly to the Lord. He recognizes that everything depends on God's grace and favor, which from the human standpoint is his response to faith and obedience. Obedience does not secure God's blessing in some semiautomatic way; rather it is an expression of the humility that keep the channels open for God's grace to keep flowing into our lives. Arrogance is a great enemy of the undivided heart. To think that I have a hotline from Heaven, a special word, or a particular gifting can so easily divert my fickle heart from humble trust to pious self-assertion. Caleb's humility is revealed in his total dependence on the Lord and the Lord's "delight."

"Delight" is a relational, almost emotional description of how the Lord wants to view his people. The heart that wholly follows him is one that is constantly deepening its love for him and rejoices in his presence, which brings joy to God's heart. It is because he has first loved us that we are able to love him in any measure at all. The center of his great plan of redemptive love is to restore his image within his people and for them to be the apple of his eye. That was why he designated Israel his "treasured possession" back at Sinai (Exodus 19:5), his personal treasure-chest, his investment portfolio, in which he finds joy. Humility is a key to our reciprocal enjoyment of all that God wants to give us. Every significant work for God depends on a relationship of humble dependence on God. "Unless the LORD builds the house, those who build it labor in vain" (Psalm 127:1). Caleb had learned the vital lesson that trusting Yahweh's promises and obeying his commands, living by his priorities and following his blueprints, is the only way to enjoy God's grace and favor as he wholeheartedly followed his delighted King.

All this underlines for us the third and perhaps greatest element of Caleb's vision, which was his faith, expressed in a simple, uncluttered trust that God would be all that he declared himself to be and thus would keep the promises that he had made. It comes through with great clarity in the Numbers 14 account. There is not a shadow of doubt there. Caleb said in essence, "The Lord will give us the land. It is already his. The Canaanites have no protection before their sovereign Creator." And that same quality of faith is foremost forty-five years later as he says to Joshua, "You know what the LORD said to Moses . . . concerning you and me" (14:6). All through the years his faith has been in the Word of God and thus in the God of the Word. That has kept him believing that he will indeed see the land since God is the one who gives life and breath, and that he will not only see it but possess his inheritance. "So now give me this hill country of which the LORD spoke on that day" (v. 12).

Faith is the antidote to fear. The ten spies were transfixed by the giants and the human impossibilities of their task, but Joshua and Caleb had their eyes on the God of promise, and thus they were able to live the life of faith. Fear said, "We cannot," but faith replied, "God can and will." This is a clear Biblical principle taught throughout the Scriptures, but perhaps with unusual clarity in Isaiah 51:12, 13. Israel is sunk in despondency caused by unbelief, facing the coming Babylonian exile and unable to believe that God has gracious purposes beyond it that will be richer and more glorious than anything they have known. God addresses them through the prophet: "I, I am he who comforts you; who are you that you are afraid of man who dies, of the son of man who is made like grass, and have forgotten the LORD, your Maker, who stretched out the heavens and laid the foundations of the earth, and you fear continually all the day because of the wrath of the oppressor, when he sets himself to destroy?" In essence God is saying, "You are afraid of man (who would not be terrified of the Babylonian war machine?), but that is because you have forgotten the Lord." Forget the eternal Creator God and his part in your affairs, and you will soon capitulate to the fear of man. Fear and faith cannot coexist. Faith may be assailed by doubt, as with the father of the demon-possessed boy who cried out to Jesus, "I believe; help my unbelief!" (Mark 9:24), but the very act of turning to God in faith begins to give fear its marching orders.

Our reaction to Caleb's story is often to elevate him to a position far above ourselves, which we fear is ultimately unattainable for us. But that is precisely because we lack faith. "How wonderful it would be to have a faith like Caleb's" becomes our stock response. But then we either settle back into our comfortable mediocrity (he was a great Bible hero and we are not) or we go on a quest to try to find a greater "faith," as though it is an abstract entity that we can acquire, perhaps through some overwhelming emotional experience. But faith is like a muscle. The more it is exercised and stretched, the stronger it will become; yet in the end it is the object of faith, rather than merely its exercise, that determines our spiritual condition. Think of a gymnast swinging on the bars. He may have an iron grip, but if the equipment is defective or wrongly assembled, the result will be disaster. What we need is not greater faith, subjective confidence, but faith in a great God. The essence of faith is holding on to a God who is faithful. Our grip may sometimes be very weak, which is perhaps why Jesus described faith as "like a grain of mustard seed" (Matthew 17:20), but it is to whom that feeble faith looks that determines the outcome.

If I take my young grandson down to the beach on a busy summer day, I will say, "Hold on to Grandpa's hand." I know he trusts me, and I want to teach him to be obedient, because I want him to be safe and to enjoy a great time. I know there are plenty of distractions to cause him to wander off and get lost or even come to harm. So because I love him, I tell him to hold on to Grandpa. But I hold on to that little hand a hundred times more firmly than the little one holds on to me. My grandchild's safety and delight depends on the firmness of my grip, not his. Yes, hold on to the God who is faithful; but his grip is infinitely stronger than ours. So faith's outcome is to know and prove that he is "able to do far more abundantly than all that we ask or think" (Ephesians 3:20). That was the secret of Caleb's vision, as it must be of ours too.

Caleb's Vigor

What an inspiring figure he is as he steps forward to claim what God has promised and what he has fought for—indeed, what he will yet have to fight for to make it fully his own! Listen to him. "I am still as strong today as I was in the day that Moses sent me; my strength now is as my strength was then, for war and for going and coming" (v. 11). Eighty-five years old and still storming forward in God's purposes to enter fully into the fulfillment of the promised blessings! What was the secret of his vigor? Obviously it was Caleb's wholeheartedly following the Lord. Spiritual vigor is the fruit of an undivided heart. The physical strength he enjoyed seems to have been the spiritual gift of God, probably shared by Joshua himself, in order to preserve them for the conquest and so to fulfill a special role at this unique point in God's redemptive history. It is not necessarily the case that all who follow the Lord wholeheartedly will be preserved into a physically strong and active old age, though many are. Paul's observation in 2 Corinthians 4:16 is the more normal human experience: "our outer self is wasting away." Our bodies do age, and many of our faculties decline. But in the context of that verse Paul also says, "Our inner self is being renewed day by day." That is why "we do not lose heart." Instead our heart is to be devoted to wholly following the Lord. It will be a daily battle, as I'm sure it was with Caleb. But if we are really dependent on the Lord, whatever our physical limitations may be, there is no reason for a Christian believer to quietly slip downhill spiritually when we should and could be storming on to glory!

Nor is Caleb's statement an idle boast. He is not saying, "I feel as well as I've ever felt," in order to keep a positive outlook. He knows there are still pockets of the Anakim (the giant race) to be driven out from his inheritance. But he is still strong and vigorous. The Lord has promised—so "give me this hill country" (v. 12a). The second half of verse 12 is typical of the man. "It may be that the Lord will be with me, and I shall drive them out just as the Lord said." Woudstra points out that "may be" "need not express fear or doubt. Usually it signifies hope," albeit a hope that is mixed with difficulty.[1] But the "I shall" of Caleb's faith ensures that the vision of his realistic, humble faith will be fulfilled in victory, and that is precisely what happens. Joshua's blessing (v. 13) indicates the approval of this servant of the Lord for the granting of Caleb's request, and so Hebron becomes his legal inheritance, "because he wholly followed the Lord, the God of Israel" (v. 14b).

The outcome is recorded for us in 15:13–19. Picking up the detail of the gift of Hebron, our narrator reminds his readers that its name at that time was Kiriath-arba, named after Arba, the father of Anak and a great man among the giant race (v. 13). But with Caleb's arrival, no less than three descendants of Anak are driven out by this vigorous octogenarian (v. 14). These were the next generation of those powerful Canaanites who had made Caleb's co-spies feel like grasshoppers and tremble in fear before them. There is a textual issue here, since 11:21 tells us that Joshua had cut off the Anakim from Hebron and Debir, so that none of the Anakim were left in the land (11:22). However, some apparently escaped outside of the area of Israel's rule and joined others of their tribe who were living in the Philistine cities of Gaza, Gath, and Ashdod (11:22). Here in chapters 14, 15 some Anakites had returned and assumed control over Kiriath-arba and the surrounding area again, although 10:36–39 indicates that it too had already been captured. The point is, one victory did not necessarily establish the settlement. The geographical range of the conquest, escapees from the cities, and the battles and constant pressure on Israel both to push on as well as to conserve their gains made for a fluid situation, in which the land is gradually coming under Israelite control, but which will take many years to establish, as the events of the book of Judges will make only too clear.

For now, however, Caleb's faith is justified. With Hebron under his control, he pushes on to Debir and offers his daughter, Achsah, to the man who will lead a successful attack to win the city. Othniel, his nephew, steps forward to win both prizes (v. 17). The Caleb qualities are being evidenced in the next generation, and through Othniel's campaign the family inheritance is enlarged still further. Later Othniel appears in Judges 3:9–11 as the first of the judges, empowered by the Spirit to rule Israel. It seems that Achsah's request for a field (probably made through Othniel) and then for springs of water with which to irrigate it are best seen as a wedding bounty (a "blessing," Joshua 15:19). This illustrates that the land is now Caleb's to dispense to his family and underlines the title-deeds and family rights that the allocation of the land, which we are about to witness, would confer on all the Israelites.

Before we leave Caleb's story, we need to consider the proper balance it helps us to strike between what is an outstanding example of Biblical faith and the big picture of God's redemptive purposes in salvation-history, within which it is so firmly set. The story of Caleb, as he bursts onto the scene, is both dramatic and inspiring. Our danger is that we may use it simply as an example, thus moralizing or spiritualizing the text. We need to recall the fundamental principle that God is the hero of the narrative and not wrest it from its context so as to turn it into merely a motivational talk.

> God uses Caleb's loyalty and faith to bring about the realization of his promise of the land. The story begun here has for its ultimate fulfilment the inheriting of salvation in Christ (see also Matt 25:34; Eph 1:14; Col 3:24; Heb 9:15). This provides the Joshua material with the necessary perspective as well as with eschatological depth, and leads to a much more dynamic and effective "application" than the example method. . . . The main thrust of the biblical text . . . is the development of the line of the history of redemption. Within that larger context, "examples" of faith may be given due prominence.[2]

This is a pertinent observation and warning, not least because it recognizes the exemplary value of a figure like Caleb but is also set firmly in the wider redemptive context, so that we do not have to identify ourselves with Caleb, since our circumstances and life-experiences are so different, but with Caleb's God in whom he placed his faith, which enabled him to follow wholeheartedly. In that sense he has provided us with a great pattern, applicable to whatever age and stage of life we may be at, and we should certainly seek to follow in his footsteps. But for us our greater and greatest exemplar is our Lord Jesus Christ, who won for us far greater victories and a more lasting inheritance and who is the object and content of our faith.

> Oh let me see thy footprints,
> And in them plant my own;
> My hope to follow duly
> Is in thy strength alone.
> O guide me, call me, draw me,
> Uphold me to the end;
> And then in Heaven receive me,
> My Savior and my Friend.[3]

17

The Allotment of the Land

JOSHUA 15:1—19:51

THIS PASSAGE STANDS at the center of a long unit that extends from 13:8 to 21:42, dealing with the distribution of the inheritance. It occupies a key position. Chapters 20, 21, while strictly part of the distribution narrative, can also be treated as a separate unit since they deal with the cities of refuge and the provisions made for the tribe of Levi. So for the purposes of this chapter we will pick up the Joshua text at 15:1 and follow it through to the end of chapter 19.

With the inheritance to Reuben, Gad, and half of Manasseh already established east of the Jordan (13:15–31), attention now turns to Judah, preceded by the story of Caleb (14:6–15), which takes priority due to the Lord's specific promise to him long before the allocation by lot. The last sentence of chapter 14, concluding the Caleb narrative, "And the land had rest from war" (v. 15b), echoes the last sentence of chapter 11, which rounded off the conquest section. Now with that testimony to all that Yahweh has achieved for his people echoing in our ears, we are ready to turn our attention to the tribes who will inherit west of the Jordan. Which parts of the land that is now at "rest" will be allocated to each tribe, clan, and family?

We have discussed before the reason for the many details recorded in these chapters, but it is good to remind ourselves that it is all primarily a witness to the faithfulness of their God who had promised this to his people centuries before. First, we see two and a half tribes west of the Jordan, which are Judah (whose inheritance is described in the greatest detail), Ephraim, and half of Manasseh, which leaves seven tribes still to be settled, excluding Levi, and remembering also that Manasseh, while divided geographically, is essentially still one tribal unit. Howard helpfully draws attention to the fact that the lists are "not identical in structure, emphasis or length" but are composed of different elements that he identifies as: "(1) boundary lists and city lists (2) notices of cities or territories remaining to be conquered (3) stories of individuals or groups asking for and receiving their inheritances and (4) miscellaneous regularities, mostly involving stereotypical introductory and concluding statements."[1] Chapter 18, with Joshua's instructions for the land's seven divisions, then intervenes before we are shown how the allotments work out with reference to Benjamin, Simeon, Zebulun, Issachar, Asher, Naphtali, and Dan. Here then is the proof, both to Israel and to all of Joshua's readers, that Yahweh will keep the promises he has made. He has the power, and he has the righteous integrity always to do what he says he will do. As each Israelite's tribe and clan and family came up, here was the proof that what was true for the nation was also true in specific detail for him as an individual. This was why they had believed and what they had fought for, and here was *terra firma* that was theirs, proving that none of this had been in vain.

Judah

Commentators from Calvin onward have indicated that Judah comes first in the order primarily because of the special blessings conferred on it by Jacob (Genesis 49:8–12). As the Old Testament story develops, Judah assumes increasing importance among the twelve, not least because King David and his descendants come from Judah, as does great David's greater son, the Lord Jesus Christ (Matthew 1:1). After the division of the kingdom, it is Judah by which the southern kingdom is known, with its capital in Jerusalem and the Lord's temple there, so that in every way this tribe has the supremacy among the brothers. In 15:1–12 its boundaries are carefully and clearly set out with regard to all four points of the compass. The southern boundary extends from the southern end of the Dead Sea westward to the Mediterranean. The eastern boundary is the western shores of the Dead Sea, while to the north it stretches from the northern end of the sea, beyond Jerusalem, to the area of Ekron and so westward to the Mediterranean. After the digression regarding Caleb's inheritance (15:13–19), the allocation continues (15:20) with the list of the Canaanite towns included in it, beginning with the Negev in the south (15:21–32), followed by the foothills of the west (15:33–44) and the Philistine settlements at the coast (15:45–47). The list then moves to the hill country (15:48–60) and concludes with the desert (15:61, 62).

As the list develops, the number of towns and villages is totaled to give an escalating sense both of the size and scope of the conquest and also of all that still needed to be done. As a reminder of those realities, verse 63 honestly records the fact that they could not drive out the Jebusites from Jerusalem, although Joshua had killed its king and defeated its army in the battle of Gibeon (10:22–27). This is one of a series of ominous notes that occur throughout these chapters, pointing to the incomplete nature of the conquest and the problems this will create for Israel in the future. In Judges 1:21 the failure is attributed to the tribe of Benjamin, probably because Jerusalem was situated on the border between the tribes, although it seems from Judges 1:8 that Judah may have had some temporary, limited success. A comment by John Calvin may strike us as somewhat severe, but its theological acumen is surely justified.

> Had they exerted themselves to the full measure of their strength, and failed of success, the dishonor would have fallen on God himself, who had promised that he would continue with them as their leader until he should give them full and free possession of the land. . . . Therefore, it was owing entirely to their own sluggishness that they did not make themselves masters of the city of Jerusalem . . . their own torpor, their neglect of the divine command from a love of ease, [these] were the real obstacles.[2]

Joseph

Again the favor of Jacob's blessing (Genesis 49:22–26) seems to be the reason why the two sons of Joseph, Ephraim and Manasseh, feature next in the allocation. With half of Manasseh already settled on the east of the river, the remaining half, along with Ephraim, are given large territories in the central part of the land, including many of the place names that become increasingly familiar to us as the Old Testament unfolds. After the quite detailed delineation of the southern boundary (16:1–4), 16:5–10 gives the details of territory for Ephraim, followed by those for western Manasseh in 17:1–13. The point is made that although they were reckoned as two tribes they drew only one lot, which is the reason for the complaint made in 17:14–18. "Why have you given me but one lot and one portion as an inheritance, although I am a numerous people, since all along the LORD has blessed me?" (v. 14). It seems that they are accusing Joshua of using their common descent from Joseph in order to deprive them of more territory that they claim should rightly be theirs. His reply is masterly. If they are such a great and numerous company, why do they not go out and attack the enemy whose territory has been allotted to them but not yet taken (v. 15)? The implication is that they have been allocated more than adequate space, but they must exercise energy and determination to make it their own. The territory was not insufficient, but their energy and faith seemed to be, as their reply indicated. There was a great deal of forested land in the hill country to be won and then presumably cleared, but it would be a demanding project.

Their response is to quibble about the unsuitability of their allocation (17:16), which will confine them to the plain, where the Canaanites are still dwelling, and they have "chariots of iron" (17:16). But Joshua will not move an inch further. If they are so numerous, let them use their numbers and strength to subdue the land and drive out the Canaanites, whatever their weaponry (17:17, 18). It is as though he is asking them, "Have you learned nothing from the whole experience of the conquest?" Provision is made for them to have more territory, but they will have to subdue and settle it by their own energy and persistence (17:17). The question as to whether they will have the faith of Joshua to accomplish the project is left hanging in the balance.

There is one other curious incident in this section, concerning the five daughters of Zelophehad (17:3–6). Here again there is a back story recorded in Numbers 26:33 where they are first named and Numbers 27:1–11 where their circumstances are revealed. Their father had died in the wilderness, and they had no brothers; so they appealed directly to Moses and Eleazar that their family name should not be removed, but that they should be given an inheritance among their father's brothers, in the tribe of Manasseh. The Lord himself instructed Moses to grant their request and established laws of inheritance that enabled its transfer to a man's daughter(s) if he died having no sons. Much like Caleb, the five women come forward now to claim their God-given and promised inheritance. They are another example of trust in the promises of Yahweh, confirmed by the award of a personal inheritance to each of them as daughters of Manasseh. Like Rahab and Achsah before them in the book, because of their faith they are not to be excluded from God's blessing on the basis of gender.

Shiloh

The establishment of the tabernacle at Shiloh is now the focus, at the center of this section dedicated to the distribution of the land. We have heard the provisions for the five tribes, or four if Ephraim and Manasseh are to be considered as one unit. That would mean that Levi would then be rightly considered as the twelfth tribe, but because no allocation of territory is to be made to Levi we can treat Ephraim and Manasseh as distinct in terms of the twelve tribal groups among whom the land is distributed. Here we are at the halfway point with seven more tribes to be covered. This all happens in a relatively short compass in chapters 18, 19, which we are encouraged to see as a unit by the marker-posts or bracketings at the beginning (18:1) and end (19:51) by reference to Shiloh.

Joshua moves his center of operations from Gilgal to Shiloh, situated in the middle of the country. This signifies a shift from being on a war footing, with the main camp at Gilgal, to being at rest. Until that point the tabernacle and the ark have either been adjacent to the camp, or possibly peripatetic as at Jericho. But now there is sufficient rest for a convocation of the whole congregation to gather at Shiloh and to establish the shrine of God's manifest presence there on a more permanent basis. It was still there at the time of Samuel's birth and childhood, indeed until the ark was captured by the Philistines at the time of Eli's death (1 Samuel 1—4). We must not lose the significance of 18:1. The people of God are established in the land, and the presence of God is located in their midst, at Shiloh, northwest of Jericho, in the territory of Ephraim.

The occasion is used by Joshua to stir the people to renewed effort in taking possession of those parts of the land over which they did not yet exercise control. He accuses them of growing slack in their prosecution of the conquest (18:3), reminding them again that the land is God's gracious gift to them. Much of the land that had been allocated already was in their hands, but this was either the settlements east of the river or the central and southern areas allocated to Judah and Ephraim/Manasseh. As the allocations began to move out further and further across the country, more and more would need to be done to make these territories their own. So to ensure the fair and just distribution of the land when the lots were cast, Joshua appoints twenty-one surveyors, not spies but reconnaissance officers, three from each of the seven remaining tribes, to "go up and down the land . . . [and] write a description of it" (v. 4). Reminding them of the allocations already made, which will not change, and also of the fact that Levi is excluded, Joshua commissions them to divide the land into seven portions and to describe it fully, bringing their findings in written form back to him (vv. 5–7). The plan is activated, and eventually the men return with "a description of it by towns in seven divisions," written in "a book" (v. 9). On receiving this information Joshua is ready to cast lots for the seven tribes, and the result is recorded for us in the rest of the section. The task was accomplished, and the unity of the nation was preserved and perhaps even enhanced by these provisions.

Benjamin is the first of the seven to whom the lot falls (v. 7). Again, as with Judah, the boundaries are described in considerable detail (vv. 11–20), followed by a listing of the cities, twenty-six in all (vv. 21–28). Benjamin's northern boundary is the same as Ephraim's southern. Simeon is next, and "their inheritance was in the midst of the inheritance of the people of Judah"

(19:1), as a sort of enclave. We are told in 19:9 that this was because Judah's share was too large for them, although it had been already indicated by lot. However, this later amendment had equal divine authority, and Simeon received seventeen cities with their villages (19:1–9). Since the patriarchal blessing of Jacob in Genesis 49 seems to have a shaping role in the order of the allocation of the land, it is worth noting that Genesis 49:7 states about Simeon and Levi, "I will divide them in Jacob and scatter them in Israel." Certainly the subsequent listing of Simeon is one of declining numbers and loss of identity.

The third lot came up for Zebulun, mentioned before his older brother Issachar, as in the order of Genesis 49:13, 14. The territory assigned is in the north of the country, bounded by Asher to the west, Naphtali to the north, and Issachar on the south (19:10–16). Issachar comes next (19:17–23), with more detail given to their cities than to the boundaries. Asher is fifth (19:24–31, where again the focus is on their twenty-two cities). Naphtali follows (19:32–39), with territory situated between Asher and upper Jordan. "His land included attractive, densely forested mountains and fairly fertile lower areas. Through this heartland of Galilee ran the major trade route between Jezreel and points north."[3]

Last came Dan (19:40–48), and again the emphasis is on the cities, which indicate its general location between Judah and Ephraim, to the west of Benjamin, which includes the coastal region of the Mediterranean Sea. Verse 47 is an interesting but ominous interpolation, from the time perspective of the narrator writing after the days of Joshua. The bald statement is that their territory was "lost to them" or literally "went out from them." Perhaps it never was properly taken, or perhaps the Danites occupied it only briefly, but the fact of their northern migration to Leshem, which they captured and renamed Dan, is well documented in Judges. "The Amorites pressed the people of Dan back into the hill country, for they did not allow them to come down to the plain" (Judges 1:34). In fact, it was the house of Joseph that subjugated the Amorites, which may indicate some lack of commitment or effort on behalf of the Danites. The full account of their migration north recounted in Judges 18 makes very sad reading, culminating in their setting up their own shrine, carved image, and independent priesthood to rival the house of God at Shiloh.

Joshua

Joshua 19:49–51 concludes the narrative of the allocation by focusing on Joshua's own personal inheritance, given to him by the people of Israel, in accordance with the command of Yahweh (v. 50). During the whole process of the distribution Joshua has been a wise, motivational, and impartial leader with no apparent concern for himself. Like Caleb he had received God's promise back in Numbers 14:30 that he would dwell in the land, and he was probably content to rest in that. Certainly his inheritance here at the end of the unit is intended to balance the inheritance given to Caleb at the beginning. In fact, these three verses bring a sense of completion to the section. Being from the tribe of Ephraim, he asks for a city in their territory, to settle back among his people at Timnath-serah in the hill country. This is where he would die and be buried (Judges 2:9). The uniqueness of his life of service is matched, in the gracious kindness of the Lord, with the unique gift of a city as his personal possession, even if it had to be rebuilt, since as Calvin surmises it was "a mere heap of stones."[4]

Joshua 19:51 closes the unit in an appropriately formal way. The agenda is completed. The meeting is closed. The task is finished. "So they finished dividing the land." The Shiloh convocation has done its work. It had all taken place at the command of the Lord, at the entrance to the tent of meeting and thus before the Lord, and he had providentially overruled in his sovereign distribution of the lots. The land that was his alone to give he has granted to his people, not just in a general sense, but in specific detail, town by town, tribe by tribe. That gift had now to be received by faith and turned into reality by continuing trust and energetic obedience as Israel committed herself to possess her possessions indeed. Those same qualities are still required in the people of God today if we are to enter in more deeply and fully to the potential of all that we already have in Christ.

How firm a foundation, you saints of the Lord,
Is laid for your faith in his excellent Word!
What more can he say than to you he has said,
You who unto Jesus for refuge have fled?

"Fear not! I am with you, O be not dismayed,
For I am your God and will still give you aid;
I'll strengthen you, and help you, and cause you to stand
Upheld by my righteous omnipotent hand."[5]

18

Refuge and Residence

JOSHUA 20:1—21:45

IT IS CUSTOMARY FOR the opponents of Biblical revelation to present the events of the conquest in extreme terms, as evidence of primitive bloodthirsty slaughter and xenophobic genocide. They see those battles as belonging to a far distant and now totally discredited era of human history when civilization had not yet had its calming effects and when the human species had not yet evolved socially to its present "sophistication." The next step is to be able to reject all that made up that culture, especially its law code, as outdated and irrelevant to modern life. Interesting antiquarian evidence is then the sum total of the Old Testament's significance for us today, it is claimed.

As with so many arguments of this sort, there is a small element of truth in what is said. We believe in progressive revelation, which does not mean that the earlier revelation is in any way defective or inferior to the later, but that there is a development of God's self-disclosure along the timeline of the Bible. What was embryonic and sometimes hidden and obscure in the earlier parts of Scripture becomes ever clearer and more complete, culminating in the coming of the Word made flesh. A key example would be the clarification, and indeed the intensification, of the Law's demands contained in Jesus' Sermon on the Mount in Matthew 5:17–48. He came not to abolish the Law or the prophets but to fulfill them, and the famous formula "You have heard that it was said . . . but I say to you . . ." illustrates what that means in a variety of references to the law code. These culminate in verses 43–45: "You have heard that it was said, 'You shall love your neighbor and hate your enemy.' But I say to you, Love your enemies and pray for those who persecute you, so that you may be sons of your Father who is in heaven." There is a shift of focus here, which moves us away from any concept of holy war or retaliatory action against those who abuse us. It also reminds us that, in Luther's famous dictum, while we read the Bible forward we can only understand it backwards. The later revelation is the lens through which we understand the former. The person and work of Christ is the key to the interpretation of the Old Testament.

However, the point that needs to be made, against its detractors, is that there is no rejection or abolition of what went before in the teaching of Christ and his apostles. Revelation is progressive in the sense that it builds on what has preceded it, but it never contradicts or nullifies it. It is also important to point out that what is sometimes called the Judeo-Christian ethical tradition is the real foundation on which modern civilization has been built, rather than on some abstract concept of social evolution. There is a cruel irony in contemporary atheists' claim to the advancement of civilized sophistication in light of the history of the twentieth-century and twenty-first-century world. Atheistic tyrants have been guilty of human slaughter on a sickening and unprecedented scale.

By contrast the record in Joshua is ordered and disciplined because the conquest is revelatory of God's character. We must not forget the antecedent revelation. God has already revealed himself as Creator of all, and he exercises sovereign authority over all that he has made. He has already declared himself to be in a covenant relationship of grace toward Abraham and his descendants. He has already activated that covenant in redeeming the sons of Jacob not only from their slavery in Egypt but also from his own righteous wrath through the provision of the Passover lamb. He has already revealed his character of righteousness, truth, and justice in the law code given to Israel at Sinai. And now he has confirmed his promises to Abraham, Isaac, and Jacob not only by multiplying their descendants to make of them a great nation but also in the provision of a land for them in which to live. All of this antecedent revelation determines the conduct of the conquest and the boundaries of the settlement. That is what justifies the destruction of the Canaanite strongholds. It is not by Israel's strength or superiority of technique or numbers that the land became theirs, but because the Lord gave it to them. Nor was this a capricious action, but rather the outworking of his eternal righteousness in judgment on the gross and prolonged iniquity of the Amorites. The cleansing of the land is a judicial act of Yahweh, and his own redeemed people are taught that they too will be expelled from the land if they fail in their consequent covenant obligations. This is not the stuff of racial phobia, but the righteous control of the supreme Creator over the creatures to whom he alone gives life and breath.

Throughout Joshua's narrative we have been reminded that he and the leaders of Israel are in effect following a script. It had been written by Moses, as instructed by God. As such it reveals the blend in God's character of his perfect justice and his gracious mercy. As the later New Testament revelation, through the Apostle John, will teach us, "God is light, and in him is no darkness at all. If we say we have fellowship with him while we walk in darkness, we lie and do not practice the truth" (1 John 1:5, 6). But the same letter equally affirms that "God is love, and whoever abides in love abides in God, and God abides in him" (1 John 4:16). It is significant that both declarations of God's attributes and nature are immediately applied to our behavior in God's world. The Biblical principle is clear. God's self-revelation has demanding implications for how we are to live. So the constant revelation of his justice and his grace, throughout Joshua, summed up in the steadfast love of his covenant faithfulness, is to have major implications on life within the land. And that script, that set of directions, already exists in "the law that Moses my servant commanded you" (Joshua 1:7), from which Joshua is not to deviate.

Cities of Refuge

Chapter 20 deals with a gracious provision of God for life in the land that is grounded both in his justice and his mercy. Verse 2 brings us back to the Mosaic script, with regard to the provision of "the cities of refuge." Back in Deuteronomy 4:41–43, as part of the settlement of the eastern tribes, Moses set apart three cities (one each for Reuben, Gad, and Manasseh) to serve this purpose. The shedding of blood (i.e., the killing of another person) cried out for satisfaction in every situation. Where the action was murder, intentional and perhaps premeditated, clearly forbidden by the sixth commandment (Exodus 20:13), the Law was clear about the punishment—"life for life, eye for eye, tooth for tooth," and so on (Exodus 21:23–25). This was both to restrict the taking of vengeance beyond the magnitude of the crime, so that feuds would not develop and fester, and also to teach the principle of punishment proportional to the original offense. But what if the killing was unintentional, what might today be defined as manslaughter rather than murder? The manslayer could flee to one of the designated cities to save his life. The procedure is further elaborated by Moses in Deuteronomy 19:1–13, at which point he passes on the instruction that following the conquest an additional three cities are to be designated west of the Jordan, one in each major area (Deuteronomy 19:2, 3). This instruction is now activated in Joshua 20.

The passage in Deuteronomy 19 illustrates the circumstances in mind, such as an accident in the forest with an axhead (Deuteronomy 19:5). Because justice demands settlement at the hands of the "avenger of blood" (v. 6), the city of refuge is to be nearby so the manslayer may run to it without being struck down.

Provision is granted for an extra three cities "if the LORD your God enlarges your territory" (Deuteronomy 19:8). Joshua 20:4 adds the detail that the manslayer is to be assessed by the elders at the city gate, and they are to afford him protection until his case can be properly heard "before the congregation" (v. 6). If his case is proved genuine, he must stay in the city until the death of the current high priest, after which he can return to his original home (v. 6). The three new cities are then designated (Kedesh, Shechem, and Hebron), and the closing verse summarizes what has been decided and its purpose (v. 9).

For us perhaps the major interest focuses on the provision about the death of the high priest, before which the manslayer could not return home. One suggestion is that the high priest's death was regarded as the end of an epoch and therefore provided an amnesty for offenses committed within his lifetime, to enable a new start with a new high priest. Woudstra suggests, "Perhaps a certain atoning effect was produced by the death of the chief sacerdotal functionary."[1] It is difficult to see quite how this would fit with the principle of the sacrifice rather than the offerer providing atonement, but one can see its attraction for the Christian interpreter. Howard agrees to the same significance in his comment, "For Christians, the typological associations with the death of Jesus Christ—the great High Priest whose death atones for their sins—are certainly visible here."[2] Whatever the true significance was, we can certainly be thankful that in the mercy of God we have a refuge to which to run, where the guilt of all our sins, unintentional or not, can be assuaged through the offering of Jesus Christ once for all as both priest and sacrifice.

Residence for Levi

With the conclusion of the allocation to the tribes, all that now needs to be added, to make the record complete, is the detail of the arrangements put in place for the Levites. This is the content of chapter 21, which begins with the Levites taking the initiative as they come to the distribution "board" at Shiloh to claim their lawful share in the provisions dictated under Moses (vv. 1, 2). We have already been told that the Levites have the Lord for their inheritance and portion (13:33), expressed further in the offerings made by fire (13:14). But still they had to live somewhere, and they also needed pasture for their livestock as part of their support. So now they come to make their appeal on the basis of the Mosaic script, much as Caleb did in chapter 14.

A connecting text is Numbers 35:1–8. There are to be forty-eight designated cities, including the six cities of refuge, and considerable detail is also provided about the size of the pasturelands immediately outside the cities, which are also to be theirs. The larger tribes with the larger populations are to provide the larger number of cities; so the allocation is to be in proportion to the resources. On this basis the heads of the tribe approach Joshua and Eleazar, and the allocation is made by lot as with the other tribes. This is intended to underline the Lord's sovereign involvement in their provision, as much as for all the others. This allocation has equally binding significance and is not to be resisted, since it is already clearly part of God's revealed will in principle and now is to be so in practice. As with Judah due to its prominence heading the allocation of land west of the Jordan, so now the priestly line of Aaron is the first for whom the lot is cast (v. 4). Levi had three sons—Kohath, Gershon, and Merari; so the division follows these three family strands (vv. 4–8). The descendants of Aaron receive thirteen cities from Judah, Simeon, and Benjamin (v. 4), while another ten cities are given to the rest of the Kohathites (v. 5), who were not of the Aaronic line. These came from the tribes of Ephraim, Dan, and Manasseh. The Gershonites received thirteen cities from the tribes of Issachar, Asher, Naphtali, and half of Manasseh (v. 6). The number of forty-eight is completed by twelve cities for the Merarites from Reuben, Gad, and Zebulun (v. 7). The cities are then named in the same order of allocation (vv. 9–42), with the interesting additional comment that in the case of Kiriath-arba (Hebron) Caleb retained "the fields of the city and its villages" as his possession (v. 12). Calvin rather quaintly comments that Caleb "with great equanimity allowed himself to be deprived."[3] Of course, all the tribes had to recognize this arrangement as part of the divine provision for the nation as an entity. But as with the other tribal allocations, the designation of the cities does not mean that they were all already under Israelite control, or that the Levites eventually settled in all of them.

The reasons why the Levites did not inherit a section of the land as their own may be both practical and symbolic. It was clearly a great advantage to have them scattered throughout the country, represented in all the other tribal territories. The blessing of Moses in Deuteronomy 33:10 affirms, "They shall teach Jacob your rules and Israel your law; they shall put incense before you and whole burnt offerings on your altar." So while the focus of their being separated to priestly office is inevitably on the tabernacle and its ministries, at this point established at Shiloh, this could only require their services on a rotational basis. For the rest of their time they are a source of teaching and interpretation concerning God's Law for all the people in their home areas. This could clearly augment and strengthen the spiritual life of the people, much more than if they only attended the tabernacle for the great annual feasts. There was, however, a symbolism in all this too. The priestly tribe, set aside to minister before the Lord on behalf of the people, was a continual reminder in Israel of the spiritual values transcending the physical and the eternal eclipsing the temporal. The Levites not being tied to the physical land may also have served to lift the eyes and hearts of the whole congregation to the unseen, eternal realities. The tenor of Hebrews 11 would certainly seem to indicate that this was a characteristic of the faithful. "[Abraham] was looking forward to the city that has foundations, whose designer and builder is God" (Hebrews 11:10). Acknowledging that they were strangers and exiles on the earth, "people who speak thus make it clear that they are seeking a homeland . . . they desire a better country, that is, a heavenly one" (Hebrews 11:14–16). The Levites provided a living example of holding the ties of earth and the constraints of territory loosely, which might enable the rest of the nation to sharpen its own spiritual perspective. Godly ministry can surely have a similar effect in the contemporary church.

Theological Reflection

The closing verses (43–45) of Joshua 21 can easily be overlooked, but they are in fact one of the high spots of the whole book. More than a summary of what has happened, they provide a theological key to all that we have witnessed. In the biggest picture of the book, they form a concluding bracket with 1:6 at the start. There it was a word of promise: "Be strong and courageous, for you shall cause this people to inherit the land that I swore to their fathers to give them." Now it is a glorious assertion of fulfillment. "Thus the LORD gave to Israel all the land that he swore to give to their fathers" (v. 43a).

The verbs hold the key to this majestic paragraph. "The LORD *gave* . . . the land" (v. 43). "The LORD *gave* them rest" (v. 44a). "The LORD had *given* all their enemies into their hands" (v. 44b). Not one promise "failed" (v. 45). These are all activities of God, and that has been the strongest motif all the way through the story. Everything is dependent on him. But each benefaction of God is also remembered in terms of the effect it has had on the everyday lives of his people. "They took possession of it, and they settled there" (v. 43). "Not one of all their enemies had withstood them" (v. 44). Everything God had promised "came to pass" (v. 45). These dominant notes reflect the book's great themes of God's promises and the people's inheritance, both coming together in the allotment of the land. It may be objected that this final paragraph is sweepingly optimistic, but the fourfold repetition of "the LORD" (Yahweh, the covenant-keeping God) reminds us that any later disappointments or failures are due to Israel's lethargy or lack of faith, not to any sort of deficiency in the Lord's purposes or in his ability to achieve them. And he does not change!

19

Unity Reaffirmed

JOSHUA 22:1-34

WE COME NOW TO the final section of the book (chapters 22—24), which takes the form of three farewell occasions. First, in this chapter Joshua dismisses the two and a half tribes whose homes are east of the Jordan, sending them back to "the land where your possession lies" (v. 4). He has some parting words of blessing for them, giving due acknowledgment to their faithful obedience in joining forces with their brothers west of the river, as commanded by God, to enable them to make these lands their own. But this apparently peaceful parting soon generates traumatic difficulties with great potential for lasting damage, as we shall see. In chapter 23 Joshua speaks his farewell words to the elders and heads, judges and officials of Israel in the presence of a wider congregation (23:2), while the final chapter addresses the whole nation ("all the tribes") at Shechem (24:1) and renews their commitment to the covenant and so to the Lord.

The book ends with a strong forward look, which is always the controlling perspective of Scripture. Prophecy is the way in which God reveals his sovereign knowledge and authority to men, and faith is the human response, which demonstrates its trust by acts of appropriate obedience. "Now faith is the assurance of things hoped for, the conviction of things not seen" (Hebrews 11:1). So the Bible's pattern is always that we live in the present, informed and challenged by the past, but motivated and energized by the eternal values of God's glorious future. We must not lose our future perspective because "our citizenship is in heaven, and from it we await a Savior, the Lord Jesus Christ" (Philippians 3:20). However, it is looking to the temporal future that causes the problems that are the subject matter of Joshua 22.

Job Well Done

The first nine verses of the chapter start things off on a high note. Joshua has nothing but commendation for Reuben, Gad, and the half-tribe of Manasseh. Detailed obedience, whatever the cost, has always been a priority in this book, and Joshua is able warmly to approve their unstinting support in helping the nine and a half tribes to acquire land in which they themselves will not have a share. Once again the script had been written by Moses, at God's instruction, back in Numbers 32:6ff, when he challenged them not to sit in their homes while their brothers went to war, which would bring massive discouragement to Israel. Rather, they agreed to fight alongside the rest of the nation (Numbers 32:16–19), returning to their home territory only when the mission was completed. They were allowed to settle their families and livestock first in the cities of Gilead, but the fighting men would remain west of the river until the land was subdued (Numbers 32:20–27). The requirement and the promise were repeated and reinforced before the conquest began (Joshua 1:10–18), and now the moment has come for Joshua to release them with an exemplary record of obedient service "these many days" (22:3).

Joshua's parting words in verse 5 prefigure what he will say to the whole nation in the next two chapters and reecho the charge under which he has lived his whole life and exercised his extraordinary leadership. These heartfelt words underline the priorities of their relationship with Yahweh, which must undergird their future lives. Careful obedience to all the laws that Moses commanded lies at the heart of this commitment that will be evidenced by walking in all his ways. They are to be loyal and faithful to the covenant requirements. But the root of this will be in the other commands here to "love the Lord," to "cling to him," and to "serve him with all your heart and with all your soul." Israelite devotion was never a matter of cold conformity to a code of rules, any more than Christian discipleship is. It is not external but deeply personal at root. Keeping Yahweh's rules is an expression of love for Yahweh's person. That too has always been the center of Mosaic instruction. "You shall love the Lord your God with all your heart and with all your soul and with all your might" (Deuteronomy 6:5)—with everything you are and have. Nothing less is required of Christian believers, for the Lord Jesus himself designated this as the first and greatest commandment, to which was added, "and your neighbor as yourself" when he approved the lawyer's answer in Luke 10:25–28. "Do this, and you will live" (Luke 10:28).

To these words of blessing, Joshua also added the temporal blessings of "much wealth and . . . very much livestock, with silver, gold, bronze, and iron, and . . . much clothing" (v. 8). The spoils of the conquest were to be shared equally by all its participants. So we have the picture of these battle-weary fighting men looking forward so much to the reunion with their wives and children and coming home loaded. It must have been a very satisfying conclusion for all concerned. Their whole community would benefit from their loyal service. But . . .

Good Intentions Misread

On their way home the warriors came to the region of the River Jordan, which forms the boundary line of the tribal territories. The dramatic way in which the story is told is a fine example of narrative art, as the reasons for what happens are only given later. The effect is that we, the readers, are as perplexed as the rest of the Israelites were, for there by the Jordan they built "an altar of imposing size" (v. 10). Later we are told that this was an action of great loyalty to Yahweh, but at this point all the warning lights are flashing. Its imposing presence means it is intended to stay there and is not to be ignored. But this is in direct contravention of Deuteronomy 12:4ff. where, warning them against any assimilation toward Canaanite pagan religious practices by setting up alternative shrines or worship centers, God commands, through Moses, "Take care that you do not offer your burnt offerings at any place that you see, but at the place that the LORD will choose in one of your tribes, there you shall offer your burnt offerings" (Deuteronomy 12:13, 14). This alternative altar must therefore be an abomination to the Lord, and that is precisely how the western tribes construe things. So indignant are they and so insistent that the problem must be dealt with once and for all that they gather together at Shiloh with the intention of launching a civil conflict against their brothers (Joshua 22:12). Those who had fought together now look destined to destroy one another. It's a terrible situation. The motivation is godly and honorable, since it involves obedience to God's Word, but the potential consequences of a conflict are devastating. We know there are groups of scattered Canaanites only too ready to regroup and reassert themselves at the least sign of Israelite weakness or disunity.

However, wisdom prevails. A delegation, headed by Eleazar and his son, Phinehas, with representatives of all the ten tribes, is sent to Gilead to see what can be done to resolve the matter before resorting to physical conflict (vv. 13–15). Their approach is direct and uncompromising, describing the building of the altar as a "breach of faith . . . committed against the God of Israel" (v. 16). This is the term that was used to describe Achan's sin in 7:1 and is used again about him at the end of this speech in verse 20. What the speech reveals is that they had learned the lessons about God's righteous judgment down the years, which now inspired in them a holy awe. Reference is made to "the sin at Peor" (v. 17), characterized by idolatry and immorality when Moab seduced Israel (see Numbers 25:1–9). On that occasion the same Phinehas had caused the death, with his spear, of an Israelite man and a Moabite woman, which stayed the Lord's judgment by plague that nevertheless produced the death of 24,000 people. One can hear the tones of frustration and incredulity in the question of verse 17, "Have we not had enough of the sin at Peor . . . ?" They knew that God's wrath would be turned against the whole nation if this act of rebellion went unchecked. Wasn't that the lesson of Achan they had learned at Ai (v. 20)? They even offer land west of the Jordan from their own inheritances if the eastern tribes consider the territory they have received as "unclean" (v. 19). West of the river was where the tabernacle was, and that was the only altar God would recognize. Anything else would be rebellious (v. 19). A powerful and impressive case is presented—both as a warning and as an exhortation. It is something of a high spot in the spiritual life of the nation when its leadership is so united in its desire to be fully obedient to the Lord's instructions, so much in awe of God's righteous wrath, and so concerned to preserve the many blessings that he has poured out upon them. But it is even better than that . . .

Problem Resolved

The reply of the tribes east of the Jordan is heartwarming and enormously encouraging (vv. 21–29). They begin with an ascription of glory to God, repeated for solemnity and emphasis—"The Mighty One, God, the Lord!" (v. 22a). At the very start of their reply the eastern tribes affirm that their confession of Yahweh as God of gods is exactly the same as their western brothers. He is the one before whom they stand, and their loyalty to him is total. "He knows; and let Israel itself know!" (v. 22). In other words, "What we want you to hear and understand about our position or actions is something that is clearly known by God and open to his all-seeing eye." He knows the integrity of their hearts, and they are able to call on him as a witness to the truth of the explanation they are about to give. If their intention had been to set up a rival shrine to the tabernacle or an alternative to the sacrificial system, they freely admit, they deserve to die (vv. 22b, 23a), and they would fully expect the Lord to take vengeance (v. 23b). That was neither their motivation nor intention.

The following verses explain the real reason for the altar's construction. Because the River Jordan formed such a significant physical barrier between them and the rest of the nation, they were afraid it might create a division between them in future generations. Their service on behalf of the western tribes could easily be forgotten when their generation had passed on; so they thought that some visible reminder was needed. If later generations west of the river began to imagine that the easterners had no right to worship the Lord at the tabernacle ("no portion in the LORD," vv. 25, 27) because they did not live in the land, then their children would be excluded from fellowship with Yahweh, with all the obvious disastrous results that implied (v. 25). The altar then was built not as a place of sacrifice but as a witness. At last the skilful storyteller brings us to the narrative's climax, which resolves the problem. The building of an altar as a memorial was not in any way meant to diminish the tabernacle but to show that these tribes were equally a part of Israel, equally dependent on the sacrificial system, and equally committed to the worship of Yahweh. This would be the ultimate answer to the questioning of their Israelite legitimacy by any future generations. The copy of the altar of the Lord is proof of their total integration within Israel, with their full covenant rights and privileges (v. 28). Their purpose was therefore the very opposite of what the eastern delegation had feared. Rather than rebellion, it was intended as a mark of loyalty and unity.

After their detailed explanation, the relief is almost palpable (v. 30). For the delegation "it was good in their eyes," exactly what they wanted to hear. Phinehas expresses their joy not only because the issue has been resolved but also because this happy and peaceful outcome is certain evidence that "the LORD is in our midst" (v. 31). The catastrophe has been averted; the loyalty of the eastern tribes is established beyond doubt; the wrath of God no longer hangs over the people. The delegation reports back to the western tribes, and it is "good in [their] eyes" too (v. 33). The threat of war is dropped, and the altar is allowed to stand. Indeed, it is given a more formal and enhanced status by the name that Reuben and Gad confer upon it—"Witness" (v. 34), or more fully, "it is a witness between us that the LORD is God." In this way it became a symbolic reaffirmation of the national unity of the twelve tribes, which is created and sustained by the fact that for them all Yahweh is Lord.

That is also the only source of unity for the contemporary Christian church, under the Lordship of Jesus Christ. True unity exists not through church councils or synods, not through resolutions or political bargaining, but in the simplest and most basic creed that is the heart of the gospel, namely that "Jesus is Lord" (1 Corinthians 12:3). That is the incontrovertible proof of the Holy Spirit's work. No other confession can unite sinners than that which is expressed by bowing to Christ's Lordship in every area of our life and experience. It is not even in Christ as Savior that the deepest unity is found, but when the Savior is exalted and worshipped as Lord. Indeed, it is only because he is the Lord that he can prove himself to be the Savior. When the rivalry to God's rule, which is endemic in our human nature, is finally laid at the feet of the crucified Lord, a unity between God and his people is created that is deeper and more lasting than the strongest earthly ties.

Of course, the ultimate fulfillment of that hope will be in the eternal kingdom. Our Christian unity will never be perfect on this earth since we still battle against the world, the flesh, and the devil. But the church needs a sharpened vision of what is possible, even in this world, as we submit to Christ and turn our backs on all rivals. In Bruce Waltke's acute and searching words, "If the absence of apostasy is a cause to praise God for his presence with his people (22:31), then its presence ought to prompt believers to investigate possible cause(s) of his disfavour."[1] The presence of apostasy in so many forms within the visible church in the West must precipitate an increasing absence of God's presence and power in its life and witness. Where God is sidelined and his Word disregarded, his Spirit is grieved and may well withdraw until his people come to their senses in renewed repentance, loyalty, faith, and obedience. The Israelites were determined to deal with the issue because the continued presence of God in their midst was both their greatest blessing and their greatest need. Is our responsibility any less?

Hark, my soul, it is the Lord!
'Tis Thy Savior, hear His Word;
Jesus speaks, and speaks to Thee,
"Say, poor sinner, lovest Thou me?"

Lord, it is my chief complaint
That my love is weak and faint;
Yet I love Thee, and adore:
O for grace to love Thee more.[2]

20

Priorities for the Future

JOSHUA 23:1–16

FAMOUS LAST WORDS have become something of an institution, aided by a variety of Internet sites. There is something peculiarly absorbing about people's final words. They may be disparaging, as in the case of Karl Marx, who is said to have told his housekeeper, sitting at his bedside, eager to record his last pearls for posterity, "Last words are for fools who haven't said enough." Sometimes they are tragiccomic, like those of General John Sedgwick, a Union commander killed in battle during the American Civil War in 1864, who remarked to his aide-de-camp as he surveyed the enemy lines, "They couldn't hit an elephant at this distance." But the last words, or farewell speeches, of the Bible have much more serious content and far deeper significance. One has only to think of the final speeches of Jacob, Moses, or David for the point to be clear, and indeed John devotes chapters 13—17 of his Gospel to the last words of the Lord Jesus on the night in which he was betrayed.

Last words do matter, and in these concluding three chapters of the book that bears his name we have Joshua's own parting discourses. We have already heard his comparatively brief words as he bade farewell to the two and a half tribes returning east over the Jordan to rejoin their family units in the land the Lord had already given them. In this chapter we are told that he "summoned all Israel," but it seems as though they were represented by the "elders and heads . . . judges and officers" (v. 2), and they undoubtedly passed on the contents of his speech within their tribes and clans. However, the major content here seems to be on the responsibilities of leadership, while 24:1 emphasizes the gathering of "all the tribes . . . to Shechem," and 24:2 specifically states that Joshua spoke "to all the people." So the final chapter is more widely ranging and of more challenge to everyone within the nation. It is also significant that Joshua 24 ends with a renewal of the covenant on a national level since the whole nation has been explicitly addressed. Chapter 23 is less formal; it is very pastoral, and it seeks to alert the leaders and bring them face-to-face with Joshua's concerns, using lessons from the past to secure a warm and godly orientation toward the future. In this way there is a balance between the exhortations to trust and obedience with which the book opened and that now become once again the focus in these final chapters.

Verse 1 sets the scene and the timing as "a long time afterward," but after what? The most obvious reference might seem to be to the exit of Reuben, Gad, and eastern Manasseh in chapter 22, but the fact that the Lord had given rest and also that Joshua was "old and well advanced in years" has a more natural link back to 13:1 (where the same phrase was first used) and so to the whole episode of the distribution of the land. Some commentators, Woudstra among them, suggest that the bracketing effect of these chapters drives us back to chapter 1 and the pre-conquest position. Each of these suggestions has validity, but what is described in 22:3 as "these many days" indicates that the conquest was over a prolonged period; so we should probably have the whole of that time (chapters 1—12) in view. We shall learn that Joshua died at the age of 110 (24:29). Assuming that he and Caleb were of similar age, we are probably looking at twenty to thirty years now since Israel first set foot in the land and set up the twelve memorial stones at Gilgal. However, far more important than the dating is the focus on "rest" in verse 1. Having given the land, the Lord has also given rest, but how will that rest be used, and what will be its fruit? That will be the focus of Joshua's address. In many ways the dangers associated with the peace will be harder and more challenging than the energy required for the conquest. The future will produce even greater tests than anything they have yet experienced. So as Joshua sees the end of his race, he is concerned to pass the baton to reliable successors and to do it well by passing on his God-given insights to the leaders of the nation.

Before we look at the text in more detail, it may be helpful to note the way in which it seems to be constructed. I have found it helpful to divide it into three main sections—verses 3–8, 9–13, and 14–16. Like many effective preachers after him, Joshua repeats his big idea or central thesis in each of the three paragraphs. At the beginning his strong theme is looking back in thanksgiving and appreciation of what God has done, but as the speech develops, each successive section delivers increasingly strong warnings about the dangers that will predominate in the coming days. As we look at this fine example of Old Testament preaching from its theological perspective thematically, we shall see more clearly its unchanging lessons for God's people today and so will be able to apply it more effectively to our own Christian living.

What You Have Seen

Not surprisingly, at the end of his long and eventful life Joshua begins by looking back. He seems to separate himself, by contrast, from his hearers as he reflects on all that he has experienced and achieved, compared with all that remains to be done in the next generation. Here is the baton-passing moment. "He referred to himself—*As for me, I am old*—in order to contrast himself with his addressees, to whom his first words were *As for you, you have seen*."[1] He calls upon the leaders to review their common experience of God's goodness, to remember what incredible things the Lord has achieved and the immense changes they have witnessed and from which they daily benefit. It is always a sound spiritual instinct to follow the later psalmist's exhortation, "Bless the Lord, O my soul, and forget not all his benefits" (Psalm 103:2). Sometimes people question why the Bible so frequently exhorts us to praise God and, especially in the epistles, to be thankful. I remember being asked once why God "needed all this praise." Was he not sufficient in himself without any human ascriptions of glory? Of course, that is true. God needs nothing from us. But we need to be praising, thankful believers both because God is worthy of all praise and also for our own benefit.

We articulate our appreciation and delight in something—a beautiful vista, a glorious sunset, a piece of music, a delicious meal; so we say "thank you," and as we express that thankfulness (which is praise) our delight deepens and our enjoyment is enriched. Similarly, when we express our gratitude to our fellow human beings for their talents and skills or kindness and concern, we deepen our relationship with them. Mutual trust develops, and from that comes a lasting interaction of friendship and affection, even love. There is no difference in terms of our relationship with God. Thanksgiving keeps us focused on him as the one from whom all our blessings and benefits come. It develops our appreciation of him and our dependence on him, so that new faith is generated to meet the new challenges of the future. We look back and see that all the blessings we now enjoy have been God's gracious gift, which makes us realize how dependent we are on him and how much we need to keep trusting him for all that we face in the future.

They had seen moments of great advance and outstanding answers to prayer. Joshua tells them to look back—to the crossing of the Jordan, the fall of Jericho, the great victory through the hailstorm at Gibeon, and more. But there had also been many days of solid plodding, which required just as much faith and courage to keep on keeping on in claiming the promises and being obedient to the Word. While we are not Joshua and we are not conquering Canaan, nevertheless in our equally real spiritual battles to grow in godliness, to bring the gospel to others, and to be used to encourage one another to life-long, progressive discipleship, all the unwritten stories of individual faithful endeavor are similarly dependent on the Word of the Lord and the power of the Spirit.

It is in this context that Joshua draws special attention to the "nations" (v. 4), a term that occurs six times in this chapter. It acts as an almost technical term for those outside of God's covenant grace shown to Israel, the "Gentiles" of the New Testament. Because of their opposition to God's purposes for Israel, they have fought tooth and nail against the conquest, blinded by their idolatry and rebellion. But verse 4 also tells us that many have already been defeated and "cut off." Israel could never have achieved any of this on her own, "for it is the LORD your God who has fought for you" (v. 3b), committed by covenant oath to give them the inheritance promised so many generations earlier to Abraham and his descendants. They had proved to be very active and largely obedient agents, but the battle belonged to the Lord. Now they could see the outcome. They each had God-given territory to possess with their families as their inheritance in the land. In many parts the nations, or their remnants, were still entrenched. But looking back at what had been accomplished would be a powerful stimulus to go on believing the great promise of verse 5: "The LORD your God will push them back before you and drive them out of your sight. And you shall possess their land, just as the LORD your God promised you." There is neither shortage of commitment nor lack of ability with Yahweh. What he has done, he will continue to do. The shape of the tasks may change, but his work never stops. Whatever the different phases may present, he is the same God, undiminished in faithful, steadfast love and limitless power to achieve his purposes.

The theme is expanded on in the second cycle beginning at verse 9. The nations were numerous and powerful, but they were no match for the Lord. Indeed, verse 10 introduces an element of effortlessness about the description of his victories. Israel has proved to be a thousand times stronger than her opponents, but for one reason only: "It is the LORD your God who fights for you, just as he promised you." If the promise-keeping God of limitless power is fighting for his own, then well might Jericho and the whole land tremble. No wonder the hearts of the Canaanites melted in terror! As Paul would later write, "If God is for us, who can be against us?" (Romans 8:31). The answer for them, as for us, is that there are innumerable enemies, but when the Lord takes the field, the outcome is beyond question. Notice that the emphasis is not just on God's power ("I know that he can do it") but especially and crucially upon his promises ("I am convinced by his Word that he will do it").

That is the point Joshua underlines in the final section beginning at verse 14. "Not one word has failed of all the good things that the LORD your God promised concerning you." Joshua turns to them and says in essence, "You know, deep down in your hearts and souls, that the Lord has never let you down, never reneged on even one of his many promises, never failed to meet all your needs. He is utterly dependable!" The point is historical, of course, but it is also hugely motivational. The lessons learned in the conquest are to have a profound and lasting effect on their conduct of life within the land. May we grasp this teaching to our own benefit, because the same is true for us. Think back on all you have experienced of God's rich mercy and awesome covenant grace thus far. Think of where you were when God found you, the circumstances of your new birth, the assurance of sins forgiven, your increasing deliverance from the world, the flesh, and the devil, your growth in grace and godliness, the progressive restoration of the image of God in you. They are all testimony to what the Lord our God has done for us in Christ. But they also motivate us to recognize that no faith can be strong if it is not growing, no virtue will be safe if it is not enthusiastic, and none of us will be secure if we are not daily dependent on God's mercy and grace, made ours in the Word and by the Spirit. Joshua's backward look is not an exercise in nostalgic self-indulgence. His theme song is not "I believe in yesterday." His call is to find fresh courage and focus from the past, to keep trusting and obeying the God of battles already won for his continuing victorious provision in all that lies ahead.

What You Must Understand

The danger that Joshua wants to emphasize stands out very clearly in verse 7. Israel "may [must] not mix" with the remaining unconquered people groups, for that will lead to their taking on those peoples' pagan gods, with all that is involved in swearing by them and bowing down to them. The detail is strikingly specific. Later history was to prove how appropriate the warning was. The subsequent decline in the spiritual health of God's people, as the Old Testament unfolds, can all be traced to this basic cause. Whether it was the period of the judges, the division of the kingdom, the fall of the northern kingdom to the Assyrians, or the collapse of Judah and Jerusalem before the Babylonians, with the ensuing exile, the story was always the same. Mixing with the pagan peoples around them always predisposed Israel to idolatry accompanied by its accompanying immorality. The two always run closely together in Scripture, as in life. The attractions of other gods were, and still are, numerous. They are so much more tangible and apparently accessible, so much more easily influenced and paid off, far less demanding than the God of truth and righteousness. They appeal because they are made-to-measure and therefore entirely under the manufacturer's control. But they are merely lifeless artifacts, pieces of wood and lumps of stone, and they can do nothing ultimately but mock their devotees since they exist only as the product of their human imagination.

Joshua wants his hearers to understand not only the nature of the danger they face but also how stealthily and imperceptibly it will conquer them. A good proportion of the land has been taken, but there is much more still to be possessed. God is committed to fight for his people, but they have also to be committed to active trust and obedience in order to accomplish his purposes. That will require razor-sharp clarity and massively enhanced energy if it is going to be actively pursued. All the energy and dynamic for victory certainly belong to the Lord, but they can only be appropriated as his people "fight the good fight" (1 Timothy 6:12). In human terms they are much more likely to settle for a comfortable level of compromise that will not require such continuing discipline or sacrifice or single-mindedness. As a result, complacency becomes endemic, and the process of verse 7 gets underway. Even as I am writing these words, I am struck by how closely parallel to all this the normal experiences of the Christian life often prove to be. This battle must be fought every day.

As Joshua returns to this theme in verses 12, 13, the warning focuses now in some detail on the outcome of complacent assimilation. It begins with "turn back" (v. 12), a term that deliberately recalls the history of Israel since the exodus. Many times over the intervening years they have talked about and have even begun to plot their return to Egypt. In 24:14 we learn that Egyptian idols can still be found in their tents and knapsacks. But to turn back to Egypt is to turn away from Yahweh's purposes, since these began with him calling Abram out of Ur and continued with his deliverance of Israel from Pharaoh. To attach themselves to the nations, especially through marriage, would be to turn their backs on both God's call to be a distinctive people through their relationship with him, which set them apart from all others, and also on all that his mercy had provided for them in the miraculous deliverances he had won for them. The consequences (v. 13) would be dire. All that Yahweh had already done and purposed yet to do for them would be stopped. Instead of driving out the nations before Israel, he will leave Israel to her own devices;

and as they should know by this time, they have no ability in themselves to deal with the matter at all. The Canaanites will reassert themselves, reducing the Israelites to slavery, trapped and ensnared, and the nations will be able freely to exert whatever painful cruelty they wish upon them, culminating eventually in the loss of the land and exile. The desire to go back to Egypt or to be like the other nations will eventually open up the route to the Babylonian captivity.

Further explanation accompanies the last part of the third cycle of the address, in verses 15, 16. We are reminded of the familiar teaching about covenant blessings and covenant curses, dependent on obedience or rebellion, as taught by Moses in Deuteronomy 28. The land does not belong to Israel; her tenancy is given by the Lord. It can be in perpetuity if they remain faithful to the covenant, but there is no inherent right to God's blessings come what may. The God who has given the land is equally at liberty to take it away. This is important, reminding us that Israel is in no way ethnically superior to the other races. All are equal before God, as all are equally his sovereign creation. In his grace and mercy he has purposed a special relationship with the sons of Abraham as a revelation of his heart of love and blessing to the whole world. But if such grace and patience are ultimately met with determined and repeated, stubborn rebellion, his judgment must ultimately fall. "Then the anger of the LORD will be kindled against you, and you shall perish quickly from off the good land that he has given to you" (v. 16b). There really are only two ways to live, and Joshua wants the next generation to be in no doubt about the seriousness of the issue.

There can be no compromise or complacency about the battle that is joined between truth and falsehood. "We do not wrestle against flesh and blood," Ephesians 6:12 reminds us, but we do wrestle. The default position of the human heart will always be to worship ourselves, to be our own god, under the influence of our idols, which we exalt to the supreme position in our lives. All around us and often deceptively attractive, they appear to offer us freedom and fulfillment, but in the end they will consume us. If we recognize the Lord Jesus as our rescuer and submit to him as our ruler, he will brook no rivals to his throne in our lives. Yet submission only to him is what is constantly under attack in the citadel of our own individual minds and hearts, in our closest relationships, family circles, and friendships, in our church fellowships, and in all our interactions with the culture in which we live. Every day the battle is joined—in the workplace, at the school gate, in the lecture hall or the shopping mall, whenever we surf the Net or turn on the television. All the time our culture is parading its idols, insisting that this is what we must have, how we must look, what we really need. Money, sex, and power are still the greatest idols of our age, as in every period of human history, and we are fools if we imagine that any of us is immune from their magnetism. But they are pseudo-satisfiers, empty idols, and in the end they destroy those who succumb to them. How then can they be overcome?

How You Must Live

We can thank God that the practical instruction of Joshua's speech is so clear and applicable, even though our context is quite different, living as we do on the fulfillment side of the cross. There are three enormously important positives within the chapter, the first of which is in verse 6, and it is almost so familiar at this stage in Joshua's book that we might easily be tempted to take it for granted. But let us hear it once again and take it deep into our hearts. "Be very strong to keep and to do all that is written in the Book of the Law of Moses, turning aside from it neither to the right hand nor to the left." As the book began (1:7), the context posed the question as to whether Joshua would prove a worthy successor to Moses and leader of Israel. Now, looking back on his wonderfully fruitful and successful life, this could well be the summary of it all. His final obituary in 24:29 will in fact confer on him exactly the same title as Moses had, "the servant of the LORD." If he has indeed proved a worthy successor to Moses, it is because verse 6 has been his life's motto, and the reasons are not hard to unpack. Spiritual strength is found in obedience to the Word of God without deviation. This is what leads to the separation from idolatry that we see being preached in verse 7. Only the Word of God can break the hold that idolatry will otherwise have on all of our lives by revealing the folly of false gods and stimulating faith in the living God that is obedient to his will. And every victory won in these battles will make us stronger to fight on the same ground with the same resources the next time. The way to conquer idolatry is to make this Lord our God, and the way to do that is to be obedient to all that he says in Scripture. That practiced conviction is what will keep us from idols.

But verse 8 takes the response a little deeper. "You shall cling to the LORD your God just as you have done to this day." This verb is used frequently by Moses in Deuteronomy and by Joshua in 22:5. It is perhaps the strongest adhesive verb in the Old Testament and is used in Genesis 2:24 to describe marriage. The man is to "hold fast to his wife," cling to her, stick fast to her, so that they become "one flesh." The word speaks, then, of total commitment, loyal devotion, and deep personal affection. That is how Israel has been living during these golden days of the conquest, and that is how they are to continue.

The Lord expects his redeemed people to give themselves unreservedly to him. But there is a shocking use of this same verb in verse 12, where, as we have seen, Joshua foresees the possibility of Israel turning back to "cling to the remnant of these nations remaining among you." The idea is horrific. To think that God's special possession, Israel, could go back to paganism and be no different from the prevailing Canaanite culture all around them is almost beyond belief. And yet which of us does not know how readily and easily that drift can happen? That is surely why Joshua immediately reminds them of all the victories they have already experienced—"No man has been able to stand before you to this day" (v. 9). Everything they already have is proof positive of the Lord's faithfulness and ability; so they are to keep trusting and obeying. The future circumstances will never be beyond the reach of God's grace or the range of his power. There can be no complacency, but neither need there be apprehension, much less despair. Clinging to the Lord is surely what Jesus meant when he told his disciples, "Whoever abides in me and I in him, he it is that bears much fruit, for apart from me you can do nothing" (John 15:5).

This leads us to the third instruction and the heart of our whole response in verse 11. "Be very careful, therefore, to love the LORD your God." We need to note how highly intentional this has to be. There is nothing automatic about it. It requires attention and energy ("be very careful"). It needs to be at the heart of the life-experience of all God's people. Once again Moses had written the original script (Deuteronomy 6:5), and centuries later the Lord Jesus would endorse and underline it (Matthew 22:37, 38). The heart of our faith is our heart relationship with our God. This should be our greatest life aim—to love God more and more. For us, as New Testament Christians, that love is generated by God's great love for us, which finds its focus in the gift of his Son. "In this the love of God was made manifest among us, that God sent his only Son into the world, so that we might live through him" (1 John 4:9). It is through his death on the cross that life has come to us. It was there that he conquered all our enemies—sin, death, and the devil—when he fought the battle for us and achieved our rescue, so that we may enter into his rest. Through his substitutionary sacrifice, he has brought us into all the blessings and privileges of the new covenant, our promised land, and he will safely bring us home to his everlasting kingdom.

All this has become ours as the Holy Spirit granted us repentance toward God and trust in our Lord Jesus Christ, so that in Martin Luther's famous words regarding faith, we have been enabled to say, "Yes, this is for me!" Yet even that faith is God's gracious gift, which is why its exercise can never be divorced from a deep-seated, heartfelt love for the Lord. We love him because of all his love for us, and that love is revealed in the avalanche of blessings that he pours into our lives. We love him because in Christ we have ceased from our own works, from trying (and failing) to justify ourselves or make ourselves acceptable to God. We love him because our confidence in time and for eternity lies not in our record but in Christ's. We love him because, as the hymn quoted below puts it, we have been "ransomed, healed, restored, forgiven." We have been made citizens of a heavenly country, adopted into the family of the King of kings. We love him because we already enter into a measure of his perfect rest here and now and anticipate the eventual fulfillment of all that we now have as a down payment in his immediate presence with light and love and joy forever and ever. Our faith is entirely relational. To love God is to embrace his proclaimed Word, to live in repentance and faith every day, to cultivate daily, detailed obedience, to enter his rest now by believing his great and precious promises, and to live here in the light of eternity and the consummation of all things at the end of this age.

If we really love God we will express it in praise and worship and will experience it in assurance of faith and resonant, deep gratitude, and we will want to speak well of him whenever we can, wherever we go. We will want to please him, to serve him, to live for him, to suffer and even to die for him. That is the challenge Joshua presented to the up-and-coming generation, and it is the challenge the Holy Spirit still puts before us today. Love conquers everything because it is the currency of God's eternal kingdom. When everything else disappears, love endures (see 1 Corinthians 13:8–13). So, beyond whatever we might seek to do in God's service, what will outlast it all will be our love for him, because he has loved us with an everlasting love. "Be very careful, therefore, to love the LORD your God" (Joshua 23:11). Only that will keep us from turning back. Only that will keep us pressing on to glory.

Praise, my soul, the king of heaven,
To his feet thy tribute bring.
Ransomed, healed, restored, forgiven,
Evermore his praises sing.
Alleluia! Alleluia!
Praise the everlasting king.[2]

21

The Inescapable Choice

JOSHUA 24:1-33

TIMES OF TRANSITION often serve as markers in our personal histories. We tend to look back on them and measure our lives by these key events—leaving school, getting that first job, getting married, moving into our first house, retiring. These significant events encourage us to look back and take stock, so that as we review the past we can set our sights for what lies ahead. As we come to the end of the book of Joshua, we are in that kind of country, as much of this final chapter is devoted to a speech made by Joshua to the whole people of God. We might call it a "state of the nation" address, in which their human leader calls them to a significant moment of renewed dedication in the light of their shared history and as a direction for their future. The challenge of the famous fifteenth verse does seem to be the center around which everything else revolves. "Choose this day whom you will serve" (v. 15).

Once again our narrator takes time and trouble with the setting of this very important encounter since it shapes the whole event he describes. Verse 1 tells us that Joshua "gathered all the tribes of Israel" ("all the people," v. 2), but not to himself. As always throughout the book, he is Yahweh's agent first and foremost, since all his leadership has been given to him by the Lord. So they are not just coming to hear Joshua. "They presented themselves before God" (v. 1b). The parallel of the New Testament assembly or local congregation, meeting together regularly, needs to carry with it the same implications. We are coming not merely to hear a human leader but to present ourselves together as a corporate entity to the Lord himself.

They came "to Shechem" (v. 1). The very name pulsates with significance in the Old Testament story. It was here, at the oak of Moreh, that the Lord appeared to Abram and promised to give the land to his offspring (Genesis 12:6, 7). Here he built an altar as an expression of his faith in the promise. It was here that Jacob bought a piece of land from the sons of Hamor after his reconciliation with his brother Esau and built an altar in the name of the God of Israel (Genesis 33:18–20). He too believed the promise. And it was here, in the shadow of Mount Ebal and Mount Gerizim, back in chapter 8 of this book, that Joshua led the nation in its renewal of its covenant commitment to Yahweh, following the debacle at Ai. So as the nation gathers at Shechem, we are prompted to recognize that the wheel has turned full circle, that the promises have been fulfilled. The great nation God had promised to Abram now gathers to meet him, at the very place in the land where he first promised that the land would be theirs—and now it is! The land has been distributed to the tribal inheritances, although much of it still remains to be possessed, and so it has been given "rest" by its owner, the Lord (23:1). The formal assembly of the nation before God at Shechem is living proof that not one word has failed of all the good things that he had promised. It is highly appropriate, then, that all God has done for his people should now be matched by their loving, wholehearted, and exclusive devotion to him as they finally commit themselves to taking formal possession of the land in a covenant-renewal ceremony (v. 25).

What is happening in chapter 24 is their signature on the contract, a recognition and acceptance of their rights and responsibilities within the land. Commentators point out that the shape of the chapter reflects the form of a treaty between an overlord and his people common in the ancient Near-Eastern world. But our interest is not antiquarian. As twenty-first-century Christians we know that this is the living and enduring Word of God; so it is full of encouragement and challenge as we review with great thankfulness all that God has already done and trust him for all that is yet to be. Supremely this is not a chapter about Israel, much less about Joshua, but about God himself and especially about his grace. Our task is not so much to find some point of comparability, real or imagined, with Israel, for we live in a very different context. Rather, our first and greatest benefit will be to remind ourselves of the nature and character of our God, who has bound himself to us with promises that can never be broken and has confirmed his covenant of redemptive grace with us through the blood of his Son. Paul told the Corinthians that "all the promises of God find their Yes in him [the Son of God, Jesus Christ]. That is why it is through him that we utter our Amen to God for his glory" (2 Corinthians 1:20). As we "utter our Amen," we choose whom we will serve. We commit ourselves to the God of the promise and resolve by his grace and in his strength to live the life of faith. That will be the benefit of allowing Joshua to teach and challenge us in the verses that follow.

The Past Is Defined by God's Grace

This is the predominant thrust of the opening section of Joshua's address (vv. 2–13). Traditionally the author of the covenant-treaty or agreement introduces himself and then reviews his relationship with the other party. In the case of a conqueror setting out his terms of subjugation, this was a unilateral imposition of his will upon those who had no voice in the matter. If they did not submit to his terms, they would perish. Though the outward structure may be similar, it is striking how different the God of Israel is from all other over-lords. Speaking on his behalf, Joshua introduces and defines him as Yahweh, the God of covenant faithfulness, who revealed his character of grace in the deliverance of the exodus. This was the same name Jacob had used for God when he built his altar at Shechem. He is the God who makes and keeps his promises, whose name reveals his nature. The history of Israel is the covenant's most eloquent proof since from the very beginning and on every page ever since it is and always has been all about Yahweh's unmerited favor—his mercy and grace. We have only to glance at all the first-person singular verbs as Joshua speaks for God to get the point. "I took your father Abraham" (v. 3a). "I gave him Isaac" (v. 3b)—the son of the promise. "To Isaac I gave Jacob and Esau" (v. 4). "I sent Moses and Aaron, and I plagued Egypt . . . I brought you out" (v. 5). "I brought your fathers out" (v. 6). "I brought you to the land" (v. 8a). "I gave them into your hand" (v. 8b). "I delivered you out of his [Balaam's] hand" (v. 10). Their entire history is the record of God's overflowing covenant grace, as is ours.

Joshua's review of the story can be divided into four main sections, each of which we will examine briefly. In verses 2–4 the story begins with the patriarchs, but first reminding us that before God called Abram, "your fathers . . . served other gods" (v. 2b). Beyond the Euphrates, the memory of the one true and living God was growing dim when the Lord chose to break into Abram's life, remove him from his settled existence in Ur, and to call him to the life of a nomad. He was led by God's hand throughout the whole land that his descendants now possess. In fact the story of Genesis 12—21 is summarized in verse 3. There was the promise of the land and the promise of a nation. As so often with God's promises, there were times when it seemed as though they would never be fulfilled, because that is how God grows our trust and increases our faithful dependence on him. Eventually Isaac was born, then Jacob and Esau. Esau had a land, but Jacob's sons had none. Instead they experienced a long period in Egypt, where it looked as though they would never inherit the land since all their circumstances seemed to deny their destiny. Yet God's grace was secretly and silently at work all the time, waiting for the iniquity of the Amorites to be complete, as he had predicted in Genesis 15:16. We know from the start of Exodus that their condition seemed beyond hope, and then suddenly verse 5 bursts into focus—"I sent Moses and Aaron."

The second section (vv. 5–7) recalls the exodus and the forty years in the wilderness. Again one verse summarizes a whole sweep of Israelite history. Exodus 1—12 is covered in verse 5! "I sent Moses . . . I plagued Egypt . . . I brought you out." Verse 6 recalls the crossing of the Red Sea, but with a dramatic shift of focus. Suddenly the past ("your fathers") is moved into the present with the direct address to "you," which alternates with "they" in verses 6, 7 and then becomes the exclusive pronoun through the rest of the speech. The transition embraces the generation who had experienced forty long years in the wilderness. They were the "little ones," under the age of twenty when the spies were sent out to report on the land (Numbers 14:28–31), whose parents never did enter God's rest because of their unbelief and rebellion. The seniors of the community, Joshua's hearers, are now brought to the heart of the story. They knew about God's grace firsthand in their own life experience, as does every believing Christian.

Verses 8–10 deal with the third period of God's gracious provision before they crossed the Jordan to enter the land. We move from the promise through the rescue to the blessing of the victories God gave them over the Amorite kings Sihon and Og (see Numbers 21:21–35), in the land east of the Jordan, settled now by Reuben, Dan, and half of Manasseh. This was a sort of firstfruits of the victories they were later to experience within Canaan itself. It was these famous victories that also struck fear into the hearts of the people of Jericho (Joshua 2:10, 11). "I gave them into your hand . . . and I destroyed them before you" (24:8). But there was also another deliverance from a more hidden and subtle foe, the false prophet Balaam, who was hired by King Balak to curse Israel (v. 9). Numbers 22—24 describes the whole saga and how Balaam, in the end, could only bless Yahweh's people. "I would not listen to Balaam. . . . I delivered you" (Joshua 24:10). Our tendency is to shrug off the importance of this event since we tend to regard curses as vacuous superstition. But Woudstra helpfully observes:

> This episode left a deep mark upon Israel's memory; even the New Testament speaks of Balaam (2 Pet 2:15; Rev 2:14). . . . Had God allowed Balaam to curse Israel, this curse would have had its effect. But God did

not allow such a thing (cf Num 22:12; 23:8, 23). Instead of cursing there was nothing but blessing. This almost ironical way of speaking shows the complete mastery of the God of Israel over all forces that would seek to harm his people.[1]

We can hear Paul's ringing assurances to the Romans that nothing in all creation will ever be able to separate God's people from his love in Christ (Romans 8:31–39), and we too can rejoice.

The final section, verses 11–13, brings the hearers up-to-date with all the victories of the conquest, which we have witnessed in this book. The list of enemies in verse 11 is impressive and daunting, but now they know that "I gave them into your hand" (v. 11b). There is a rather mysterious reference in verse 12 to "the hornet" that God sent before the Israelites and "which drove them out before you." The reference to "the two kings of the Amorites" at this point seems to confirm that the most likely meaning is metaphorical. The liquidation of Og and Sihon produced terror and panic among the Canaanites equivalent to an invasion of hornets, when everyone would seek cover to protect themselves. There is nothing in the battle texts to indicate a literal meaning, but several references (2:9–11, 24; 5:1; 6:27) show that Canaanite morale was at rock bottom. An alternative view would be to identify the two Amorite kings as Adoni-zedek (10:1), head of the southern coalition, and Jabin (11:1), head of the northern coalition, which is certainly true to the actual history but makes the reference to the hornet more obscure. However, the main point of verse 12 is unmistakably clear: "it was not by your sword or by your bow." Of course, their swords and bows were used a great deal, but that was not the reason for their success. These great victories were not achieved by human tactics, skill, or strength. The conquest was entirely due to God's power, as this whole book has made clear, and verse 13 sums it all up. It is all of grace—both the gift of the land and the quality of the gift ("cities . . . vineyards . . . orchards"). Everything they now possessed and enjoyed had been given to them by God. And this is because the Lord is compassionate, full of mercy and steadfast love, keeping the promises he has made, so that he *can* be trusted; indeed he *must* be.

As we review Israel's history, we can recognize that spiritually it is ours as well, since "[God's] purpose was to make him [Abraham] the father of all who believe without being circumcised, so that righteousness would be counted to them as well" (Romans 4:11). There is no alteration in the character of grace since there is no deviation in the character of the God whom it reveals. So this passage must surely encourage us to review our spiritual heritage, as Paul does in his majestic opening to the letter to the Ephesians when he exclaims, "Blessed be the God and Father of our Lord Jesus Christ, who has blessed us in Christ with every spiritual blessing in the heavenly places" (Ephesians 1:3). It would be a spiritually health-giving application of Joshua 24 for us to review the blessings that have been purchased for us through Christ's victory on the cross and in his resurrection. Ephesians 1 reminds us of our election, adoption, redemption, forgiveness, knowledge of God's will, and the inheritance of the eternal kingdom. None of this came to us by sword or bow. They are all only the product of the grace of God in the gospel. We contribute nothing to them and can add nothing to them. We are people of undeserved but abundant mercy from start to finish. It is grace alone that defines who we really are.

The Present Demands of God's Grace

We have often noted, in the course of our study of Joshua, the careful balance or blend of two factors in terms of God's covenant relationship with Israel. These are privilege and responsibility, or blessings and obligations. God's covenant of grace is not a *quid pro quo* arrangement since it is not made between two equal parties. Rather it follows the ancient world's treaty format, in which the requirements of the subordinate party are clearly spelled out. Although in today's culture the clamor is for rights over responsibilities, we are all aware that if things are to function harmoniously, both need to be in place. Privileges do incur obligations. When I was a teacher in a traditional boys' school in southern England, I remember the headmaster regularly addressing the boys' behavior outside the school, since they were wearing a distinctive uniform and their school could be easily identified. "Boys of this school (and you are privileged to be here)," he would say, "do not eat or chew gum on the buses, nor do they behave in a riotous manner in public." But, of course, the fact of the matter was that they did, and that was why he was addressing the matter, having received another complaint, no doubt. It was his way of trying to impose the demands of privilege on the irresponsible or recalcitrant among his charges, usually to little effect, it must be said. Something like that is happening in verse 14, which begins a new major section, running to the end of verse 18.

"Now therefore" picks up the privileges of verses 2–13, in order to demand the equivalent obligations that follow. They are expressed in four imperatives, all in verse 14—"fear the LORD and serve him," "put away the [foreign] gods . . . and serve the LORD." Fear is to be the underlying response to all that the Lord has done for them thus far. What he had done to Egypt, to Sihon and Og, and to the alliances of Canaanite kings was awesome, even terrifying. Yet fear here is not a paralyzing horror but a reverent awe. It is the proper attitude of a redeemed sinner before a holy God, a humble submission that recognizes that he is God and we are not and that therefore submits every area of our lives to his authority. This inner response, at the control center of the personality, will evidence its genuineness in the outward response of service, "in sincerity and in faithfulness" or more literally "completeness" or "fullness." The core idea is integrity, which is not just the knee-jerk reaction of a moment but the steady, persevering direction of a lifetime. It is the appropriate and equivalent response to a God whose characteristic behavior to us is true and faithful. Joshua is exhorting them to make a single-minded response to God, the sort of wholeheartedness that we saw exemplified in the story of Caleb back in Joshua 14.

That sort of sincerity carries with it the pressing requirement of verse 14: "Put away the gods that your fathers served. . . ." There are three references to prior spiritual unfaithfulness—first to the Abrahamic generation beyond the Euphrates, then to the generations who lived in Egypt and assimilated their idols (v. 14), and finally to the Canaanite gods where they are now (v. 15). These are all examples of how the exclusive loyalty of God's people was tested, often, sadly, to the point of capitulation. The record is not encouraging, and these old pagan deities seem still to be among them. Syncretism had always been a part of their history, and it is still one of the greatest challenges and most threatening dangers facing the contemporary church. However, Joshua's crucial purpose is to bring his hearers to a critical, decisive action now and for the coming years. He calls them to make a solemn and binding choice to have no other gods but Yahweh and so to be done with the idols of the pagan peoples in the land. Yet he knows, very realistically, that there will be a resistance, or at the very least a hesitation, to narrowing down their options in this way. We can imagine their internal dialogue very readily because we are so used to hearing it played out in our own hearts. Do we really want to give up our comfort blanket of idol worship that we all treasure? After all, no one would actually believe in idols if they didn't offer some comfort and provide some help, would they? Do we really want to go out on a limb and let God be the ultimate authority in every part of our life? Do we actually want to yield the control of our life to an authority outside of ourselves?

That goes some way toward explaining what seems such a curious idea in verse 15, that it might even seem "evil in your eyes to serve the Lord," to be fully committed to his will. It was a day of decision for Israel, but there is a sense in which each new day is a decision day for each of us as we understand the present demands of God's grace. The challenges come to us in all sorts of contexts with a variety of options, but they always call on us to leave behind our past and to resist the peer group pressures of the present in order to invest in our eternal future. The certain reality is that we all serve either the living God or ourselves through the medium of our idols. Think of some of them. Are we really prepared to give God the reins of control over our marriage and our family, or do we expect our spouse to give us what only God can give and try to control our family so they will fulfill our ambitions for them? Whom will we serve? Are we prepared to put our career into God's hands, to be content for him to guide us, to govern our time and priorities, so that we are not consumed by our work-idol—its status or power or success? Are we willing to put our future in God's hands, to trust him for whether we marry and if so, whom? Will we ask him to give us his wisdom about where we should live, how we are to be using our resources, our money and time, our skills and gifts? Whom will we serve? And will we be prepared to put our Christian service in his hands as well, content to fulfill the roles he has for us and not forcing our way into greater public recognition, trying to be a celebrity or a Christian empire-builder? These are real challenges, aren't they? Make no mistake, we all serve something or someone. So then, whom will we serve?

If this book of Joshua has done its work and achieved its goal, it will find its readers responding, "But as for me and my house, we will serve the LORD" (v. 15b). Joshua leads by example, from the front, and the people respond with passion and zeal. They are willing to renounce all alternative gods since they recognize the utter uniqueness of the Lord through his redemption from Egypt, his daily providential care, and his constant, generous provision (vv. 16–18). "Therefore we also will serve the LORD, for he is our God" (v. 18b). The logic is impeccable. If the Lord is your God, then it is total folly not to serve him. We too understand the message of the saying, attributed to Augustine, that if Jesus Christ is not Lord of all (in my life), then he is not really Lord at all. There is no negotiation possible here about a shared loyalty. "You cannot serve God and money" Jesus taught us (Matthew 6:24), but in place of "money" you could easily substitute anything or anyone, for as the start of the verse in Matthew tells us, "No one can serve two masters." Not "should" but "can"; it is a logical impossibility. We might think that Joshua would be overjoyed by the people's response, but the forty years in the wilderness and the duress of the conquest have made this hardened old warrior more of a realist than we often are.

The Future Is Dependent on God's Grace

The response of verse 19 is a staggering comfort, staggering because it is so unexpected. "You are not able to serve the LORD." Joshua is in essence telling them, "What you have promised is impossible." But Joshua is not just turning the tables or playing games with them. The rest of the verse explains what he means. God is "holy" and "jealous." He is set apart from all the petty, false, pagan deities and also from his own people by his righteousness and moral purity. There is no flicker of deviation in his character, which is why he will not share Israel's devotion with any rivals. He is jealous, like a faithful partner in a marriage whose love for his or her spouse is so constant and so uncompromising that reciprocal undivided love is the only appropriate response in return. Yahweh's response underlines the absolute demands and awesome nature of God's grace, seen in his holiness and jealousy. It is not a light choice to refuse to genuinely surrender to his Lordship (v. 20).

But just as there is no one like him, so there is no real choice for the people. I am reminded of Peter's words to the Lord Jesus when many were turning back and no longer walking with him: "Lord, to whom shall we go? You have the words of eternal life" (John 6:68). So Joshua's hearers affirm, "No, but we will serve the LORD" (v. 21). Having encouraged them to count the cost and to enter into this renewed covenant seriously and thoughtfully, aware of their own weakness and inability, Joshua accepts their choice and calls them to witness against themselves that this is the solemn resolve to which they have come, which they do (v. 22). That means getting rid of the idols, their counterfeit gods, once and for all, which is the essence of all true repentance. This must be followed by a daily life of discipleship, described here as "inclin[ing] your heart to the LORD" (v. 23b), which is the object of all saving faith. Again the people affirm their desire to serve Yahweh by obeying his voice (v. 24).

On that basis the covenant is made, with its stipulations and implications being recorded "in the Book of the Law of God" (v. 26a). Once again the written testimony is to have priority of place in the future life of the nation, and that corpus of divine inspiration is growing. Also a witness stone is again set up (vv. 26b, 27a) as a perpetual reminder of the covenant now signed and sealed as the people accept "all the words of the LORD that he spoke to us" (v. 27b) and commit themselves to a life of loyal service. It confirms what they have promised, and it will testify against them in any future breach. With these words Joshua dismisses the convocation, and they return to their newfound homes within the land to live out what they have solemnly chosen and promised to do. The same grace that has provided every man with his own inheritance will be sufficient for all the trials and testings, opportunities and possibilities that the future will offer, if only they will continue to trust and obey.

The story is complete. Joshua's work is done, and the narrative draws to its conclusion (vv. 29–33). The son of Nun is now accorded the ultimate accolade of the same title as that by which Moses was dignified—he is "the servant of the LORD" (v. 29). At the age of 110 Joshua dies and is buried in his own personal part of the land at Timnath-serah, in Ephraim (vv. 29, 30). Verse 31 provides a suitable epitaph and a wonderful summary of the long-lasting impact that his servant leadership had upon his nation. He influenced a whole generation for God and for good, so that while that generation lived "Israel served the Lord." Sadly, the book of Judges will tell a very different story, but it was no small achievement to have kept Israel on track so assiduously and so fruitfully during the many years of his influential leadership. Yet all this was due solely to God's grace and power, mediated through the Word of God and prayer.

Two other brief notes round the record off. The bones of Joseph, brought up out of Egypt and carried through the wilderness and conquest, are at last laid to rest in Shechem "in the piece of land that Jacob bought" (v. 32). Just as the death and burial of Joshua in his part of the land are a confirmation of God's faithfulness in keeping his promise, so here the same spiritual point is being made. Huge steps forward have been made in the fulfillment of God's salvation-history since Jacob bought that piece of land in faith and also since Joseph "made the sons of Israel swear, saying, 'God will surely visit you, and you shall carry up my bones from here'" (Genesis 50:25), again by faith, as Hebrews 11:22 confirms. The third grave is that of Eleazar, who had been to Joshua as Aaron had been to Moses, also buried in the north country of Ephraim, where his son, Phinehas, lived (v. 33). It is the passing of an era, but the mention of Phinehas and the elders who outlived Joshua reminds us that though human leaders come and go, the work of God continues. The next generation is already in place, greatly privileged in what they have witnessed and all that they have received. The question of this last chapter has been, what will they do with these present blessings and about their great expectations? That was Joshua's concern as he passed on the baton to the elders, the heads, the judges, and the officers. The people have made their resounding affirmative response, "We will serve the LORD" (vv. 21, 24). The issue will be whether the heritage Joshua has left them will be developed or squandered.

Come, Thou fount of every blessing,
Tune my heart to sing Thy grace;
Streams of mercy, never ceasing,
Call for songs of loudest praise.
Teach me some melodious sonnet,
Sung by flaming tongues above.
Praise the mount! I'm fixed upon it,
Mount of Thy redeeming love.

O to grace how great a debtor
Daily I'm constrained to be!
Let Thy goodness, like a fetter,
Bind my wandering heart to Thee.
Prone to wander, Lord, I feel it,
Prone to leave the God I love;
Here's my heart, O take and seal it,
Seal it for Thy courts above.[2]

Epilogue

ONE OF THE GREAT STRENGTHS of the book of Joshua is the clear way in which it blends God's sovereign ability and Israel's obedient activity together in the narrative of how the conquest was achieved. This serves to make it an excellent tool for teaching practical theology.

From the Godward side, the faithfulness of Yahweh is the outstanding theme of the book. When God says he will do something, his word is his oath, and he sees that promise through to fulfillment. Joshua represents the first generation of Israelites who have to rely on the written Word, already given to and through Moses, by which to guard and govern their progress. For them (and us) this lesson is of first importance—namely, that the Word of God is 100 percent reliable. This is not only so in seeing what God has done, but also because he speaks before he acts (he is the God of promise), and his subsequent great deeds confirm his power and his faithfulness, thus increasing trust and reliance. His word carves out his way forward. It prevails over all human factors. To learn that is one of the greatest steps forward we can make in our lives of discipleship.

We see this at the very start of the book, when Moses, the great leader, has just died. Can this possibly be the time for a new forward movement into Canaan (1:1, 2)? Yes, if God says so. The challenge is to trust his faithfulness and not to try to sort things out in our own way. The word of God is not only something for his people to rely on, it is the main cutting edge of their advance. Joshua is a great book for demonstrating how God's word does God's work. The Spirit of God still uses the word of God to accomplish the purposes of God. Jericho was already defeated by the penetration of the truth of what God had already done (2:8–11). In several other examples (5:1; 9:24; 10:1, 2) the same principle is being taught. God's word is the sharpest weapon of all, and it was because Joshua lived by it that he conquered (1:8). At almost every point he set himself to discover God's will and do it—to obey God's word. If we do not know his word, we shall not prove his faithfulness. So studying the Bible, and not least the book of Joshua, is not merely an intellectual pursuit but is the essential weapon-training for a life of victory. There can be no spiritual maturity independent of the Word, for "faith comes from hearing, and hearing through the word of Christ" (Romans 10:17).

This brings us to the other side of the big picture in Joshua, the necessity of obedience as the required human response. This was the hallmark of Joshua's own personal life and the secret of his success. Naturally he appears to have been comparatively insecure, perhaps even timid, certainly needing a lot of encouragement (1:6, 7, 9, 18). But God made him a conqueror because of his careful obedience, which sprang from a living, vital faith. The key is summarized in 1:8. "Meditate . . . be careful to do . . . then you will have good success." Both ingredients matter. When we receive God's Word and then obey it, we have something to give to others (1:9, 10; 3:8, 9; 4:1–4). But, of course, Joshua had his failures. He was the man of faith and obedience except when he wasn't! Yet even what happened with Ai and Gibeon was overruled for good by the grace of God. However, we are clearly being taught that obedience is the way to blessing, since it is the road to godliness.

The nation had to learn it too (6:17–19). When Jericho fell, the spoils were to be dedicated totally to God, so they would realize that all their advance was dependent on God's power, given only to those who depend on him exclusively. From the very start it was clear that if they were to see amazing things done by God, there must be wholehearted consecration to him (3:5; 7:13). All the idols have to go (24:23), for God is looking for practical, down-to-earth holiness, expressed in detailed, daily obedience. Even today with these two principles interacting—faith claiming the promises and obedience fulfilling the commands—there is no limit to what God can and will do, both for and in his people, since we are people of God's purpose.

Soli Deo gloria!

Notes

Chapter Two: A Double Commissioning

1. See, for example, David A. Dorsey, *The Literary Structure of the Old Testament* (Grand Rapids, MI: Baker Academic, 2004), p. 90ff.

2. *Africa Bible Commentary* (Grand Rapids, MI: Zondervan, 2006), p. 258.

3. See "Argument of the Book of Joshua," in Calvin's Commentaries, vol. 2, *Joshua and the Psalms*, trans. H. Beveridge (Grand Rapids, MI: A P & A, n.d.), pp. 8–10.

4. Horatius Bonar (1808–1889), "Blessed Be God, Our God."

Chapter Three: Inside Ememy Territory

1. Calvin's Commentaries, vol. 2, *Joshua and the Psalms*, trans. H. Beveridge (Grand Rapids, MI: A P & A, n.d.), p. 18.

2. See "Excursus: On Rahab's Lie," in David M. Howard Jr., *The New American Commentary: Joshua* (Nashville: Broadman & Holman, 1998), pp. 106–112.

3. M. H. Woudstra, *The Book of Joshua* (Grand Rapids, MI: Eerdmans, 1981), p. 75.

4. For a full discussion of these issues see Howard, *The New American Commentary: Joshua*, pp. 115–117 and Woudstra, *The Book of Joshua*, p. 75.

Chapter Four: Wonders among You

1. M. H. Woudstra, *The Book of Joshua* (Grand Rapids, MI: Eerdmans, 1981), p. 78.

2. Alexander MacLaren (1826–1910) was a Baptist pastor in Southampton and Manchester. His printed sermons are produced in numerous volumes.

3. Joseph Hart (1712–1768), "How Good Is the God We Adore," in *Lancashire Sunday School Songs* (1857).

4. Calvin's Commentaries, vol. 2, *Joshua and the Psalms*, trans. H. Beveridge (Grand Rapids, MI: A P & A, n.d.), p. 26.

5. Ibid., p. 27.

6. Gordon D. Fee and Douglas Stewart, *How To Read the Bible for All Its Worth* (Grand Rapids, MI: Zondervan, 2003), p. 85.

7. William Williams (1717–1791), "Guide Me, O Thou Great Jehovah."

Chapter Five: A Memorial Forever

1. R. Polzin, *Moses and the Deuteronomist* (New York: Seabury, 1980), p. 101.

2. David M. Howard Jr., *The New American Commentary: Joshua* (Nashville: Broadman & Holman, 1998), p. 133.

3. M. H. Woudstra, *The Book of Joshua* (Grand Rapids, MI: Eerdmans, 1981), p. 92.

4. For this view in detail, see Howard, *The New American Commentary: Joshua*, p. 136.

5. "Ebenezer" refers to another memorial stone, celebrating God's victory for Israel over the Philistines and meaning "Till now the LORD has helped us" (see 1 Samuel 7:12).

6. John Newton (1725–1807), "Begone, Unbelief; My Saviour Is Near."

Chapter Six: Essential Preparations

1. J. A. Motyer, "Circumcision," *The Illustrated Bible Dictionary, Part 1* (Leicester, UK: Inter-Varsity Press, 1980), p. 289.

2. David M. Howard Jr., *The New American Commentary: Joshua* (Nashville: Broadman & Holman, 1998), p. 158.

3. Ibid., p. 160.

4. Words by Jean-Baptiste de Santeüil, 1686, trans. Isaac Williams, 1836, with two lines as altered in *Hymns Ancient and Modern.*

Chapter Seven: The Battle That Wasn't

1. M. H. Woudstra, *The Book of Joshua* (Grand Rapids, MI: Eerdmans, 1981), p. 109.

2. For a fuller and very helpful discussion of these issues, see "Excursus— Destruction and Devoted Things in Joshua," in David M. Howard Jr., *The New American Commentary: Joshua* (Nashville: Broadman & Holman, 1998), pp. 180–187. Also P. Copan, *Is God a Moral Monster?*, Chapter 15: "Indiscriminate Massacre and Ethnic Cleansing?" (Grand Rapids, MI: Baker, 2011), pp. 158–168. I am indebted to both these sources for help in understanding these issues.

3. Howard, *The New American Commentary: Joshua*, p. 186.

4. Keith Getty and Stuart Townend, "O Church Arise," copyright 2005 by Thankyou music.

Chapter Eight: Tragedy Strikes

1. M. H. Woudstra, *The Book of Joshua* (Grand Rapids, MI: Eerdmans, 1981), p. 120.

2. Ibid., p. 126.

3. Charles Wesley, "Jesus, Lover of My Soul," 1740.

Chapter Nine: Conquest Resumed

1. David M. Howard Jr., *The New American Commentary: Joshua* (Nashville: Broadman & Holman, 1998), p. 187.

2. J. I. Packer, *Hot Tub Religion* (Wheaton: Tyndale, 1987).

3. M. H. Woudstra, *The Book of Joshua* (Grand Rapids, MI: Eerdmans, 1981), p. 142.

4. For a fuller treatment of this theme see my *Teaching Isaiah*, Proclamation Trust Media (Fearn, Scotland: Christian Focus, 2010), esp. pp. 240–249, 279, 280.

5. John H. Sammis, "Trust and Obey," 1887.

Chapter Ten: Covenant Renewed

1. M. H. Woudstra, *The Book of Joshua* (Grand Rapids, MI: Eerdmans, 1981), p. 145.

2. See, for example, Ephesians 2:11–18 or Romans 5:1, 2.

3. Isaac Watts, "When I Survey the Wondrous Cross" 1707.

Chapter Eleven: Flattering to Deceive

1. David M. Howard Jr.,*The New American Commentary: Joshua* (Nashville: Broadman & Holman, 1998), p. 220.

2. See footnote 154 in ibid., p. 222.

3. Howard, *The New American Commentary: Joshua*, p. 231.

Chapter Twelve: No Day Like It

1. John C Lennox, *Seven Days That Divide the World* (Grand Rapids, MI: Zondervan, 2011), p. 36.
2. Ibid., p. 17.
3. Ibid., pp. 21–27.
4. David M. Howard Jr., *The New American Commentary: Joshua* (Nashville: Broadman & Holman, 1998), p. 239.
5. M. H. Woudstra, *The Book of Joshua* (Grand Rapids, MI: Eerdmans, 1981), p. 176.
6. See detailed exegesis in Howard, *The New American Commentary: Joshua*, p. 248.
7. Hugh J. Blair, "Joshua," in *The New Bible Commentary*, 3rd edition (London: Inter-Varsity Press, 1970), p. 244.
8. Dale Ralph Davis, *No Falling Words* (Fearn, Ross-shire, UK : Christian Focus, 2005).
9. Howard, *The New American Commentary: Joshua*, pp. 241–248.
10. Ibid., p. 247.
11. Isaac Watts, "Alas! And Did My Saviour Bleed?" in *Hymns & Spiritual Songs*, 1707–1709, Book II.

Chapter Thirteen: The Southern Conquest

1. See David M. Howard Jr., *The New American Commentary: Joshua* (Nashville: Broadman & Holman, 1998), pp. 256, 257.
2. M. H. Woudstra, *The Book of Joshua* (Grand Rapids, MI: Eerdmans, 1981), p. 184.
3. *The New American Commentary: Joshua*, p. 259.
4. Paul Copan, *Is God a Moral Monster?* (Grand Rapids, MI: Baker Books, 2011), pp. 170–173.
5. Quoted in ibid., p. 163.
6. Nahum Tate and Nicholas Brady, "Through All the Changing Scenes of Life," 1696.

Chapter Fourteen: The Northern Conquest

1. David M. Howard Jr., *The New American Commentary: Joshua* (Nashville: Broadman & Holman, 1998), p. 271.
2. See Bruce K. Waltke, "Joshua," in *The New Bible Commentary*, 4th edition (Leicester, UK: Inter-Varsity Press, 1994), p. 249.
3. M. H. Woudstra, *The Book of Joshua* (Grand Rapids, MI: Eerdmans, 1981), p. 196.

Chapter Fifteen: Receiving the Inheritance

1. David M. Howard Jr., *The New American Commentary: Joshua* (Nashville: Broadman & Holman, 1998), p. 292.
2. For details and discussion see ibid., p. 294.
3. Quoted in ibid., p. 82.
4. Bruce K. Waltke, "Joshua," in *The New Bible Commentary*, 4th edition (Leicester, UK: Inter-Varsity Press, 1994), p. 251.

5. "The Acts of the Apostles," in *The New Bible Commentary,* 3rd edition (London: Inter-Varsity Press, 1970), p. 974.
6. Calvin's Commentaries, vol. 2, *Joshua and the Psalms,* trans. H. Beveridge (Grand Rapids, MI: A P & A, n.d.), p. 78.

Chapter Sixteen: Wholehearted Following
1. M. H. Woudstra, *The Book of Joshua* (Grand Rapids, MI: Eerdmans, 1981), p. 230.
2. Ibid., p. 231.
3. John E. Bode, " O Jesus, I Have Promised," 1868.

Chapter Seventeen: The Allotment of the Land
1. David M. Howard Jr., *The New American Commentary: Joshua* (Nashville: Broadman & Holman, 1998), p. 315.
2. Calvin's Commentaries, vol. 2, *Joshua and the Psalms,* trans. H. Beveridge (Grand Rapids, MI: A P & A, n.d.), p. 85.
3. Bruce K. Waltke, "Joshua," in *The New Bible Commentary,* 4th edition (Leicester, UK: Inter-Varsity Press, 1994), p. 255.
4. Calvin, *Joshua and the Psalms,* p. 95.
5. John Rippon, ed., "How Firm a Foundation," in 1787.

Chapter Eighteen: Refuge and Residence
1. M. H. Woudstra, *The Book of Joshua* (Grand Rapids, MI: Eerdmans, 1981), p. 301.
2. David M. Howard Jr., *The New American Commentary: Joshua* (Nashville: Broadman & Holman, 1998), p. 386.
3. Calvin's Commentaries, vol. 2, *Joshua and the Psalms,* trans. H. Beveridge (Grand Rapids, MI: A P & A, n.d.), p. 98.

Chapter Nineteen: Unity Reaffirmed
1. Bruce K. Waltke, "Joshua," in *The New Bible Commentary,* 4th edition (Leicester, UK: Inter-Varsity Press, 1994), p. 257.
2. William Cowper, "Hark, My Soul, It Is the Lord," 1768.

Chapter Twenty: Priorities for the Future
1. David M. Howard Jr., *The New American Commentary: Joshua* (Nashville: Broadman & Holman, 1998), p. 420.
2. Henry F. Lyte, "Praise, My Soul, the King of Heaven," 1834.

Chapter Twenty-One: The Inescapable Choice
1. M. H. Woudstra, *The Book of Joshua* (Grand Rapids, MI: Eerdmans, 1981), p. 348.
2. Robert Robinson, "Come, Thou Fount of Every Blessing," 1758.

Scripture Index

General Index

Index of Sermon Illustrations

bank balance and everything to do
with purposes of the living God being
fulfilled, 28
You don't get the benefit of $1,000 by
framing the check, putting it up on
your wall, and looking at it from time
to time, 29
Alexander MacLaren quote, "God often
opens his hand one finger at a time,"
42
Hymn, "Guide Me, O Thou Great Jehovah," 49
M. H. Woudstra: "The notion of remembering in Hebrew is more than a calling to mind. It involves a remembering with concern; it also implies living
reflection and, where called for, a
corresponding degree of action," 52
Hymn, "O Church Arise," 76
John H. Sammis hymn, "Trust and Obey,"
93
One of the most popular recorded songs
in recent decades is "My Way," 99
Isaac Watts hymn, "When I Survey the
Wondrous Cross," 102
We cannot worship truly at the cross, our
altar, and then go on living in disobedience, because the two attitudes are
mutually exclusive, 102
David Howard, quoting T. C. Butler, on
how the Joshua narrative stands "as a
monument to the great faithfulness of
Joshua to the Mosaic law," 131
Obedience does not secure God's blessing
in some semiautomatic way; rather it
is an expression of the humility that
keeps the channels open for God's
grace to keep flowing into our lives,
147
Author taking young grandson to beach
on a busy summer day and saying,
"Hold on to Grandpa's hand," 148–49
Hymn by John E. Bode, "O Jesus, I Have
Promised," 151
Hymn, "How Firm a Foundation" (John
Rippon, ed.), 159

Obligations
A headmaster regularly addressing
students' behavior outside of school,
since they were wearing a distinctive
uniform . . . "Boys of this school . . .
do not eat or chew gum on the buses,
nor do they behave in a riotous manner
in public," 188

Peace
Trotsky quote, "Whoever longs for a
quiet life has been born in the wrong
generation," 103

Praise
Hymn, "Jesus, Lover of My Soul," 86
Hymn by Henry F. Lyte, "Praise, My
Soul, the King of Heaven," 182
Hymn by Robert Robinson, "Come, Thou
Fount of Every Blessing," 193

Prayer
King Canute ordered the sea waves not to
encroach on his throne sitting on the
beach, 120

Presence of God
Bruce Waltke: "If the absence of apostasy
is a cause to praise God for his presence with his people, then its presence
ought to prompt believers to investigate possible cause(s) of his disfavor,"
172

Promises of God
This is why the book of Joshua is of
such great potential benefit to the
twenty-first century church. The God
of Joshua is our God. He does not
change his purposes or renege on his
promises. So we can learn from this
book great principles of Christian life
and faith, for our edification, 24
Thanksgiving keeps us focused on him as
the one from whom all our blessings
and benefits come. It develops our appreciation of him and our dependence

on him, so that new faith is generated
to meet the new challenges of the
future, 175

Repentance
Isaac Watts hymn, "When I Survey the
Wondrous Cross," 102

Responsibility
The story of a man who wanted to know
greater victory in his Christian walk
so he cut out the six letters L-E-T-G-
O-D, 89
A headmaster regularly addressing
students' behavior outside of school,
since they were wearing a distinctive
uniform . . . "Boys of this school . . .
do not eat or chew gum on the buses,
nor do they behave in a riotous manner
in public," 188

Revelation
Author quote, ". . . it is a major principle
of Biblical interpretation that later
revelation provides the interpretive key
to a right understanding and application to the former," 73

Rhetoric
Paul Copan quote that the book of Joshua
uses "the language of conventional
warfare rhetoric," 126

Satan
The perspective of the Bible is that whatever rope he may be allowed is only
given so that the greater purposes of
God may be fulfilled, to the greater
praise of the glory of God's grace,
104

Science
Galileo popularized and developed the understanding of a sun-centered universe
and was opposed by the Christian
orthodoxy of the day, 114

Luther quote, "The fool wants to turn the
whole art of astronomy upside-down.
However, as Holy Scripture tells us,
so did Joshua bid the sun to stand still
and not the earth," 114
Warning by John C. Lennox that in the
dialogue between the Bible and science
two extremes must be avoided, 114

Scripture
John Calvin on Rahab: "It is indeed a
regular practice with the Rabbins
[sic] when they would consult for the
honor of their nation, presumptuously
to wrest Scripture and give a different
turn by their fictions to anything that
seems not quite reputable," 34
Gordon Fee and Douglas Stewart: "No
Bible narrative was written specifically
about you. . . . You can always learn
a great deal from these narratives,
but you can never assume that God
expects you to do exactly the same
things that the Bible characters did, or
have the same things happen to you
that happened to them," 47
Galileo popularized and developed the understanding of a sun-centered universe
and was opposed by the Christian
orthodoxy of the day, 114
Luther quote, "The fool wants to turn the
whole art of astronomy upside-down.
However, as Holy Scripture tells us,
so did Joshua bid the sun to stand still
and not the earth," 114
Response of an elderly minister accused
of extremist views on the authority of
Scripture, 114
Warning by John C. Lennox that in the
dialogue between the Bible and science two extremes must be avoided,
114
Paul Copan quote that the book of Joshua
uses "the language of conventional
warfare rhetoric," 126

Atheistic critic Richard Dawkins labeling the conquest of Canaan as genocide or ethnic cleansing, 127

David Howard, quoting T. C. Butler, on how the Joshua narrative stands "as a monument to the great faithfulness of Joshua to the Mosaic law," 131

John Calvin quote, [Calvin] "would not be very exact in delineating the site of places, and in discussing names, . . . because great labor would produce little fruit to the reader," 136

Luther's famous dictum: while we read the Bible forward we can only understand it backwards, 162

Hymn by William Cowper, "Hark, My Soul, It Is the Lord," 172

Sin

Sin always blurs our vision and distorts our view of God, so that we become aggrieved and peevish. Defeat shows us that we are not strong in and of ourselves, and like Joshua we imagine that our enemies are stronger than they are, so strong that even God will not be able to defend his name against them. What rubbish! But how incredibly true to our experience in the paralysis and paranoia that swiftly follow when our whole world seems to come crashing down around us, 81

Hymn, "Jesus, Lover of My Soul," 86

How often the Lord is waiting for us to seek him, to pray that he will direct our steps and govern our decision-making through the light of his Word and the grace of his providence. Yet how often we snatch our lives back into our own control. We sample the moldy bread, and we act foolishly because we have been deceived by what we see and what people say, by flattery and pride, 107

M. H. Woudstra quote, ". . . the sovereignty and majesty of the divine counsel is not limited by the will of man," 132

Trust

Alexander MacLaren quote, "God often opens his hand one finger at a time," 42

Author taking young grandson to beach on a busy summer day and saying, "Hold on to Grandpa's hand," 148–49

Victory

The story of a man who wanted to know greater victory in his Christian walk so he cut out the six letters L-E-T-G-O-D, 89

Isaac Watts hymn, "Alas! And Did My Saviour Bleed?" 121

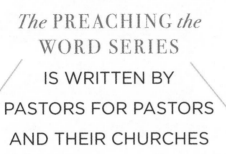

The PREACHING *the*
WORD SERIES

IS WRITTEN BY

PASTORS FOR PASTORS

AND THEIR CHURCHES